Making a European Welfare State?

Convergences and Conflicts Over European Social Policy

Edited by
Peter Taylor-Gooby

Blackwell
Publishing

BLACKWELL PUBLISHING
350 Main Street, Malden, MA 02148-5020, USA
108 Cowley Road, Oxford OX4 1JF, UK
550 Swanston Street, Carlton, Victoria 3053, Australia

First published 2004 by Blackwell Publishing Ltd

Library of Congress Cataloging-in-Publication Data has been applied for

ISBN 1-4051-2116-5

A catalogue record for this title is available from the British Library.

Set by Graphicraft Limited, Hong Kong
Printed and bound in the United Kingdom
by MPG Books Ltd, Bodmin, Cornwall

The publisher's policy is to use permanent paper from mills that operate a sustainable
forestry policy, and which has been manufactured from pulp processed using acid-free and
elementary chlorine-free practices. Furthermore, the publisher ensures that the text paper
and cover board used have met acceptable environmental accreditation standards.

For further information on
Blackwell Publishing, visit our website:
http://www.blackwellpublishing.com

Making a European Welfare State?

CONTENTS

ACKNOWLEDGEMENT

This volume derives mainly from the work of the EU COST A-15 programme, working group 3 on Subsidiarity, Convergence and Trajectories. The contributions of other members of the group to the development of these papers is gratefully acknowledged.

NOTES ON CONTRIBUTORS

Wienke G. W. Boerma is Professor at the Netherlands Institute of Health Services Research (NIVEL).

Denis Bouget is Professor at the Maison des Sciences de l'Homme Ange Guépin, Nantes.

Luís Capucha is Professor in the Department of Sociology, Higher Institute for Business and Labour Studies, Lisbon.

Anne Daguerre is a freelance researcher.

Maurizio Ferrera is Professor in the Department of Social and Political Studies, University of Pavia, and Director of the Centre for Comparative Political Research, Bocconi University, Milan.

Karl Hinrichs is Senior Research Associate at the Centre for Social Policy Research at the University of Bremen, and Adjunct Professor of Political Science at Humboldt University in Berlin.

Björn Hvinden is Professor in the Department of Sociology and Political Science, Norwegian University of Science and Technology, Trondheim, and Senior Advisor, The Welfare Research Programme of the Research Council of Norway.

Mads Meier Jæger is Researcher at the Danish National Institute of Social Research, Copenhagen.

Olli Kangas is Professor of Social Policy and the Head of the Department of Social Policy at the University of Turku, Finland.

Jon Kvist is Senior Researcher at the Danish National Institute of Social Research, Copenhagen.

Manos Matsaganis is Assistant Professor in the Department of Economics, University of Crete.

Luis Moreno is Senior Research Fellow in the Comparative Policy and Politics Research Unit, National Research Council, Madrid.

Ileana Neamtu is a member of staff at the Research Institute for the Quality of Life, The Romanian Academy, Bucharest.

Ana Rico Gomez is Research Fellow at the European Observatory on Health Care Systems, Madrid.

Richard B. Saltman is Professor at the European Observatory on Health Care Systems, and Emory University.

Dimitri A. Sotiropoulos is Lecturer in Department of Political Science and Public Administration, University of Athens and the Hellenic Observatory, The European Institute, The London School of Economics and Political Science.

Maya Stoyanova works at Bulgarian National Radio, and at the Department of Political Science and Public Administration, University of Athens.

Peter Taylor-Gooby is Professor of Social Policy at the University of Kent.

1

Introduction:
Open Markets versus Welfare Citizenship: Conflicting Approaches to Policy Convergence in Europe

Peter Taylor-Gooby

Welfare states in Europe face common pressures from a range of factors that include economic globalization and enhanced economic competition, population ageing, family change, and labour market shifts that reduce opportunities for the less-skilled. One argument is that common pressures should produce policy convergence, and this has been a central concern of the EU, from the ambitions of harmonization in the 1980s and the 1993 Green Paper through to the more cautious Open Method of Coordination (OMC) and the issues of European citizenship, fundamental rights and tax harmonization advanced in the draft EU constitution (EU 2002). Social policy is complex, involving government policies in health care, education, social security, housing and poverty directly; it is indirectly associated with economic, fiscal, labour-market and family policies. Governments wish to promote growth as well as citizen welfare. Not surprisingly, social policy convergence processes are not simple, uniform and consistent. They involve tensions between different policy objectives, and the most obvious and intractable lies between economic and welfare policy objectives.

This volume provides a detailed analysis of welfare convergence in Europe, through theoretical and cross-national examination of developments at the European level and through case studies of particular policy areas and regional developments. It shows that arguments which distinguish convergence and divergence risk over-simplifying processes in which developments in both directions coexist. Different national economic and social contexts ensure that common measures produce different responses, even when goals are similar. This introduction reviews the key themes of the papers and goes on to show how a basic tension between economic and social goals shapes policy-making at the European level. This tension ultimately reaches back to fundamental differences in the understanding of how capitalist societies work and of how they deliver welfare to their citizens.

The two opening papers examine theoretical issues. Jæger and Kvist point out the ambivalent consequences of the current pressures for different welfare states. While it is sometimes claimed that economic pressures imply welfare cutbacks, the argument shows that, in particular contexts, an expansion of provision to support growth may be more appropriate. Hinrichs and Kangas seek to expand understanding of restructuring processes and demonstrate that policy redirection can take place through the cumulating of minor incremental shifts, rather than high-profile and abrupt changes. Thus the identification of convergence cannot rest on set-piece policy reform, but requires the careful analysis of developments over time.

Rico, Saltman and Boerma present a detailed analysis of the role of primary care reforms in European health-care restructuring, which indicates that institutional structures may promote a convergent reform model in some socio-political contexts, whereas path dependency in the existing system may prove stronger in others. Hvinden analyses disability policies to show that common EU approaches are more likely to develop in areas where governments have not already established strong policy directions. Thus Europe-wide strategies are most viable in areas where national positions are not entrenched. Daguerre and Taylor-Gooby show that some common features can be identified in responses to labour-market change in the very different policy regimes of France and Britain: governments are keen to enhance the employability of unskilled, especially younger people and women with childcare responsibilities, but very different national traditions set strict limits to how far convergence can go.

Other papers examine developments in particular European regions. Matsaganis, Ferrera, Capucha and Moreno show that anti-poverty policies are developing across the Mediterranean EU members, but that provision remains uneven and that the context of strong supportive families plays an important role in substituting for government services. Conflicts between the goals of political legitimacy (which implies expanded social provision) and economic growth (which implies restraint) affect policy development in the Southern accession states (Sotiropoulos, Neamtu and Stoyanova). Finally, Bouget completes this collection by showing that, while a trend to convergence in social spending can be identified across EU countries, the process is interrupted by pressures for austerity which are most marked at times of economic downturn. It is an intermittent process, proceeding at a different pace in different European countries.

Thus convergence exists, as a goal and in the actual trajectory of policy in some areas, but in a context where some developments imply divergence. It is a process fraught with tensions, of which the most basic lies between the economic and the welfare concerns of government. This division emerges clearly in policy at the European level, and in the rest of this paper we examine in more detail the dilemmas that result. On the one hand, Europe invented the welfare state, and current EC policies imply substantial direct involvement in welfare state issues (in relation to public health, the needs of young, old, disabled, unemployed and poorer people, social inclusion and ethnic minorities). They also imply indirect involvement through policies on what are primarily work-related issues—the equal treatment of men and women and of other groups in employment, health and safety at work, working conditions, employment rights and the likely outcomes of enhanced social dialogue and worker participation in management. The free movement of labour within Europe also has implications for welfare. On the other hand, the development of an open market across Europe in goods, services, labour and finance, the restrictions on individual governments' fiscal policy implied by the Growth and Stability Pact, and the fact that the European Central Bank is charged with managing monetary policy and foreign exchange with the primary objective of maintaining price stability, all imply a shift towards a more market-oriented and less interventionist role for government. This contradicts the traditional approaches of welfare states in seeking to manage national economies to contain unemployment and to provide a high level of public services.

The tension between open market and welfare state in Europe reflects a division in understanding of how to advance human welfare in modern capitalist market societies. This cleavage is neatly summarized in the conflicting theories of Schumpeter and Polanyi, published at the end of the Second World War. These approaches contrast the view that capitalism develops through a chaotic and fitful process of creative destruction, led by entrepreneurial risk-takers, who require minimal interference from government and other social institutions to be able to pursue innovations and invest resources where they can best be used, with an alternative: the view that free market systems may create rapid growth, but in doing so destroy the human and social fabric on which they depend, and that economic institutions must be embedded in a social and cultural framework in order to operate in a way that promotes human welfare. The implication is that state welfare is essential to sustain the framework that civilizes the market. At the most basic level, open market and welfare state approaches to European policy-making derive from analyses that may be traced back to these alternative conceptions. This paper describes the two approaches and examines how they are reflected in current European policy-making. It concludes that policy, direct and indirect, at the European level, is moving in the direction of a Schumpeterian approach to social risk, but that the door to a shift in the direction indicated by Polanyi is still open.

Open Market versus Welfare State

Schumpeter

Capitalism, Socialism and Democracy (1943), a book written to defend the liberal model of capitalism against the "Marxian revival" that Schumpeter identified in the Western political economy of the 1930s and 1940s, argues that the great merit of liberal capitalism is its ability to deliver expanding wealth and thus enhance the welfare of citizens over time. The "first test of economic performance is total output" (p. 63), and Schumpeter is able to demonstrate convincingly that total output has increased over time (ch. 5) in the USA, his paradigm for a developed capitalist country, at an average conservatively estimated to be 2 per cent a year during the previous century (p. 67). "Broadly speaking, relative shares in national income have remained substantially constant over the last hundred years", so that, over time, a rising tide lifts all boats and "if capitalism repeated its past performance for another half century . . . this would do away with anything that according to present standards could be called poverty" (p. 66). He points out that "supernormal unemployment is one of the features of the periods of adaptation that follow . . . those industrial revolutions that are so characteristic of the capitalist process" (p. 70), but such phenomena are temporary (although often exacerbated by "anti-capitalist policies beyond what . . . need have been . . . and economically irrational methods of financing relief"—p. 71). However, if capitalist development continues, it should be possible to provide for unemployed people during temporary restructurings of the market system at a level which would ensure that the misery associated with unemployment in the 1930s would enter the "limbo filled by the sorry spectres of child labour and the 16-hour day" (p. 70). Society will realize the "possibilities held out by capitalist evolution for the care of the aged and sick, for education and hygiene and so on" (p. 71).

He acknowledges the arguments accepted by Marxists and others (and traced back to Ricardo), that capitalist market systems achieve greater allocative and cost efficiency in the use of resources by a competitive process that drives down prices and wages, leading to gloomy predictions of immiseration and increasingly bitter class struggle. However, he suggests that these claims miss a crucial point: markets do not just direct resources to where they command the highest marginal return and drive down prices to those of the cheapest competitor, they also promise substantial rewards for the successful innovator or entrepreneur, who leads the way in offering something that is more attractive than what is produced by competitors. The real reason, he argues, why capitalist economies are able to deliver ever-higher living standards is through the economic growth achieved as a result of the inherent and ineluctable pressure to innovate:

> Capitalist economy . . . is incessantly being revolutionised from within by new enterprise . . . by the intrusion of new commodities or new methods of production, or new commercial opportunities into the industrial structure as it exists at any moment . . . Economic progress in capitalist society means turmoil . . . In order to escape being undersold every firm is in the end compelled to . . . invest in its turn, and in order to be able to do so, to plow back part of its profits . . . to accumulate. Thus everyone . . . accumulates. (p. 31)

The vital element in the "turmoil" of "creative destruction" is the entrepreneur:

> the function of entrepreneurs is to reform or revolutionise the pattern of production by exploiting an invention, or, more generally, an untried technological possibility for producing a new commodity or . . . an old one in a new way, by opening up a new source of supply of materials or a new outlet for products, by reorganising an industry and so on . . . To undertake such new things is difficult . . . This function . . . consists in getting things done. (p. 132)

4

Growth comes from innovation driven by individuals, and the benefits of this process outweigh the competitive pressure to cut the proportion of resources going to workers. Market capitalism is a positive-sum game in which both sides of industry benefit, not a zero-sum game between capitalists and working class. The logic of this argument stresses the importance of expanding the opportunities available for entrepreneurship and for permitting the chaotic vitality of capitalism to operate untrammelled. The approach supports the advocacy of a liberal market-oriented model of capitalism and the limitation of state intervention.

Polanyi

An alternative position that accepts the essential dynamism of capitalism, but views the impact of free markets from a bleaker standpoint is offered by Polanyi. His most important work: *The Great Transformation* (published in 1944—the year after *Capitalism, Socialism and Democracy*) is concerned to analyse the basis of what he saw as the economic glory and human disaster of nineteenth-century civilization. He argues that this system represented a new departure in economic arrangements, and one that was ultimately unsustainable:

> The font and matrix of the system was the self-regulating market . . .
> The idea of a self-adjusting market implied a stark utopia. Such an institution could not exist for any length of time without annihilating the human and natural substance of society; it would have physically destroyed man and turned his surroundings into a wilderness. (p. 1)

Liberal capitalism, based on the self-adjusting market, unregulated by external social institutions, such as government interventions or social and cultural norms, is a historical anomaly. He points out, on the basis of the anthropological work of Thurnwald, Malinowski and others, that market exchange has been an important feature of society since the later Stone Age. However, in all previous forms of society, markets had been regulated through norms of redistribution or of reciprocity. "When reciprocity rules, acts of barter are usually . . . embedded in long-range relations implying trust and confidence, a situation which tended to obliterate the bilateral character of the transaction" (p. 61). In the nineteenth century, however, the relationship was reversed—market principles attained dominance and social relations were defined by them. The institutional embedding of market relationships was irreversibly destroyed. This is at once the success and the failure of the liberal system—it generates the conditions for rapid accumulation but, in the long term, self-regulating capitalism is not viable, since it would simply consume the social and human fabric of society. His evidence for this is the treatment of the destitute under Speenhamland and the 1834 Poor Law (which imposed the brutal logic of the market by ensuring that conditions in the poor house were worse than the minimum the lowest-paid labourer outside could afford) and the disasters of the great famines in Ireland and India as a result of the ruthless imposition of market principles that denied relief on the grounds that it disrupted market forces.

The book traces the various social and political changes which set the stage for the operation of the free market—the expansion of long-distance trade, separated from the regulating institutions in which market exchange had developed, the growth of mercantile regulation by a centralized state and its decline, the construction of a free market in labour through the operation of the Poor Law and the movement to international free trade with exchange regulated by an automatic gold standard. Polanyi argues that the "great transformation", which wrenched economic relationships away from their restraining context, also generated a controlling response:

> for a century the dynamics of modern society were governed by a double movement: the market expanded continuously, but this movement was met by a counter-movement checking the expansion in definite directions . . . in the last analysis, it was incompatible with the self-regulation of the market and thus with the market system itself. (p. 130)

A large part of the book is concerned to trace the operation of efforts to control free-market forces by various interests—trade protectionism in the Corn Laws, the development of Chartism, of Owenism, and then of a politicized labour movement, and imperialist conflicts generated by trade rivalries. Ultimately, "nineteenth century civilisation was not destroyed by the external or internal attack of barbarians . . . It disintegrated as the result of the . . . measure which society adopted . . . not to be . . . annihilated by the action of the self-regulated market" (p. 249). Free markets are unable to operate successfully in the long run, because they undermine the conditions of their own success; more generally, economic relationships must be embedded in a fabric of regulation through cultural norms, social institutions and political controls. Unlike Schumpeter, Polanyi believes that the structures that may be provided by an interventionist welfare state are necessary to enable market capitalism to flourish in the long term.

More Recent Developments

The contrasting models of capitalist development—liberal versus interventionist, with their different implications for the future of the European welfare state—are often seen as instantiated in the different national economic systems of the modern world. Soskice and others distinguish between

> two types of advanced industrial economies—coordinated market economies (CMEs) and liberal market economies (LMEs). CMEs such as Germany and Sweden are characterised by networks of formal and informal linkages between firms and between firms and other economic actors (such as banks and trade unions), which facilitate the supply of collective goods involved in production . . . [including] the supply of transferable skills . . . long-term finance, technological innovation and industrial peace. LMEs such as the UK on the other hand, involve no

comparable level of capital coordination, and in consequence are unable to supply similar collective goods. (Wood 2001: 376–7)

The USA also fits the LME model. Thus, the industrial organization of most of the leading European economies is contrasted with that of the USA and the UK. The approaches of Schumpeter and Polanyi lead in different directions—to the advocacy of a society based on liberal market relationships or to one based on the regulation of the free market as the best way to serve human interests under capitalism. There are, of course, substantial bodies of work on both sides. The liberal market agenda is of great importance in a more globalized world where a number of changes drive the rapid expansion of international trade. These include: the development of technologies that enable cheaper and more rapid communications, both in moving physical goods and in transferring information and finance; the breakdown of the barriers to trade provided by the ending of the division between state socialist and capitalist nations in Europe and the greater participation in international markets of China; the growth of smaller Asian industrialized economies such as Korea and Malaysia; the expansion of trade among large developing countries such as India; and the establishment of institutions designed to promote free trade, most importantly the World Trade Organization. Even critics of the globalization thesis accept that transnational trade now exceeds the level of the nineteenth century (Hirst and Thompson 1999). The liberal market agenda is also contained in the development of freer trade across NAFTA countries and in Europe, and the process whereby barriers to the movement of goods, labour, services and capital are gradually being removed.

The move towards greater liberalism in market institutions has, from this perspective, gained ascendancy in Europe and in the world. Distinguished economists such as Baumol (2002) continue to promote the argument that it is the relatively free operation of liberal market institutions that lays the foundations of growth through the provision of opportunities for the promotion and adoption of innovation.

Recent EC policy directions, from the 1993 White Paper on Growth Competitiveness and Employment (EC 1993b), which stresses flexibility and compares European performance in job-creation unfavourably with that of America, to the establishment of an integrated transnational marketplace, constitute a move away from heartland European traditions towards a more liberal approach, with the aim of making European industry more adaptable, productive and competitive. The shift is away from the Polanyian logic of a market system, in which economic relationships are sustainable because they are embedded in other institutions, towards a Schumpeterian system which promotes the dynamic role of the liberal entrepreneur. The question arises as to whether European welfare systems will follow the open market in the direction of the USA, and to what extent they will retain their distinctive concern with social protection and inclusion.

Recent developments imply a move away from the Keynesian welfare state. The process of denationalization has been pursued across all European countries. The Growth and Stability Pact strictly limits the deficit financing of state provision. Everywhere there is a move to increase the proportion of private services in the welfare mix, most noticeably in the measures to expand private pensions in France, Germany, Sweden and the UK (Taylor-Gooby 2001, ch. 8). Everywhere, state welfare spending is under constraint. However there are also counter-indications. The EU has consolidated the social rights (mainly related to employment) of the Maastricht Social Protocol in the 1997 Amsterdam Treaty and extended them in relation to combating discrimination. Pochet, Rhodes and others point out that collective negotiations remain highly significant so that "the market is clearly more important than in the past and international constraints have increased . . . but . . . we are witnessing . . . a concerted process of adaptation in which the core principles of the European social model may be sustained" (Rhodes 2001: 193, 194; see also Fagertag and Pochet 2000).

The changes imply strict limitations on governments' ability to manage their economies to promote employment or to deficit-finance public provision. The welfare state and the economic context in which it is set will be more constrained than under Keynesianism, and an outcome of public spending restrictions, privatization and a narrower targeting of services is expected. We move on to consider how liberal and interventionist approaches to making capitalism work are reflected in European welfare policy.

Liberalism and Interventionism in EC Welfare Policy-making

The founders of the European common market were initially concerned to establish a trading partnership which would promote economic development and would have the larger aim of reducing military conflict. In this the EU has been spectacularly successful. The progress towards "ever-closer union" has culminated in the integration of monetary systems for most members, the surrender of major economic policy-making powers (setting interest and exchange rates) to a central bank divorced from immediate political control, and substantial progress towards freedom of trade in goods and services and movement of labour or capital across the union. States bordering the union are keen for membership and the process of expansion continues, so that the EU will soon become the richest as well as the largest consumer market in the world. The soldiers of member states have not been engaged in national wars within the territory of the EU.

Welfare issues take second or lower place. Social protection or inclusion is not included among the four principal objectives on the opening page of the Europa website (http://europa.eu.int/abc-en.htm), although the link on job creation leads to discussion of such issues as non-discrimination, equal treatment in the labour market and employment. Social policy has entered the EU agenda almost entirely through its relevance to labour-market policies, although the range of areas covered has expanded through the continuing efforts of the European Commission to enlarge its sphere of competence, reinforced by judgements of the European Court of Justice. Structural funds were initially established to promote "harmonious development . . . economic and social cohesion . . . and reduce regional disparities" (Single European Act [SEA], Article 130a), and programmes to promote particular objectives were created. The most relevant funds are the Social Fund and the Regional

Fund. Over two-thirds of the resources in the funds (totalling about 120 billion Euros in 1989–93 and about 150 billion in 1994–9) was allocated to meeting the needs of the poorer regions (Geyer 2001, table 6.1). Specific programmes have been established within the Funds to promote such interests as vocational training (Euroform), the labour-market integration of disabled people (Horizon) and women's opportunities (NOW). The Social Action Programmes are smaller initiatives designed to advance particular social objectives, but with an increasing stress on labour market issues.

During the 1980s strenuous efforts were made by the Commission to establish social policy concerns alongside economic issues as EC goals, as a "social dimension" to EU policy. This led to the development of a Social Charter, which listed fundamental rights for workers and was passed as a non-binding "solemn declaration" (with the UK government voting against) at the 1989 Strasbourg summit. The Charter influenced the 1989 Social Action Programme, but was overshadowed by the issue of monetary union in the debates about the Maastricht Treaty. The Social Protocol of the treaty included a number of social policy advances, including qualified majority voting in the Council for health and safety, working conditions, workers' consultation, equal opportunities and treatment and the integration of those excluded from the labour market, although the UK was permitted to opt out. A series of political developments (the UK presidency immediately afterwards, the Danish referendum, the economic pressures resulting from the requirements for monetary union) delayed subsequent social policy development.

The 1993 Green Paper on Social Protection was issued as a "consultative document". This identified a number of objectives at the European level, which included solidarity and integration, equal opportunities, establishing common social standards, and social cohesion alongside growth, human capital and high employment (EC 1993, part III). However, the employment White Paper in the same year advanced a different set of priorities, promoting monetary stability and an open and decentralized labour market characterized by greater flexibility, leaning more towards the Schumpeterian approach (EC 1993: 12–16). In 1994 the Council initially refused to adopt the Fourth Poverty Programme (funded at more than double the level of the previous programme), and instead expanded the Third Programme, but limited it to employment and training (Geyer 2001: 163). The Amsterdam Treaty in 1997 finally incorporated the full Social Protocol and ended the UK opt-out. The treaty addressed discrimination (Article 13) but made no new spending commitments, and measures for improving the position of the elderly and of disabled people were dropped from the final text. The Fourth Social Action Programme (1998–2000) reflects the labour-market orientation of EU social policy: it stresses "jobs, skills and mobility" and "the changing world of work", with "an inclusive society" as the third priority. EU social policy has followed an uneven path of development but has expanded and been consolidated. It is mainly linked to employment rights, and various related activities concerned with specific programmes on poverty, disability, youth and women's opportunities in employment.

In the main, EU policy-making is not interventionist. Acceptance of the principle of subsidiarity in the Maastricht and Amsterdam treaties means that Union competence is restricted to areas where national governments cannot meet policy objectives through their own actions, but EU intervention can achieve these aims. The difficulties encountered in the promotion of the "social dimension" has led to the abandonment of any direct attempt at the "harmonization" of national policies and the shift to an "open method of coordination". Increasingly, the EU seeks to set benchmarks or indicators for national policy outcomes which may be achieved by diverse means, in order to promote "levelling-up". Certain areas (public health, gender equality and, to some extent, disability) have attained "mainstream" status, so that they are included in the general process of policy-making and discussion and are covered in the statistics and reports prepared by the EC as a matter of course—although this may imply that issues in these fields become subsumed within the concern for improved economic performance. Both open market and social protection logics can be detected in EU activities. The questions that arise are whether these are compatible in the long run and how the member states of the Union will manage the tension between them in the future.

EC action in specific areas

Table 1 summarizes the current status of EC social policy and related areas, and indicates where there has been substantial development and there is a likelihood of future expansion. All the areas covered have implications for welfare because the circumstances and conditions of employment affect individual life-chances, but an attempt is made to group the areas into those where the emphasis is on welfare issues, an intermediate group which straddles welfare and labour-market concerns and a third group concerned primarily with employment issues. Those policies where the grounds for intervention are to do with individual or citizenship needs fall into the first, policies where the grounds are the needs of the economy into the second, and those where the grounds apply to both into the intermediate group. The first area thus includes public health, poverty and the needs of older, disabled and younger people. The intermediate group comprises policies which developed from both labour-market and welfare concerns: employment (already implicit in that much of policy for young and disabled people is concerned with labour market participation), the equal treatment of men and women and policies combating racist discrimination. The third group consists of measures that are chiefly concerned with direct labour-market issues, but which have social policy implications—the free movement of labour, the enhancement of social dialogue between unions and employers, stronger employment rights, working conditions, worker participation, and health and safety in the workplace. The divisions between these groups are a matter of judgement, partly because issues that originated with concerns in one area may expand to have important implications for another.

The table shows the areas where EC intervention has been strongest, judged by the criteria of being subject to qualified majority voting (which prevents individual member states blocking policies), having access to both structural funds and specific programmes to advance EU-wide reform in the area, having a substantial amount of legislation in the field, and having a

Table 1

EU social policy and related measures

	QMV status	Significant access to structural funds	Funded action programmes	Legislative acts	Probability for future expansion	Consolidated treaties—Articles
Mainly welfare-related						
Poverty	Maastricht SP (Art. 2)	Yes	No	0–5	Low	136, 137
Elderly	Unanimous voting	Yes	Yes	0–5	Low	13
Disability	Unanimous voting	Yes	Yes	0–5	Low	13
Youth	Maastricht (Art. 126–7)	Yes	Yes	10+	High	149, 150
Public health	Maastricht (Art. 129)	No	Yes	5–10	Medium	3, 152
Market/social welfare-related						
Employment	Amsterdam (Art. 109)	Yes	Yes	10+*	High	2, 125–130
Gender	Maastricht SP (Art. 2)	Yes	Yes	10+	High	13, 137, 141
Racial discrimination	Unanimous voting	Yes	Yes	0–5	Low	13
Mainly market-related with welfare implications						
Health and safety	SEA 118a	Yes	Yes	10+	Medium	3, 136, 137, 140
Free movement	SEA (Art. 7)	Yes	Yes	10+	Medium	3, 14, 39–42, 61–9
Working conditions	SEA 118a	No	No	5–10	Medium	137
Social dialogue	Maastricht SP (Art. 4)	Yes	Yes	10+	Medium	136, 139
Employment rights	Unanimous voting	No	No	0–5	Low	137
Worker participation	Maastricht SP (Art. 2)	No	No	0–5	Low	137

SP = Social Protocol.

*Some of the directives included under youth or disability are primarily concerned with employment for these groups.

Source: Updated from Geyer (2000: 204–5).

medium or high possibility of further development. These areas concern: programmes to help young people, employment, equal treatment of men and women, health and safety at work, the free movement of labour, and social dialogue. They thus span all the areas of EU activity mentioned. Public health, working conditions and perhaps anti-poverty policy (which has access to structural funds) might come next, followed by worker participation. EU policies which have a bearing on welfare have made substantial progress in relation to health and safety, free movement of labour, women's rights and the needs of young people, but offer less potential in other areas. However, it is in the way in which social protection issues are addressed that the distinctive policy orientations of the EU emerge. The key question concerns the extent to which social issues are addressed through measures dominated by the demands of a liberal open market, and how far the concern of policy-makers is to create a supportive social framework which reduces the destructive impact of the working of the market.

In all the areas of EU policy-making, attempts to tackle welfare-related issues directly have tended to be ineffective, while policies that advance social ends as an adjunct to more directly economic and labour-market policies have enjoyed greater success. This is in contrast to the area of economic policy, which has produced a single currency, an open market and policies to promote a level playing field in labour markets, equal opportunities and industrial relations. Thus the aspirations expressed in the 1988 Social Chapter that workers should be entitled to "adequate" social protection and citizens to "sufficient" resources and assistance (EC 1990: 10) were omitted from the Maastricht Treaty. This instead referred to combating social exclusion, and integration of those excluded from the labour market (Articles 1 and 2). The Fourth Poverty Programme was initially rejected by the European Council in view of its concern with social exclusion, and was only finally implemented when it was limited to training and employment strategies. Policies against social exclusion only gained qualified majority voting (QMV) status on this basis in the Amsterdam Treaty. The move towards the Open Method of Coordination (OMC) in this area established common objectives at the Nice Council (2000) in which the first place goes to "facilitating participation in employment" (through equal opportunities and improving employability), followed by "guaranteeing access to resources", which includes, again, employability, and then "helping the most vulnerable". Thus poverty as an objective is intimately bound up with employment-centred policies.

The economic orientation of employment policies is illustrated by the fact that the Amsterdam Treaty adds the promotion of employment to the list of Community objectives (Article 2), provided that it does not undermine competitiveness. The goal (Article 109) is a high level of employment rather than the full employment preferred by Swedish delegates. Current policy emphasizes positive activation rather than benefits for the unemployed. Since the 1997 Luxembourg summit, policy has included the production of a series of strategy papers (EC 1997, onwards) which are increasingly concerned with making social protection more "employment-friendly" as in the National Action Plans for social exclusions (see, for example, CEU 2002, annex 2, section 1), and from the 2000 Lisbon summit onwards specifically endorse "making work pay" (CEU 2003, annex 1, proposal 8). Current OMC strategies centre on the four pillars of employability, entrepreneurship, adaptability and equal opportunities in consort with the other EU policies discussed here.

In relation to policies to meet the needs of specific groups, the EU directs its policy-making energy towards actual and potential labour-market entrants. Older people receive little attention in policy-making. Although the needs of this group are mentioned in the 1988 Social Charter and are relevant to the Social Fund and Social Action programmes, and an Observatory was established in 1993, there is little concrete policy. The Amsterdam Treaty extends non-discrimination to include age, among other areas (Article 137), but the new grounds do not have effect and require unanimity in voting. Disabled people have received rather more support, although this tends to be from a labour-market perspective. Thus the Social Fund from 1971 included rehabilitation programmes and a range of programmes (Helios onwards) in the later 1980s were developed to integrate disabled people into paid work. The group is included in Article 137 mentioned above and have achieved lobbying support and recognition in EU "soft law" chiefly on account of their potential relation to the labour market. Younger people, however, are effectively mainstreamed, since the needs of the group for education and training were included in the Treaty of Rome. By 1982, young people made up 44 per cent of Social Fund beneficiaries (Geyer 2001: 197) and were eligible for a large number of exchange and training programmes costing over 1 billion Euros between 1987 and 1995. The group's needs are reaffirmed in Maastricht (Articles 126, 127) and attained QMV status. The Essen Employment summit put commitment to youth training and easing the transition from school to work as the top priority and the group has emerged in a strong position in the employment OMC process.

Equal treatment has been well established in EU legislation in relation to work and pay since the 1957 Treaty included an equal pay principle (Article 119), interpreted through directives and ECJ judgements in the 1980s and 1990s to cover training, access to employment, working conditions, career progression and benefits and, from 1979, state and occupational benefits. The 1974 Social Action Programme introduced the theme of work–life balance in relation to women's opportunities, and this has become increasingly prominent, for example in the OMC social inclusion and employment strategies. The Maastricht Treaty (Articles 2 and 6) and the Amsterdam Treaty (Article 141) included equality, non-discrimination by gender and equal pay clauses extending to positive discrimination. The EC established a Women's Lobby to coordinate NGOs in 1990, and directives have extended to parental leave, childcare, sexual harassment and other areas. Gender equality has become embedded or "mainstreamed" in EU policy-making in relation to employment, reaching thereby into social security and domestic responsibilities that affect attainment in work, and is an example of how the employment orientation of EU social policy can achieve more wide-ranging progress. In contrast, policy in relation to racial discrimination has achieved much less, despite a Joint Declaration against Racism and Xenophobia in 1997, an Observatory in the 1990s and inclusion in Social Fund initiatives. The relevant Amsterdam Treaty article (137) requires unanimous voting. However, the recent prominence of far-right parties and national responses to refugees may prompt action.

Policy in the directly market-related areas (free movement of workers, health and safety, employment rights, working conditions, social dialogue and worker participation) is interesting because in one sense it is EU "core business", fundamental to the fair operation of an open labour market, and derived from the original EU Treaties. However, legislation may lead to conflicts with the different national approaches to labour-market management (most obviously between LMEs and CMEs) and may impact on other policy areas, such as social security, work–life balance, education and qualifications. Free movement is established in the Treaty of Rome (Article 3c) and leads the list of social rights in the pre-Maastricht Social Charter. Directives cover discrimination against non-nationals, transferability of social security, and residence and family rights, and action programmes for migrant workers were set up from the 1970s onwards. Health and safety (included in the same clause and consolidated in the SEA and the Amsterdam Treaty, with QMV status) has generated a number of directives, including the regulation of working time and more tentative approaches to the area of public health. This was broadened in the new EC Treaty (Article 152) to include health promotion and all dangers to human health, but the community's role remains subsidiary and coordinating, and policy development is limited.

Developments in other directly market-related areas have been slower: employment rights and working conditions have produced directives on redundancy and the transfer of acquired rights on company merger, but little else, despite QMV voting in the early 1990s. Proposals to include employment rights in the EU Constitution have generated further controversy. Workers' participation produced no directives until after QMV was introduced following Maastricht, but now works councils are required. Social dialogue has developed slowly and, at the European level, has been mainly concerned with sectoral agreements in areas with high public-sector involvement.

Thus the EU has a clear involvement in the obvious areas of activity that underpin an open European market, particularly the free movement of labour. In the other market-related areas, there have been some developments in relation to health and safety at work, influenced by concern for equal competition, but less activity in the other areas listed. The EU sets strict limits to the policy areas in which it will intervene. Unanimity on the Council is still required for the protection of workers against unfair dismissal and in the workplace. The EC does not address pay, the right to form unions and the right to strike or lock out.

Conclusion

EU engagement in social policy is wide-ranging. This brief review shows that it is in those areas where there is a clear relationship to employment (for example, enabling young or disabled people to participate in the labour market) or to the establishment of a competitive open labour market on equal terms (for example free movement and associated social security rights, common measures for health and safety) that most policy development has taken place. Public health, the needs of the elderly or the poor (other than in relation to employment) and racial discrimination receive much less attention. Other areas directly related to the workplace (employment rights, working conditions, workers' participation and social dialogue) occupy an intermediate position. There has been substantial legislative activity, but progress is hampered by the differences between the industrial relations regimes of member states, so that key areas such as unfair dismissal have not progressed to qualified majority voting and basic industrial relations issues (for example, the right to strike or to form a union) are simply not addressed. Equal treatment is an interesting case (bridging employment rights, the capacity of very large numbers of people to contribute to paid work and individual opportunities), and here the EU has been active in developing policies to bring women into the labour market. Across other areas national provision remains dominant, and it is uncertain how far the "open method of coordination" will produce convergence of outcomes where it is pursued. Issues such as tax harmonization (provoking intense debate as a proposal in the draft EU Constitution) seem unlikely to achieve consensus in the near future.

Social policy issues are addressed almost entirely through measures that do not conflict with policies designed to advance the market agenda, although in some areas they modify those policies to accommodate the needs of particular groups. EU policy-making departs from a crude liberal agenda in its promotion of a positive rather than a negative activation agenda, in its commitment to the development of human capital in relation to young and disabled people and the opportunities available to women, and, to a lesser extent, in its poverty policy. The dilemmas that arise when policy debates impinge on issues of the balance between work and family responsibilities (as in equal treatment or poverty policy) or national social security frameworks (as in the free movement of workers and their families) may offer opportunities for the future development of policy. Thus EU policy-making accepts the Schumpeterian argument that market freedom is essential to economic success, but does allow a social agenda to enter, so long as welfare ends do not conflict with the market, and encourages social interventions when they can be made to support movement towards the goal. Pressures for both liberalism and for a stronger interventionist role exist, and whether the balance between the two will shift in the future is at present unclear. In short, the European approach to social risks is more Schumpeter than Polanyi, but that may not be the last word.

References

Atkinson, A., Cantillon, B., Marlier, E. and Nolan, B. (2001), *Indicators for Social Exclusion in the EU*, Oxford: Oxford University Press.

Baumol, W. (2002), *The Free-Market Innovation Machine: Analyzing the Growth Miracle of Capitalism*, Princeton, NJ: Princeton University Press.

Council of the European Union Social Protection Committee (CEU) (2002), *Fight against Poverty and Social Exclusion: Common Objectives for the Second Round of National Action Plans*, Soc 508, Brussels: CEC. Available at: http://europa.eu.int/comm/employment_social/soc-prot/soc-incl/counciltext_en.pdf.

Council of the European Union (2003), *Proposal for a Council Decision on Guidelines for Employment Policies*, Barcelona: Barcelona European Council. Available at: http://europa.eu.int/comm/employment_social/employment_strategy_prop_2003/gl_en/pdf.

EC (1990), *Social Chapter (Agreement and Protocol on Social Policy)*, Brussels: EC.

EC (1993a), *European Social Policy: Options for the Union*, com (93) 551, Brussels: DG for Employment, Industrial Relations and Social Affairs.

EC (1993b), *Growth Competitiveness and Employment*, Bulletin of the EC, supplement 6/93, Brussels: CEC.

EC (1997), *1998 Guidelines for Member States' Employment Policies*, Brussels: CEC.

EU (2002), *Preliminary Draft European Constitution*, European Convention, 369/02, Brussels: European Convention.

Fagertag, G. and Pochet, P. (2000), *Social Pacts in Europe*, European Trade Union Institute (ETUI) & OSE, Brussels.

Geyer, R. (2001), *Exploring European Social Policy*, Cambridge: Polity Press.

Hirst, P. and Thompson, G. (1999), *Globalization in Question*, Cambridge: Polity Press.

Polanyi, K. (1944), *The Great Transformation*, London: Rhinehart.

Rhodes, M. (2001), The political economy of social pacts. In P. Pierson (ed.), *The New Politics of the Welfare State*, Oxford: Oxford University Press.

Schumpeter, J. (1943), *Capitalism, Socialism and Democracy*, London: George Allen and Unwin.

Taylor-Gooby, P. (2001), *Welfare States under Pressure*, London: Sage.

Wood, S. (2001), Labour market regimes under threat. In P. Pierson (ed.), *The New Politics of the Welfare State*, Oxford: Oxford University Press.

2
Pressures on State Welfare in Post-industrial Societies: Is More or Less Better?

Mads Meier Jæger and Jon Kvist

Introduction

The work of Esping-Andersen (1990) on the *Three Worlds of Welfare Capitalism* marks a turning point in comparative welfare state research. Drawing on the insights of earlier research, Esping-Andersen distinguishes the historical development of three distinct configurations of state welfare that are by now classic starting points for welfare state scholars: the Social Democratic, the Conservative and the Liberal welfare state regimes. By doing so he discards the tendency of earlier research to view the welfare state and its historical development as a universal and a one-dimensional phenomenon. Acknowledging the existence of different types of welfare states provided a new locus of interest for the importance of welfare state diversity.

This work spurred a fast-growing and by now extensive body of research that has scrutinized the diversity of contemporary welfare states, the structural and social pressures associated with different welfare state regimes, as well as the policies aimed at reforming welfare states (e.g. Esping-Andersen 1996; Kitschelt *et al.* 1999; Ferrera and Rhodes 2000; Kuhnle 2000; Kautto *et al.* 2001). The thrust of this research in recent years has been on the impact of economic and social pressures in different welfare state regimes, and in particular on investigating how pressures are "filtered" by regimes into distinct policy responses. Comparative welfare state research has tended to become the business of political scientists with the prime focus on the meso-level: political institutions, power configurations, and policy processes.

In much of this literature, pressures on contemporary post-industrial societies supposedly fuel demands and needs for welfare state reforms that imply a curtailment of state welfare (Mishra 1999; Gilbert 2002). Scholars emphasizing the diversity of welfare states have introduced the concept of welfare state "restructuring" (adaptation, adjustment, etc.) to grasp the fact that welfare reform is multifaceted and entails more than retrenchment (Bonoli *et al.* 2000; Pierson 2001a). For example, Pierson (2001b) suggests that policy reform in the three welfare state regimes takes place along three general strategies of *cost containment*, *re-commodification*, and *recalibration*. Consequently, welfare state reforms may be just as much about restructuring as about retrenchment.

While this research provides important insights into the diversity and reform paths of welfare states, a number of issues have yet to be adequately addressed. We argue that too little attention has been paid to the societal pressures themselves that may or may not facilitate welfare reform. Today it is commonplace to argue that the welfare state is somehow adapting to economic, political and social pressures in post-industrial societies. These perceived pressures stem from globalization and Europeanization, ageing populations, changing labour markets and family structures, just to mention a few of the usual suspects.

In the following sections we challenge the dominant view that the welfare state is reacting to a set number of societal pressures. Weighing the evidence on needs and possibilities for welfare state reform through a critical literature review, we make a twofold argument. First, we argue that some of the perceived pressures have little, if any, impact on the welfare state. To the extent that these do influence welfare state reform, such pressures tend, on the whole, to call for more rather than less state welfare. This is not least because social needs with respect to e.g. labour markets and families have become much more diverse in post-industrial societies compared with the traditional, industrial era. Second, we point out that most of the contemporary pressures on post-industrial societies do not relate to welfare states *per se*, but rather to post-industrial societies more specifically. Consequently, the conceptual notions that pressures are tied specifically to the welfare state institution, which are often found in contemporary research, should be widened to include a society-centred perspective.

In the first section we outline the conceptual frame of reference. Which theoretical concepts of "pressures" have been used in the literature and which ones should we use to capture the diversity of contemporary welfare state pressures? In the following sections we discuss the perceived pressures on post-industrial societies as these are found to influence current welfare state reforms.

The Short History of Welfare State Pressures

The concepts of the pressures that face welfare states have changed in content over the past four decades or so, but the idea that welfare states are continually encountering some specific kind of pressure is by no means new to comparative welfare state research (cf. Alber 1988; Esping-Andersen 1999; Jæger and Kvist 2000). The notion of "pressure" is used in this context as the theoretical term for denoting the objective forces that strain the welfare state. It includes the whole range of economic, political, and social forces both endogenous and exogenous to welfare states that have been identified in the literature. Table 1 presents the four most important theoretical concepts of welfare-state pressures evident from the literature since the 1960s.

In the 1960s and early 1970s writers like Philip Cutright, Frederick Pryor and Harold Wilensky saw the emergence of the welfare state as essentially a functional response to the new social problems that emerged with industrialism, urbanization, demographic alterations in the populations, and the maturing of the capitalist economy (Wilensky and Lebeaux 1958; Cutright 1965; Pryor 1968; Wilensky 1975). These pressures were seen as being curbed by the growing welfare states in tandem with high economic growth.

By the early 1970s economic recession and a resurgence of (neo-)Marxist (O'Connor 1973; Gough 1979; Offe 1984) and (neo-)liberal thinking (Kristol 1971; King 1975; Hayek 1994) prompted a much more pessimistic interpretation of both the pressures faced by welfare states and their possibilities of handling these pressures. Welfare states were now deemed to be in states of crisis for a number of reasons, notably because of the conflicting aims of wanting at the same time to generate tax revenues and to uphold popular support. The consequences of the crises also manifested themselves in fiscal instability, political uncontrollability, and diminishing social solidarity in the family and in the institutions of civil society. The pressures were thus viewed mostly as vested in macro-economic conditions. It was widely believed that the external pressures following the economic recessions of the 1970s would "trigger" the structural problems inherent in the Western welfare states and that these would change radically.

From the early 1990s perceptions of pressures on welfare state development changed from their being viewed as jointly endogenous and exogenous to mostly exogenous "challenges", and the question of welfare state retrenchment and restructuring as responses to exogenous pressures has since dominated the literature (Pierson 1994; Clayton and Pontusson 1998; Scarbrough 2000; Millar 2002). At the same time the effects of economic and political internationalization on states' capacities for securing and controlling their fiscal bases and political sovereignty came to be a focus of research (Katzenstein 1985; Schwartz 2001). Economic and political pressures, often in the form of economic globalization and political integration within the EU, were now treated as independent variables affecting welfare states' possibilities of reform and systemic restructuring (e.g. Bonoli *et al.* 2000; Taylor-Gooby 2001; Pierson 2001a).

Over the last 40 years, the nature and scope of pressures on welfare states have thus been conceptualized quite differently. Interestingly, the question of whether these pressures are empirically observable, and to what degree they might pertain to welfare societies more generally rather than welfare states *per se*, has not been investigated much since the welfare state itself was the primary object of study. An underlying causal assumption in the literature on welfare state pressures is that policy reform is a virtually automatic response.

However, recent research has demonstrated that, even in the light of persistent problems of low economic growth and high unemployment during the past decades, the many European welfare states have in fact been remarkably resilient to profound retrenchment and that state welfare in some areas is even expanding. What is more, countries least exposed to "permanent austerity" (Pierson 2001b) have expanded state welfare; that is "change without challenge" (Goul Andersen 2002). Such findings challenge the causal assumption found in earlier research, and we need to reconsider which pressures on welfare states are more important than others. As a consequence, in this review article we introduce the concept of "controversy" in addition to the familiar

Table 1

Four concepts of welfare state pressures

Concept	Adaptation	Crisis	Challenge	Controversy
Time period	1960s/1970s	1970s/1980s	Mid-1990s	Late 1990s–
Societal context	Industrial society	(Post-)Industrial society	Post-industrial society	Post-industrial society
Notion of pressure	Exogenous objective pressures of industrialism	Pressures are symptoms of structural contradictions/deficiencies in welfare states	Pressures pose calling for political action	Objective implications of pressure contested
Policy impact	Gradual reform/adaptation	Radical systemic reform imminent/required	Gradual adaptation, retrenchment/restructuring	Status quo—irrelevant, expansion
Welfare state context	Emerging/expanding	Consolidating/mature	Mature	Mature
Proposed response pattern	More state welfare	Radically less state welfare	Less and/or more efficient state welfare	Mostly more state welfare

vocabulary of "crisis" and "challenge". This concept is used when we judge that the impact of some of the alleged pressures found in the research literature has not, when reconsidered critically, been substantiated. This is, for example, our judgement in the case of the effects of globalization on welfare states. Thus, when reviewing the literature we use the notion of "controversy" in cases, first, when the specific pressure is contested theoretically, and second, when empirical consequences of pressures are ambiguous or have not been found to be of significance to welfare states. This is also the case when evidence suggests that pressures pertain to post-industrial societies rather than welfare states as such.

In the remainder of the paper we review the contemporary pressures on welfare states that have been proposed in the research literature using this analytical distinction of crises, challenges and controversies. First, the exogenous pressures of globalization and Europeanization are discussed. Second, we turn to the mainly endogenous pressures of demographic developments, changes in post-industrial labour markets, and finally the question of the persisting popularity of public welfare programmes.

External Pressures: Globalization, Europeanization and Migration

Two particular pressures that are deemed as exogenous to national welfare states and which have drawn considerable attention in recent years are those of globalization and Europeanization. Globalization is often portrayed as a multifaceted phenomenon affecting welfare states in many and diverse ways. In particular, economic globalization is highlighted in relation to social policy. The basic thrust in most of the economic globalization literature is that, as competition and deregulation in financial and capital markets have grown rapidly in the postwar period, and since national economies have increasingly become dependent on exports in internationalized markets, states have effectively both lost control over their means of revenue and rendered fiscal policy instruments ineffective (Cosh *et al.* 1992; Mishra 1999). As a consequence, economic globalization has triggered a "race to the bottom" of social spending in that national welfare states, in their efforts to attract capital and cultivate markets for foreign investments, have been forced to restrain or cut back on public spending. The result of this competitive adaptation on an international scale is that welfare states enter a vicious circle of outbidding each other in terms of stimulating favourable business climates, through such policies as tax exemption or reduction, lax job protection, low environmental standards, and infrastructural advantages, creating an international trend of what is often referred to as "downward harmonization" of social protection (Martin and Schumann 1997; Greider 1997; Crotty 2000).

While pessimistic interpretations of the impact of economic globalization on welfare states are clearly dominant, alternative scenarios do exist (see Bowles and Wagman 1997; Burgoon 2001). Some writers suggest that economic globalization and welfare state policies need not be in tension, not least because increased trade openness and economic vulnerability tends to foster demand for welfare compensation (Garrett and Lange 1991; Swank 1998).

Yet others claim that the correlates of economic globalization (increased capital mobility, trade openness and deregulation of financial markets) have no significant impact on welfare states at all (e.g. Lipsey *et al.* 1995; Cline 1997). The main argument put forward in this literature is that the vast majority of all trade and economic activity still takes place within geographically close regions, and notably the USA, Western Europe, and Japan. Additionally, while financial and trade markets have surely been internationalized, so has the control and regulation of these markets through powerful international organizations and institutions (e.g. the WTO, the IMF, the EU, and NAFTA) (see Rieger and Leibfried 1998, 2001). As such, there need not be any direct causal link between economic globalization and welfare state policies.

The arguments developed in the studies of the impact of economic globalization on the welfare state remain tenuous for a number of important reasons. Firstly, a commonly accepted theoretical definition of the concept of economic globalization has yet to be developed. Different studies use different definitions of globalization which are often exceedingly abstract and sometimes mutually exclusive (Burgoon 2001; Carroll 2002). As a consequence there is little or no comparability between studies and thus no accumulative knowledge of the effects of globalization on the welfare state. Second, there is a lack of a consistent body of empirical studies of the impact of globalization on welfare state efforts (e.g. Rhodes 1996; Schwartz 2001). Early empirical studies like Cameron (1978) and more recent studies by Rodrik (1997), Garrett (1998), and Garrett and Mitchell (2001), among others, find no conclusive support for the "downward harmonization" thesis in the OECD area. Rather, while empirical studies do not find unambiguous evidence for the (either positive or negative) effects of economic globalization,[1] much evidence seems to indicate that developments within national states themselves (especially in labour markets and in demographic structures) or in technology exert far more important pressures on welfare states (e.g. Lipsey *et al.* 1995; Iversen and Cusack 2001). As such, the notion that there is a direct causal link between economic globalization and welfare state development remains contentious (Schwartz 2001). Arguably, as is highlighted by Pierson (2001a) and Scharpf and Schmidt (2000), the growing internationalization and deregulation of economies on the whole tends to reduce the number of effective policy instruments available to governments to control their political economies. This trend is well documented in comparative welfare state research, and it is much less controversial than the assumption of causal logic found in the globalization literature. Consequently, despite the popularity of the concept during the 1990s, we deem economic globalization as no more than a "controversy" with respect to its impacts on the welfare state.

Does Europe Matter?

Political concern about the impact of the EU on national welfare states is reflected in a growing literature. The interplay between the national welfare states and the supranational level in the EU is scrutinized in studies looking at the development of European integration in social policies as well as studies looking at the impact of European integration on national welfare states, the so-called Europeanization studies.

Accounts of how Europeanization and European integration affect national welfare states underline both intentional as well as unintentional aspects of this process. According to neo-functionalist integration theory intentional efforts and spillover effects at the supranational level will result in harmonization of national policies. The Amsterdam Treaty of 1997 made employment among the prime objectives of the EU and also prohibits discrimination based on gender and ethnicity, just as the Social Charter was incorporated in the Treaty itself (for the preceding development see Mosley 1990 and Leibfried 2000). This fact has resulted in three so-called European strategies for, respectively, employment, inclusion, and old age pensions, and more strategies are in the making. The strategies are backed up institutionally and financially by various funds, most notably the European Social Fund, and procedures such as setting up partnership projects and the drawing up, evaluation and monitoring of national action plans. At the same time, however, these strategies are based on the open method of coordination: member states agree on common objectives, but are free to choose how to meet them, and there are no legal or economic forms of sanctioning in case of non-compliance.

When it comes to hard law only about ten directives directly affect social policy. The maternity directive (92/85/EEC) stipulates a maternity leave of a minimum of 14 weeks, and the parental leave directive (96/34/EEC) ensures a parental leave of three months and the right to absence from work in case of serious illness or injury within the family. Eight directives prohibit discrimination on grounds of gender, ethnicity, age and disability in relation to both employment and various aspects of social policy. These directives aim to secure, for example, the equal treatment of men and women.

This lack of a fully-fledged European social policy fits well with findings in other studies of European integration since the middle of the 1980s. These studies tend to treat the EU as an international regime institutionalizing forms of collective action among nation states (for a critical review see Pierson 1996). Intergovernmentalists insist that member states are preoccupied with maintaining their sovereignty, and that the creation of supranational institutions only takes place when these are instruments for lowering transaction costs, allowing for collective action and diminishing problems of information. Consequently, member states will only give increased power to the EU "in so far as it strengthens, rather than weakens, their control over domestic affairs" (Moravcik 1993: 507).

Other authors maintain that indirect spillover effects may be transmitted from one policy area to another. This is not least due to pressures towards greater similarities in economic and fiscal policies, institutional arrangements and levels of provision in the EU member states (Streeck 1996; Hagen 1999; Leibfried and Pierson 2000). Nevertheless, a certain degree of schizophrenia can be detected as the same authors also note that the very existence of different institutions, whether polity systems or policy programmes, render the creation of European social policies unlikely (e.g. Pierson 1996). For example, the different welfare regimes in Europe are likely to hamper the development of a uniform welfare model, as is also evident from recent empirical studies (Scharpf 1997; Kautto and Kvist 2002).

Moreover, Europeanization of welfare states may also come about as a by-product of the general political and economic integration of public policies in the EU (Finnemore and Sikkink 1998). Economic and social pressures—perceived or real—from the establishment of the EU with free movement of goods, services, capital and labour may also be of significance. In fact, perhaps the most disputed EU threats to national welfare states concern social dumping and social tourism. The social dumping argument is a regional version of the globalization thesis that states that companies speculate in national labour market standards with regard to taxes, wages and job legislation, and that governments in response lower standards in order to retain or attract capital and companies (Alber and Standing 2000; Guillén and Matsaganis 2000).

There is nothing "social" nor "touristic" about the argument of social tourism which says that EU nationals from countries with poor social benefits migrate to countries with better and accessible social benefits. Currently, the coming enlargement of the EU fuels fear that such migration may come from the Eastern parts of Europe. Recent studies find that it is particularly labour markets in border regions in Austria and Germany that are most likely to be affected (for an overview, see Commission of the European Communities 2001). Estimates of the scope of migration from new to old EU members after 10 to 15 years varies between 700,000 and 2.7 million persons and, after the accession of Bulgaria and Romania, between 1.4 and 4.2 million. Despite such disagreement, coming intra-community migration from the East to the West of Europe cannot match the increased demand for labour caused by ageing populations (see Fuchs and Thon 1999 for Germany). Hence, increased intra-community migration of workers does not constitute an insurance against ageing populations in the West, but rather some threat of brain drain from the East. In this respect improved social policies may help to retain workers in coming member states (see Kovacs 2000).

While there are few signs of direct impact on social policies, the stability pact of the Economic and Monetary Union (EMU) may hinder member states from pursuing other policies. The convergence criteria damp down possibilities of leading an expansive fiscal policy even in times of sluggish economic growth and growing unemployment, as currently witnessed in France and Germany. In other words, the combination of EMU convergence criteria and the relatively modest existence of EU social policies make the pressures on national welfare states from Europe controversial.

In sum, during the 1990s reference to "external pressures" from the European context began to supplement established criticism against welfare state arrangements based on internal pressures (see Esping-Andersen 1999; Jæger and Kvist 2000; Kersbergen 2000). However, the bulk of empirical cross-national studies conclude that European integration has not progressed far in the traditional areas of the welfare state and that claims of a Europeanization of welfare policies are difficult to sustain (Kuhnle 2000; Scharpf and Schmidt 2000; Taylor-Gooby 2001; Kautto et al. 2001; Kvist 2002). The notion of European social policy or a European welfare state is very small and fragmented, and national welfare states undertake by far the most tasks of the welfare state. Europeanization thus has yet to manifest itself as a challenge to the Western European welfare states.

Ageing Populations

Ageing of the population is perhaps the biggest and least contested component of the demographic challenges. The baby boom generation of the Second World War retires within the next 5–17 years, and since they did not reproduce themselves to establish a stable population growth, the share of the working-age population will decline at the same time as the share of the elderly rises. Both the EU 15 and the 10 accession states on average will experience an increase of 8 percentage points in the population share of the elderly from 2000 to 2025 (Kvist 2002). Obviously, this puts pressure on national governments to maximize the number of potential workers.

In some countries low rates of female labour market participation have meant that efforts are made to increase the share of women on the labour market just as the EU has set a target of a female employment–population rate at 60 per cent by 2010 (see table 2). In general this calls for more rather than less state welfare in terms of child and elder care services that help women to establish a better balance between work and family life. Such a professionalization of care services, however, may be challenged by a shortage of labour. For example, in the countries that already have comprehensive public social services like the Nordic ones, where the welfare state is an important employer for women (Hernes 1987; Kolberg 1991), national studies predict that around one in four of current female students must become nurses and social workers if current levels of provision are to be kept in the future.

Shorter Working Life

The challenge of the ageing population has to be seen in the light of a tendency across countries and socio-economic groups to make a later entry into, and an earlier exit from the labour market, as well as greater longevity in European countries. In total, this means that fewer working people in the future will have to support more people outside the labour market (OECD 2000).

When people retire later they pay taxes for longer and draw benefits for a shorter period. This helps explain why the EU has set a target of an employment–population rate of 50 per cent for people aged 55 to 65 years. Table 2 shows that less than a handful of the 25 countries meet this target. The elder part of the working-age population have generally low participation rates in all countries irrespective of welfare regime. Whether a shorter working life calls for more or less state welfare is controversial. On the one hand, it may require government to make unpopular decisions to reduce early exit. This would be seen as retrenchment by most scholars, and definitely by the persons concerned. On the other hand, such retrenchment may not alone help increase labour supply among the elder part of the working-age population. More state welfare measures may also be needed, for example, to combat age-based discrimination and provide employers and the "elderly" with greater incentives and possibilities.

Table 2

EU employment–population targets and rates according to country, gender and age, 2001

	Population aged 15 to 65 years			Population aged 55 to 65 years
	Total	Men	Women	Total
EU targets for 2010	70.0	—	60.0	50.0
EU 15 average	63.9	73.0	54.9	38.5
Current EU member states				
Denmark	76.2	80.2	72.0	58.0
Finland	68.1	70.9	65.4	45.9
Sweden	71.7	73.0	70.4	66.5
Netherlands	74.1	82.8	65.2	39.6
Belgium	59.9	69.1	50.5	24.1
Luxembourg	62.9	74.8	50.9	24.4
France	63.1	70.3	56.1	31.0
Germany	65.8	72.6	58.8	37.7
Austria	68.4	76.7	60.1	28.6
Italy	54.8	68.5	41.1	28.0
Spain	56.3	70.9	41.9	38.9
Portugal	68.9	76.9	61.1	45.7
Greece	55.4	70.8	40.9	38.0
Ireland	65.7	76.4	55.0	46.8
UK	71.7	78.3	65.1	52.3
Coming EU member states				
Estonia	61.1	65.6	56.9	48.6
Latvia	58.9	61.9	56.1	36.4
Lithuania	58.6	59.8	57.4	39.1
Poland	53.8	59.2	48.4	30.5
Hungary	56.3	63.3	49.6	23.7
Czech Republic	65.0	73.2	57.0	36.9
Slovakia	56.7	61.8	51.8	22.5
Slovenia	63.6	68.6	58.6	23.4
Bulgaria	50.7	53.6	47.9	23.9
Romania	63.3	68.6	58.6	50.5

Source: Eurostat (2002).

Ethnic Minorities

In many European countries, the—in most cases increasing—share of ethnic minorities in the population is often viewed as a problem. From a sociological perspective it may, for example, be a topic for discussion whether increasingly diverse populations are able to share the core values and norms that create the normative foundation of the welfare state. If not, social cohesion in the welfare state may be problematic. However, with regard to demographically induced redistribution challenges related to the ageing of populations discussed above, the ethnic minorities constitute a possibility for securing the economic sustainability of the welfare state rather than a threat. This is because of the age profile of ethnic minorities that is generally somewhat younger than the majority of natives. Coupled with lower labour market participation among many ethnic minority groups, this may provide a potential for increased labour supply in so far as ethnic minorities obtain jobs in the formal economy. Hence, from a demographic and economic point of view, increased shares of ethnic minorities are not a threat but rather a possibility for the securing of the financial basis of the welfare state. Welfare reforms aimed at increasing labour market participation among ethnic minorities could thus be a means of alleviating part of the demographic challenge.

In sum, low fertility among the post-Second World War generation is the main reason why welfare states are currently facing an ageing of the population. This puts pressure on the welfare state due to an expected increase in outlays, but, most importantly, a decrease of revenue to finance welfare schemes. The pressure is exacerbated by the tendency of older segments of able-bodied people in the labour market to retire earlier, and, probably to a lesser degree, by increased longevity. To the extent that it is possible to increase the effective retirement age as well as the labour market participation of women and growing population shares of ethnic minorities, such demographic challenges may be met in part. However, for this to succeed more, rather than less, public welfare and policy is likely to be required.

Individualization

The need for welfare state reform is also sparked by an increased individualization in society (e.g. Giddens 1991). The traditional family pattern of a male breadwinner is being replaced with a diversity of family forms, including a greater share of single-parent and two-breadwinner households (Lewis 2001). To the extent that such families are able to balance family responsibilities with participation in the labour market, social policies may be accommodated to facilitate these new family configurations. Balancing work and family life is thus seen as an increasingly important issue confronting the welfare state on both the EU and national political agendas. In particular policies supporting the traditional family in Continental and Southern Europe are seen as constituting disincentives for female labour market participation and fertility (see Esping-Andersen 2002). The counter position in Scandinavia of encompassing and subsidized care services for children and the elderly may not only be an incentive for fertility and female labour market participation, but also come at the price of gender-segregated labour markets and penalties on women's wages (e.g. Gupta *et al.* 2001).

In general, the diversification of individual life courses, de-standardization of career and labour market participation patterns is most likely to call for more flexible social policy arrangements. In many respects welfare states have so far catered for the norms of the "traditional" social risks associated with the nuclear families in industrialized society. Such social protection is provided primarily by income transfers in events like unemployment, sickness, old age, death (for survivors), and disability, schemes that often assume couples are in stable marriages (e.g. Arber *et al.* 2001). Married couples also still tend to have advantageous protection compared to cohabiting couples with respect to, for example, taxes, parental custody, and inheritance rules. In short, women and emerging family types are often discriminated against.

Importantly, care services are also to a large extent provided by the unwaged labour of women. Child and elder care as well as active social and labour market measures are just some of the policies called for in order to, respectively, better reconcile work and family life and improve the employment prospects of, especially, vulnerable groups in the labour market.

Given the growing share of singles, atypical families and a future shortage of labour, the need to "individualize" social security and increase the service side of the welfare state has grown significantly. Consequently, a substantial challenge to contemporary welfare states lies in modernizing existing welfare arrangements to accommodate the social needs arising from individualization of life courses and de-standardization of families in post-industrial societies.

The Popularity of the Welfare State

During the 1960s and 1970s most welfare-state scholars claimed that the welfare states of Western Europe were suffering from an almost universal lack of legitimacy, and, as a consequence, they were facing a crisis of legitimacy (O'Connor 1973; Gough 1979). The "conventional" wisdom that public support for the welfare state was dangerously low persisted until the mid-1980s, when newly founded cross-national surveys documented otherwise.[2] Comparative studies have since then demonstrated quite unambiguously that the general level of support for most aspects of public welfare provision is very high in all Western European countries (see also Papadakis and Bean 1993; Taylor-Gooby 1995). Additionally, the high level of support has been found to be relatively constant (at least) since the mid-1980s, and, interestingly, positive attitudes do not differ systematically between different welfare state regimes (Svallfors 1997; Bean and Papadakis 1998). Finally, studies show that the biggest differences in attitudes towards the welfare state are not to be found between different countries, but rather within countries themselves. Most importantly, individuals' political preferences and a range of socio-economic characteristics are the main determinants of positive or negative attitudes (e.g. Papadakis 1993; Svallfors 1996).

Recent empirical findings have turned the legitimacy debate of the 1970s on its head. The decisive question today is not what the consequences of lacking public support mean for the sustainability of the welfare state, but rather which challenge its persisting popularity poses for the future of welfare. Neo-institutional theory within political science holds that the popularity of the welfare state is attributed to a self-reinforcing property in that, as increasing shares of the population have become recipients or providers of some form of welfare benefit or service, then these people will react against attempts at curtailing already-gained social rights. Consequently, the risk of electoral damage tends to make political actors and parties refrain from radical cuts and maintain the political status quo (Pierson 1994).

Still, the fact that significant reforms have actually taken place during the 1990s in the European welfare states begs additional explanations. One strand of theory argues that the opinion patterns of executive and political elites are different from, and typically more pro-reformist than, those of the general public (Sihvo and Uusitalo 1995; Blomberg and Kroll 1999). As a consequence, the propensity for carrying through policy change has increased. Furthermore, contextual factors such as the social construction of economic recession in the public sphere may ease voters' acceptance of cutbacks in dire times (Cox 2001). This means that opposition to retrenchment or restructuring of the welfare state may become easier, but by no means easy. Consequently, weighing "push" and "pull" factors we find that the popularity of state welfare in the general public constitutes an important challenge to contemporary welfare states. Political developments over the past few decades show that reforming welfare states to meet new social demands in post-industrial societies is a difficult undertaking because existing welfare state programmes maintain their popularity over time. Thus, the political task of keeping the welfare state in line with changing needs by reforming or abolishing existing or creating new welfare programmes is also likely to be a prominent challenge in the future.

Conclusion

We find that the notion of "crisis" used by some scholars as an all-encompassing condition that threatens the foundations of the welfare states has no empirical justification and should be abandoned. Current pressures on post-industrial societies are not potentially cataclysmic to welfare states. Rather we find that pressures differ in nature and in impact: challenges call for some policy response, whereas the impact of controversies remains an empirical question. Indeed, it is often difficult a priori to establish a direct causal link from pressures on post-industrial societies to welfare reform. Most contemporary pressures are often controversies in that their potential impact is long-term and relatively uncertain.

The review also shows that the impact of the alleged exogenous challenges of globalization and Europeanization on welfare states has yet to be demonstrated and must be considered as controversial. Globalization remains little more than a "buzz"-concept, mainly because its existence and impact on welfare states has not so far been established convincingly in the literature. European integration may in the longer run affect national welfare states, but not in the short- or medium-term perspective. National institutions and interests tend to prevail over the diffusion of ideas and the establishment of supranational institutions.

National endogenous pressures seem more important and less ambiguous. Demographic change is one of the most significant challenges common to the European countries. Low fertility and the increasing share of elderly in the population pose a significant challenge to economic sustainability. Furthermore, the relative decline in the working-aged population forces governments to seek new ways to increase employment, not least among the oldest segments of the labour force, women, ethnic minorities and groups on the margins of the labour market. In many of these instances extensions of welfare programmes and labour market policies, rather than curtailments, may be an appropriate solution, especially provision of childcare services, family benefits, and active labour market programmes. Activating labour "reservoirs" may be an important counterbalance to demographic and labour market challenges.

The welfare state must also handle the increasing individualization of career and family patterns in post-industrial societies. These developments, especially in the long-term perspective, are likely to exert pressures for more flexible and customized social security programmes, both with respect to transfer incomes and social services. A final endogenous challenge consists in reforming welfare programmes with entrenched popularity.

On the theoretical level, this review suggests that mature welfare states face a partly new set of challenges in post-industrial societies compared to the "traditional" problems associated with the industrial era. New diversities and social risks have emerged, and the evidence presented suggests that these new challenges should not necessarily be met with curtailment but rather with expansion of welfare programmes. Moreover, pressures on post-industrial societies not only create a need for welfare reform, but also give rise to possibilities for welfare reform. For example, increased labour shortages make it possible to direct resources away from compensation in the form of different types of benefits for the unemployed to a greater emphasis on preventive measures, also to groups that in times of high unemployment may have been neglected (for example in the current wave of European disability pension reforms). In short, the content of pressures and their relationship to welfare reform need further examination. Much of societal change seems to call for more rather than less state welfare; new types of welfare states may be needed in a post-industrial society.

Notes

The authors would like to thank Eero Carroll, John Clarke, and Niels Ploug for helpful comments on an earlier version of the paper.
1. Empirically, economic globalization is usually operationalized by e.g. the total volume of international trade, proportion of foreign direct investment relative to GDP, degree of financial openness, and low wage imports.
2. Especially important comparative data sets are the International Social Survey Programme (ISSP), The European Values Survey (EVS) and the Eurobarometer surveys. Beginning in 2003, the new European Social Survey (ESS) will continue this trend (see: http://www.europeansocialsurvey.org).

References

Alber, J. (1988), Is there a crisis of the welfare state? Cross-national evidence from Europe, North America, and Japan, *European Sociological Review*, 4, 3: 181–208.
Alber, J. and Standing, G. (2000), Europe in a comparative global context, *Journal of European Social Policy*, 10, 2: 99–119.
Arber, S., Ginn, J. and Street, D. (eds) (2001), *Women and Pensions*, London: Open University Press.

Bean, C. and Papadakis, E. (1998), A comparison of mass attitudes towards the welfare state in different institutional regimes, 1985–1990, *International Journal of Public Opinion Research*, 10, 3: 211–36.

Blomberg, H. and Kroll, C. (1999), Who wants to preserve the "Scandinavian service state"? In S. Svallfors and P. Taylor-Gooby (eds), *The End of the Welfare State? Responses to State Retrenchment*, London: Routledge.

Bonoli, G., George, V. and Taylor-Gooby, P. (2000), *European Welfare State Futures: Towards a Theory of Retrenchment*, London: Polity Press.

Bowles, P. and Wagman, B. (1997), Globalization and the welfare state: four hypotheses and some empirical evidence, *Eastern Economic Journal*, 23, 3: 317–27.

Burgoon, B. (2001), Globalization and welfare compensation: disentangling the ties that bind, *International Organization*, 55, 3: 509–51.

Cameron, D. (1978), The expansion of the public economy: a comparative analysis, *American Political Science Review*, 72: 1243–61.

Carroll, E. (2002), The clear and present danger of the worldwide "globaloney" industry: a critical review on concepts of globalization in welfare state research and social scientific opinion pieces since the mid-1990s. Paper presented at the EU COST A15 Work Group Meeting, Florence, 11–12 October.

Clayton, R. and Pontusson, J. (1998), Welfare-state retrenchment revisited: entitlement cuts, public sector restructuring, and inegalitarian trends in advanced capitalist societies, *World Politics*, 51, 1: 67–98.

Cline, W. R. (1997), *Trade and Income Distribution*, Washington, DC: Institute for International Economics.

Commission of the European Communities (2001), *Enlargement of the European Union: An Historic Opportunity*, Brussels: Directorate-General for Enlargement.

Cosh, A. D., Hughes, A. and Singh, A. (1992), Openness, financial innovation, changing patterns of ownership, and the structure of financial markets. In T. Banuri and J. B. Schor (eds), *Financial Openness and National Autonomy: Constraints and Opportunities*, Oxford: Clarendon Press.

Cox, R. H. (2001), The social construction of an imperative: why welfare reform happened in Denmark and the Netherlands, but not in Germany, *World Politics*, 53, 3: 463–98.

Crotty, J. (2000), Structural contradictions of the global neoliberal regime, *Review of Radical Political Economics*, 32, 3: 361–8.

Cutright, P. (1965), Political structure, economic development, and national social security programs, *American Journal of Sociology*, 70, 5: 537–50.

Esping-Andersen, G. (1990), *The Three Worlds of Welfare Capitalism*, Cambridge: Polity Press.

Esping-Andersen, G. (ed.) (1996), *Welfare States in Transition: National Adaptations in Global Economies*, London: Sage.

Esping-Andersen, G. (1999), *The Social Foundations of Postindustrial Economies*, Oxford: Oxford University Press.

Esping-Andersen, G. (ed.) (2002), *Why We Need a New Welfare State*, Oxford: Oxford University Press.

Eurostat (2002), *Employment in Europe 2002*, Luxembourg: European Communities.

Ferrera, M. and Rhodes, M. (eds) (2000), *Recasting European Welfare States*, London: Frank Cass.

Finnemore, M. and Sikkink, K. (1998), International norm dynamics and political change, *International Organization*, 52, 4: 887–917.

Fuchs, J. and Thon, M. (1999), Nach 2010 sinkt das Angebot an Arbeitskräften— Selbst hohe Zuwanderung werden diesen Trend nicht stoppen können, *IAB Kursbericht*, 4: 3–6.

Garrett, G. and Lange, P. (1991), Political responses to interdependence: what's "left" for the Left? *International Organization*, 45, 4: 539–64.

Garrett, G. (1998), *Partisan Politics in the World Economy*, Cambridge: Cambridge University Press.

Garrett, G. and Mitchell, D. (2001), Globalization, government spending and taxation in the OECD, *European Journal of Political Research*, 39: 145–77.

Giddens, A. (1991), *Modernity and Self-identity*, Cambridge: Polity Press.

Gilbert, N. (2002), *Transformation of the Welfare State: The Silent Surrender of Public Responsibility*, Oxford: Oxford University Press.

Gough, I. (1979), *The Political Economy of the Welfare State*, London: Macmillan Press.

Goul Andersen, J. (2002), Change without challenge? Welfare states, social construction of challenge and dynamics of path dependency. In J. Clasen (ed.), *What Future for Social Security? Debates and Reforms in National and Cross-national Perspectives*, Bristol: Policy Press.

Greider, W. (1997), *One World Ready or Not: The Manic Logic of Global Capitalism*, New York: Simon and Schuster.

Guillén, A. and Matsaganis, M. (2000), Testing the "social dumping" hypothesis in southern Europe: welfare policies in Greece and Spain during the last 20 years, *Journal of European Social Policy*, 10, 2: 120–45.

Gupta, N., Oaxaca, R. and Smith, N. (2001), Swimming upstream, floating downstream: trends in the U.S. and Danish gender wage gaps, *CLS Working Paper*, 01–06.

Hagen, K. (1999), Towards a Europeanization of social policies? A Scandinavian perspective. In D. Bouget and B. Palier (eds), *Comparing Social Welfare Systems in Nordic Europe and France*, Paris: MIRE-DREES.

Hayek, F. A. (1994) [1945], *The Road to Serfdom*, Chicago: University of Chicago Press.

Hernes, H. (1987), *Welfare States and Women Power*, Oslo: Norwegian University Press.

Iversen, T. and Cusack, T. R. (2001), The causes of welfare state expansion: deindustrialization or globalization? *World Politics*, 52, 3: 313–49.

Jæger, M. M. and Kvist, J. (2000), Skiftende forestillinger om velfærdsstatens kriser [Changing perceptions of the crises of the welfare state], *Nordisk Sosialt Arbeid*, 20, 4: 219–33.

Katzenstein, P. (1985), *Small States in World Markets*, Ithaca, NY: Cornell University Press.

Kautto, M., Fritzell, J., Hvinden, B., Kvist, J. and Uusitalo, H. (eds) (2001), *Nordic Welfare States in the European Context*, London: Routledge.

Kautto, J. and Kvist, J. (2002), Distinct or extinct? Nordic welfare states in a global and European context, *Global Social Policy*, 2, 2: 189–208.

Kersbergen, K. V. (2000), The declining resistance of welfare states to change. In S. Kuhnle (ed.), *Survival of the European Welfare State*, London: Routledge.

King, A. (1975), Overload: problems of governing in the 1970s, *Political Studies*, 23, 2/3: 284–96.

Kitschelt, H., Lange, P. and Marks, G. (eds) (1999), *Continuity and Change in Contemporary Capitalism*, Cambridge: Cambridge University Press.

Kolberg, J. E. (ed.) (1991), *The Welfare State as Employer*, New York: M. E. Sharpe.

Kovacs, J. M. (2000), Approaching the EU and reaching the US? Transforming welfare regimes in East-Central Europe, *EUI Working Papers*, Robert Schuman Centre for Advanced Studies RSC no. 2000/50.

Kristol, I. (1971), Welfare: the best of intentions, the worst of results, *Atlantic Monthly* (August).

Kuhnle, S. (ed.) (2000), *Survival of the European Welfare State*, London: Routledge.

Kvist, J. (ed.) (2002), *Velfærdspolitik i et nyt Europa* [Welfare Policy in a New Europe], Copenhagen: Danish National Institute of Social Research.

Leibfried, S. (2000), National welfare states, European integration and globalization: a perspective for the next century, *Social Policy & Administration*, 34, 1: 44–63.

Leibfried, S. and Pierson, P. (2000), European social policy. In H. Wallace and W. Wallace (eds), *Policy-making in the European Union*, 4th edn, Oxford: Oxford University Press.

Lewis, J. (2001), The decline of the male breadwinner model: the implications for work and care, *Social Politics*, 8, 2: 152–70.

Lipsey, R., Blomstrom, M. and Ramstetter, E. (1995), *Internationalised Production in World Output*, NBER Working Paper no. 5385.

Martin, H.-P. and Schumann, H. (1997), *The Global Trap: Globalization and the Assault on Democracy and Prosperity*, London: Zed Books.

Millar, J. (2002), Diminishing welfare: the case of the United Kingdom. In G. S. Goldberg and M. G. Rosenthal (eds), *Diminishing Welfare. A Cross-national Study of Social Provision*, Westport, CT: Auburn House.

Mishra, R. (1999), *Globalization and the Welfare State*, Cheltenham: Edward Elgar Publishing.

Moravcik, A. (1993), Preferences and power in the European Community: a liberal intergovernmentalist approach, *Journal of Common Market Studies*, 31, 4: 471–524.

Mosley, H. (1990), The social dimension of European integration, *International Labour Review*, 129, 2: 147–62.

O'Connor, J. (1973), *The Fiscal Crisis of the State*, New York: St Martin's Press.

OECD (2000), *Employment Outlook*, Paris: OECD.

Offe, C. (1984), *Contradictions of the Welfare State*, Cambridge MA: MIT Press.

Papadakis, E. (1993), Class interests, class politics and welfare state regime, *British Journal of Sociology*, 44, 2: 249–77.

Papadakis, E. and Bean, C. (1993), Popular support for the welfare state: a comparison between institutional regimes, *Journal of Public Policy*, 13, 3: 227–54.

Pierson, P. (1994), *Dismantling the Welfare State? Reagan, Thatcher, and the Politics of Retrenchment*, Cambridge: Cambridge University Press.

Pierson, P. (1996), The path to European integration: a historical institutionalist analysis, *Comparative Political Studies*, 29, 2: 123–63.

Pierson, P. (ed.) (2001a), *The New Politics of the Welfare State*, Oxford: Oxford University Press.

Pierson, P. (2001b), Coping with permanent austerity: welfare state restructuring in affluent societies. In P. Pierson (ed.), *The New Politics of the Welfare State*, Oxford: Oxford University Press.

Pryor, F. L. (1968), *Public Expenditures in Communist and Capitalist Nations*, Homewood, IL: Irwin.

Rhodes, M. (1996), Globalization and West European welfare states: a critical review of recent debates, *Journal of European Social Policy*, 6, 4: 305–27.

Rieger, E. and Leibfried, S. (1998), Welfare state limits to globalization, *Politics and Society*, 26, 3: 361–88.

Rieger, E. and Leibfried, S. (2001), Welfare state mercantilism: the relations between democratic social policy and the world market. In E. Rieger and S. Leibfried (eds), *Limits to Globalization*, Cambridge: Polity Press.

Rodrik, D. (1997), *Has Globalization Gone Too Far*, Washington, DC: Institute for International Economics.

Scarbrough, E. (2000), West European welfare states: the old politics of retrenchment, *European Journal of Political Research*, 38: 225–59.

Scharpf, F. (1997), Economic integration, democracy and the welfare state, *Journal of European Public Policy*, 4, 1: 18–36.

Scharpf, F. and Schmidt, V. (eds) (2000), *Welfare and Work in the Open Economy: From Vulnerability to Competitiveness*, Oxford: Oxford University Press.

Schwartz, H. (2001), Round up the usual suspects! Globalization, domestic politics, and welfare state change. In P. Pierson (ed.), *The New Politics of the Welfare State*, Oxford: Oxford University Press.

Sihvo, T. and Uusitalo, H. (1995), Economic crises and support for the welfare state in Finland 1975–1993, *Acta Sociologica*, 38: 251–62.

Streeck, Wolfgang (1996), Neo-voluntarism: a new European social policy regime? In G. Marks, F. Scharpf, P. Schmitter and W. Streeck (eds), *Governance in the European Union*, London: Sage.

Svallfors, S. (1996), *Välfärdsstatens Moraliska Ekonomi. Välfärdsopinionen i 90-Talets Sverige*, Umeå: Boréa.

Svallfors, S. (1997), Worlds of welfare and attitudes to redistribution: a comparison of eight Western nations, *European Sociological Review*, 13, 3: 284–304.

Swank, D. (1998), Funding the welfare state: globalization and the taxation of business in advanced market economies, *Political Studies*, 46, 4: 671–92.

Taylor-Gooby, P. (1995), Who wants the welfare state? Support for state welfare in European countries. In S. Svallfors (ed.), *In the Eye of the Beholder. Opinions on Welfare and Justice in Comparative Perspective*, Umeå: Impello Säljksupport AB.

Taylor-Gooby, P. (ed.) (2001), *Welfare States Under Pressure*, London: Sage.

United Nations (1999), *World Population Prospects*, New York: United Nations.

Wilensky, H. L. (1975), *The Welfare State and Equality*, Berkeley, CA: University of California Press.

Wilensky, H. L. and Lebeaux, C. (1958), *Industrial Society and Social Welfare*, New York: Russell Sage.

3

When Is a Change Big Enough to Be a System Shift? Small System-shifting Changes in German and Finnish Pension Policies

Karl Hinrichs and Olli Kangas

Introduction

After the publication of Esping-Andersen's seminal study on the *Three Worlds of Welfare Capitalism* in 1990 a great deal of intellectual endeavour has been used up in debating the existence of qualitatively different models of welfare regimes. Ever since, comparative social policy studies have almost without exception revolved around the question of welfare state models, and disputes have raged about the correct number of these models and the principles on which their differentiation should be based.

Whereas Gøsta Esping-Andersen launched the "modelling business" (Abrahamson 1999) thrust in comparative analysis of welfare states, it was Paul Pierson (1994) who initiated the "retrenchment business". Since the publication of *Dismantling the Welfare State* this business has dealt with the transformation of developed welfare states: whether a country has changed its socio-political regime as a consequence of globalization, economic crisis, ideologically motivated governments committed to a roll-back of welfare provisions and the like, and what were the institutional hindrances to recalibration.

There are, however, at least three problems that are not properly dealt with in the "modelling" and "retrenchment business". A first problem relates to the approach. If we look at the aggregate level of social spending one could conclude that, despite the strong rhetoric against expanding the public sector, in many European countries there was actually a welfare state expansion in the 1980s and 1990s (Alber 1998). However, this does not demonstrate that no restructuring or roll-back of the welfare state had taken place. Reforms in one programme may balance the impact of reforms in other policy areas and, consequently, aggregate spending level does not reveal any change at all. Moreover, spending may increase while, at the same time, benefit levels decrease. Based on UK spending levels, Pierson (1994) found no evidence supporting the hypothesis of social policy cutbacks. However, closer analyses of the benefit levels tell a completely different story: compensation levels in areas like unemployment benefits fell dramatically (Carroll 1999). Similarly, if we are interested in shares of welfare state financing, at the aggregate level one may find a strong degree of stability, but when studying trends in the distribution of taxes and social security contributions at programme level a different and considerably more complex picture may arise (Kautto 2001).

Secondly, the period or point in time studied has important consequences for results obtained. For example, in Esping-Andersen's study of 1990 the empirical data analysed relate to 1980 for all countries included. The problem may be that two countries which actually follow an identical pattern in their social policy development but vary in the timing of reforms fall into different social policy regimes in those cross-sectional examinations. If countries in their social policy development pass through different phases or several ideal types, results from short-term cross-sectional analyses are sensitive to the point in time on which the analysis is based. A short look at the Linnaean zoology clarifies the point. A butterfly may appear as a caterpillar, pupa, or a fully fledged butterfly, and without a historical perspective, we could draw the wrong conclusion that there are three different species. In order to circumvent these problems data from different points in time are needed, and analyses must be complemented by longitudinal descriptions.

Thirdly, at the level of policy domains many changes are incremental and their real impacts are not always immediately visible; rather, it takes years before the full consequences materialize (see also Kersbergen 2000). Compared to other programmes, like social assistance or child allowances, pension schemes are probably the best example for this kind of change since it is in their very nature to bridge long spans of time (Hinrichs 2000). Sometimes those schemes are thoroughly reformed in such a way that it is obvious that there is a clear shift from one system to another. More usually, they change in a gradual manner, and because of the incremental nature of policy reforms it is hard to say if and when there was a system shift. The central question we try to tackle in this contribution is: when is a change big enough to be labelled as a system shift?

Peter Hall (1993) has already suggested a hierarchical ordering of the nature of changes: first-order change refers to a mere adjustment of *levels*, e.g. the contribution rate of a social insurance scheme may be lowered or increased. A second-order change takes place when the structure and functioning of the scheme is altered, e.g. when the benefit formula or the method of indexing benefits is essentially changed. Beyond such a shift of the *instruments*, third-order changes are *goal* shifts and thus the most severe ones. They pertain to a situation where the basic philosophy upon which a welfare state programme or a social security system as a whole was based is substantially altered.

Hall's classification undoubtedly offers a useful heuristic tool. However, as will be evident later, again we meet severe definitional and measurement problems just because of the incremental fashion of the transformation. The aim of this paper is to illuminate how incremental and gradual first- and second-order changes may eventually imply a fundamental third-order change without receiving much attention in the political discourse on the issue. The illustrative focus is on pension reform policies in Germany and Finland. A comparison of these two cases in particular is interesting for at least three reasons. First, there is a first-and-last dimension: Germany has been a pioneering country in the development of social insurance while Finland, being dominated by agriculture for a long time, has usually lagged behind other European countries. Second, historically the approaches to providing income in old age were quite different, but apparently there is some convergence now. Third, reforms carried through in these two countries since the late 1980s were piecemeal, and operated at a surface level: *not that much* was altered. However, we argue that those small, "not-system-changing" first- and second-order reforms may, in fact, gradually shift the basic characteristics and goals of the retirement income system's elements in the respective countries. For the above-mentioned "Linnaean" reasons, our approach is historical, and we trace some past and present trends in the developmental patterns in both welfare states. In order to approach the data problem described above, we look at the spending levels as well as at the institutional structures of pension schemes in Germany and Finland.

The German Case

The structural reform of 1957

Right from the beginning in the last decade of the nineteenth century, benefits from the German public pension scheme were linked to preceding contribution payments. However, the level of benefits emanating from this static scheme were low and, hence, "being old" was—for low-skilled blue-collar workers in particular—synonymous with "being poor" although, partly representing remnants of Bismarck's original concept of a tax-financed flat-rate pension, the scheme still contained elements of basic security until 1957 (Döring 2000).

Different from the introduction of the employment-related pension scheme for private-sector employees (TEL) in Finland four years later, the public pension reform of 1957 had an *immediate* impact on the economic well-being of current retirees when the benefit formula and the post-retirement adjustment of benefits were made dynamic (Hinrichs 1998). Taking into account individual, lifetime earnings in relation to average earnings of all insured (thereby granting credits for military service, spells of unemployment and education) when calculating the pension amount and annually upgrading it according to *gross* wage growth made the retirees participate in economic progress. The benefit increase of more than 60 per cent in the spring of 1957 transformed public pensions as a floor of retirement income into an actual wage replacement that subsequently increased to a higher ratio. Although basic security elements were abolished completely (as was differential treatment of white- and blue-collar workers), the number and rate of elderly people dependent on (additional) social assistance benefits declined, particularly after the expansionary reform of 1972 when, among others, internal redistribution was enhanced: a revaluation of periods with earnings below 75 per cent of average favoured low-paid workers with long employment careers (and their surviving widows). It is hardly surprising that the structural reform of 1957 not only meant to be the "cornerstone" of postwar social policy reform in Germany but, due to the windfalls all current pensioners experienced, also stands out as its most popular element. It substantially contributed to the support for the new *economic order* of "social market economy" and further consolidated the legitimacy of the restored *democratic system* in general.

In conclusion, not earlier than 1957 the old-age income system attained its specific shape that is usually associated with Germany as the prototype of a conservative welfare regime: providing status maintenance at a high level for the male, full-time employed breadwinner after a full occupational career through a public scheme that is strictly earnings-related and hardly redistributing in the vertical dimension. Although features of continuity (or *path dependence*) prevailed, at the same time, the reform of 1957 meant a *new* pension system was established (Conrad 1998; Döring 2000).

General and selective retrenchments between 1989 and 1997

Increasing outlays and declining contribution revenues out of actual earnings beleaguered all social insurance schemes in Germany after the "sudden death" of full employment in 1974. In the public pension scheme, additionally burdened with the costly consequences of the reform of 1972, this pressure implied a series of discretionary interventions resulting in a *factual* net wage development of pensions after 1977 but no substantial cuts for certain categories of insured. Preceded by an, in principle, non-controversial debate on the implications of demographic ageing and the need for timely action, eventually in 1989 another structural reform passed the legislative bodies with the consent of the largest party in opposition, the Social Democrats, and both social partners. At that time the equally non-acceptable alternatives were either to exempt retirees from any benefit cuts, and then gradually have to increase the contribution rate from about 18.7 to 36.4 per cent by 2030, or to cut benefit levels by half while maintaining a stable contribution rate. The cumulative effect of the altogether incremental reform elements should reduce the increase of the expected contribution rate by almost 10 percentage points (Schmähl 1993; Sozialbeirat 1998: 242).

The difference to the pre-reform projections mainly stemmed from three changes:

1. As of 1992 benefits were automatically adjusted to the preceding year's *net* wage development. The new formula should ensure a stable net replacement rate of 70 per cent (after 45 years in covered employment and constantly earning an average wage) as well as pensioners' participation in demographically (or otherwise) induced alterations of social insurance contributions and income tax codes.
2. Federal grants were increased to 20 per cent of the scheme's expenditure in 1992 and should remain at that level.
3. Except for seriously handicapped persons, in 2012 all provisions for early retirement before age 65 without reduced benefit were scheduled to be

phased out. The permanent deduction is 3.6 per cent for each year of premature retirement and, additionally, no credits are earned for those years (or months) not spent in covered employment any more.

When this structural reform became effective in 1992, the "unification boom" was almost over in West Germany and employment in East Germany was still in steep decline. The deteriorating labour market situation resulted in a nearly exploding influx into an early retirement scheme for elderly unemployed. This development triggered another round of retrenchments of the public pension scheme, included in an omnibus bill enacted in 1996. The most important changes were an accelerated phasing-out of retirement options before age 65 without permanent benefit deductions (see above) and a reduction of various non-contributory entitlements. The latter group of cuts included the provision that periods of education after the age of 17 are credited at a lower value and for not more than three years (the 1992 reform had already stipulated a reduction to a maximum of seven years). Furthermore, three instead of the first four years of covered employment (when, for example, during an apprenticeship, earnings are regularly low) are revalued to a level of 75 per cent of average earnings (formerly: 90 per cent). The Social Democrats and the unions vehemently opposed these changes (and further elements of the omnibus bill, such as waiting days for sickness benefits). The passing of this law in parliament and the subsequent preparations for another structural pension reform by the Christian–Liberal government mark the end of the traditional "pension consensus" between the two large parties and between the social partners—although not all elements of the reform legislated in 1997 were fundamentally controversial.

For example, increased federal subsidies, financed out of an increased rate of VAT and meant to cover non-contributory components of the benefit package more completely, were not contested, and nor was a further improvement of child care credits. However, the two most momentous reform elements were, at the same time, the most controversial ones:

1. In continuation of the preceding changes aiming at a higher *actual* retirement age, individual efforts to evade permanent benefit deductions by resorting to disability pensions were made unattractive, and access to them was rendered more difficult.
2. Reduced mortality rates at higher ages imply an increasing period of benefit receipt for newly and already retired persons. Pensioners enjoying more work-free years should take part in the financial consequences.

Beginning in 1999, it was planned to integrate rising life expectancy at age 65 into the formula by which the *initial benefit level* as well as the *annual adjustment* is calculated. Further rising longevity assumed, the "demographic factor" should lower the *net* standard pension level from nearly 70 to 64 per cent, but not below that level. The unions and Social Democrats objected to both changes, arguing that those insured with lower than average earnings and/or a shorter than standard contribution record would increasingly see their pension benefits approaching or even falling below the social assistance level.

The government itself estimated that the legislative changes of 1996 and 1997 would further moderate the increase of the contribution rate: instead of 26.9 per cent in 2030 a rate of 22.4 per cent was calculated, only two percentage points more than the rate valid in 1997 (BMAS 1997: 16). Although other projections arrived at (slightly) higher rates (for example Sozialbeirat 1998: 242; Sinn and Thum 1999) and more funding out of general (and partly earmarked) tax revenues contribute to the diminished increase, it is obvious that future pensioners themselves will be the main "victims" of the ageing process. The scheduled decrease of the target replacement ratio due to the "demographic factor" would not have delivered the largest expenditure savings. Over and above this widely used indicator of benefit generosity, other, less immediately visible elements of the reform packages will display more serious consequences on benefit level of certain pensioners and the overall distribution of benefits.

Two empirical studies confirm this argument. The *AVID* study (Kortmann and Schatz 2000) is based on an investigation of the hitherto earned entitlements (and private provisions made for old age) of a representative sample of singles/couples born between 1936 and 1955. The (future employment) behaviour and (legal) parameters for the remaining years until reaching retirement age are modelled. Entitlements for *public* pension benefits will be lower for *men* of the youngest birth cohorts, particularly in East Germany. Compared to the oldest cohort in question, *women* born in the early 1950s can expect roughly the same benefit level in East Germany, whereas in West Germany, on average, they will receive a significantly higher public pension. These results reflect the changed (un-)employment and family careers of men and women born within this 20-year period as well as the extent to which the different birth cohorts will eventually be affected by retrenchments enacted so far. On both accounts (*West* German) women's entitlements will grow—particularly due to the introduction of child care credits in 1986, their extension for births after 1 January 1992 and a further revaluation enacted in 1997 (see above). The gradually improved recognition of child-raising work (again in the latest reform of January 2001) when determining the benefit amount was the only expansionary element in the reform packages otherwise geared at retrenchment and strengthening the link between own contribution payments and benefit level.

The *PROGNOS* study (1999) forecasts public pension entitlements of cohorts retiring until 2040 as compared to those already retired in 1996 and assuming identical insurance careers for all cohorts. It focuses solely on the consequences of the legal changes enacted between 1989 and 1997. Generally, the benefit level of the youngest cohorts (retiring in 2020 and later) was estimated to be about 20 per cent lower than that of their counterparts who retired in 1996 with an even larger loss for those with earnings constantly below the average. Since the study was commissioned by the association of life insurers, unsurprisingly, the conclusion is that, in order to attain the same income or replacement level in old age, the younger cohorts have to intensify their efforts for private provision.

The effects of the single reform elements legislated during the period in question are small in themselves. Their cumulative effect is much larger, but the full impact has to be evaluated in view of ongoing socio-economic changes which cause workers to earn more or less pension credits than previous birth cohorts. Those changes may include more frequent spells of unemployment during the working career and, in consequence, a retarded upward mobility of earnings, earlier/later entry into covered employment, more frequent part-time work, more continuous labour force participation of women. Most decisive for the pension benefit of individuals (or the average) of a certain birth cohort is whether the socio-economic changes are compensated for by corresponding adaptations of the entitlement rules or are aggravated when exactly those provisions aiming at social adequacy of benefits are removed.

The two studies cited above show the cumulative consequences of the incremental reforms of the 1990s much more accurately than is possible by measuring their magnitude when looking into spending data (see also Brooks 2002: 504–5). Social expenditure on "old age and survivors", as calculated by the German government, increased from 10.7 per cent to 11.9 per cent of GDP between 1991 (i.e. after unification, but before the pension reform legislated in 1989 became effective) and 2000. If corrected for the increased share of people aged 60 and over (from 20.4 per cent to 23.6 per cent), there was actually a decline in spending by 3.8 per cent. It cannot be answered from these spending data to what extent the decline is due to the reforms becoming effective during the 1990s. If one carries out similar calculations for the 1980s (only *West* Germany) the decline was even steeper—minus 12.1 per cent between 1980 and 1990 although there were no reforms, but rather recurrent manipulations with the indexing formula (causing a basis effect that ripples through subsequent years).[1]

A paradigmatic change?

As announced by the Social Democrats before the 1998 election, the Red–Green government revoked the two most controversial elements of the 1997 reform package: somewhat moderated impairments for disability pensioners went into effect according to a law enacted in 2000, and the demographic factor, blamed as "unsocial" and "pension cut", was eventually replaced by discretionary manipulations of the benefit (adjustment) formula leading to roughly the same result in the long run—a lowered standard replacement ratio. Shortly after entering office, the new government introduced a gradually increasing energy tax (*Ökosteuer*). The revenues are earmarked as a supplementary federal grant to the public pension scheme and made possible a reduction of the contribution rate to 19.1 per cent in 2001, but due to the state of the economy it had to be increased to 19.5 per cent in 2003.

However, three elements of the reform package of 2001 possibly justify speaking of a paradigmatic change in Germany's old-age security policy, although the outcome is almost negligible at present and will remain so for the next two decades or so.

(a) As in most other pay-as-you-go, defined-benefit public pension schemes, in Germany the contribution rate was and will be increased when the available funds fall below a certain contingency reserve. In future, a "revenue-oriented expenditure policy" will be applied, which means a complete reversal. It is stipulated that the government has to take action when a contribution rate higher than 20 per cent in 2020 and 22 per cent in 2030 comes within reach. Apart from increasing the standard retirement age and (further) selective cuts, there are not many options left to live up to the legally fixed cap on the contribution rate development, since the standard replacement ratio must not fall below the pre-defined threshold of 67 per cent.

(b) Among the 18 traditional OECD member countries, so far only Germany has had no special minimum protection scheme for the elderly. Persons without sufficient insurance claims were referred to the general social assistance scheme. At the beginning of this decade about 1.3 per cent of retirement-age people received those means-tested benefits. The official justification for introducing a special basic security scheme within which the subsidiarity principle (the legal obligation of adult children to support their parents) is virtually lifted was to increase the take-up rate. This might be the immediate consequence after its implementation in 2003, but in its explanation to the reform bill the government also mentioned as a justification the changing (un-)employment careers that might lead to public pension benefits lower than the social assistance level (Bundesregierung 2000: 46). Indeed, there is every reason to expect that, in combination with shifts in the labour market, leading towards more non-standard employment relationships, the lowered target replacement ratio and the effects of various retrenchments already enacted will increase the number of new retirees with insufficient insurance entitlements.

(c) Hitherto, retirement income policy in Germany was tantamount to *public* pension policy and a "one-pillar approach". At present, about 80 per cent of total retirement income stems from unfunded public sources (when the civil servants' pensions are included). Other resources during retirement regularly bear a *supplementary* character. Outside the public sector, almost nowhere have occupational pensions been an element of industry-wide collective bargaining so far. Thus, coverage is comparatively low and has been on the decline for about 25 years. Private provision (personal pensions, income from assets) is on the increase but, like occupational welfare, it is predominantly a component in the benefit package of pensioners with formerly above-average earnings.

The central elements of the Red–Green pension reform are incentives for *voluntary* private provision which is meant to *compensate* for the declining target replacement ratio. Gradually increasing to 4 per cent (in 2008) of gross earnings, certain savings arrangements are tax-privileged with a bias in favour of families with children and high-income earners. This reform element is an unequivocal expression of the turn towards a "multi-pillar approach" and an extended retirement income policy in Germany. It is so despite the fact that for those birth cohorts retiring over the next three decades the proceeds from those new subsidized savings schemes will not contribute much to their total retirement income. If contributors to the public pension system follow the recommendation to save an additional 4 per cent of their gross earnings for a personal pension and if these savings were to yield a constant interest rate of 4 per cent, the personal pension accrual would amount to no more than 11.8 per cent of the standard public pension for a worker retiring in 2030. Albeit this component of the retirement income mix will be small in the beginning, it will enlarge economic inequality in old age because, in addition to a far from complete take-up rate, the private provision is of the "defined-contribution type" and contains no redistributing elements.

The pension reform of 2001 will, according to the rather optimistic assumptions of the government, lead to a slightly lower contribution rate in 2030 than was expected by the Kohl government when it enacted its last pension reform in 1997. However, one has to add the 4 per cent the *employees* are expected to voluntarily contribute to private pensions. Unlike the public pension scheme (and to the trade unions' annoyance) the employers are exempted from joint financing. Such a higher contribution rate is unavoidable if one moves from a complete pay-as-you-go system to partial funding and represents the well-known "double payment problem". In the short run the 2001 reform contains no massive additional cuts, but in the long run a new architecture of the German retirement income system will be established. Whereas the reforms of the 1990s were first- and second-order changes which, in a socially differentiated manner, will threaten the receipt of a sufficient public pension, the latest reform package explicitly abolishes the claim of the scheme to provide status maintenance through public benefits alone. In future, the employee has to save for a complementary private pension in order to attain this goal. The approach towards a multi-pillar system clearly represents a third-order change.

The Finnish Case

National pensions: from residual to universal and back?

Finland was a late-comer in pension policy (for a general review, see Salminen 1993). The first pension scheme became effective not earlier than 1939. It represents a problem for followers of the "modelling business". Basically, the scheme was universal in coverage: all were insured. However, it strictly applied the insurance principle: every citizen was obliged to save in individual accounts kept by the public pension institution, and the size of the future pension was completely determined by the funds the claimant had accumulated. Factually, national pensions were means-tested since the long maturing period and restrictive qualifying conditions excluded the majority of elderly from benefits. By 1950, only one-fifth of the elderly above age 65 was entitled to national pensions (Kangas 1988). Besides the take-up ratio being extremely low, the benefits provided were meagre. Including all possible supplements, the full national pension amounted to no more than 15 per cent of the average industrial wage, which was one of the lowest ratios in the Western countries (Jäntti et al. 1996). In sum, this "universal", "insurance-based" scheme was clearly residual in its character (see Palme 1990).

National pension legislation was totally revised in 1956 when everybody older than 65 years became eligible. It remains a matter of definition whether this reform was a change of the second or third order. Undeniably, the previous scheme also had universality as the ultimate goal but very far away in the future, while the 1956 reform immediately made citizenship the basis for entitlement. Concretely, the national pension was divided into two separate parts: (1) a flat-rate amount paid on the basis of citizenship or residence of at least five years; (2) an income-tested supplement (Overbye 1996). Until 1985, the supplement was tested against *any* other income (employment-related pensions, income from investments or work, and so on) with a withdrawal rate of 100 per cent. Since then only pensions from the statutory employment-related schemes and from the collective occupational schemes affected the supplement. "Nordic universalism", the renunciation of income-testing, was not carried through in the Finnish pension system until 1985. In that sense one could argue that the minor reform of 1985 was again a system-changing reform.

A small step that once again, we argue, changed the whole principle of the Finnish national pension scheme was taken by Lipponen's (SDP) "rainbow coalition"—consisting of Social Democrats, Conservatives, the Greens and the left-wing alliance. In 1996, the government decided to make the universal *basic amount* subject to a pension-income test as well. In 2000, the basic amount was completely abolished. At present, the amount of national pension is fully dependent on the employment-related pension, and since more and more Finns are receiving full pensions from the now-matured statutory employment-pension schemes they are no longer entitled to the national pension at all. Thus, the traditional idea of an unconditional citizenship pension is gone. No longer being a "people's pension", nowadays the national pension scheme only supports those with no or small employment-related pensions. The "not-system-changing" reforms of a second-order quality enacted in the 1990s, which were minor in monetary terms, have in fact shifted the Finnish pension regime from a citizenship-based model towards an employment-related scheme (see figure 1).

The image of the severity of the reforms depends on the data we use. If we look at individual pensioners living on national pensions, they have not lost anything, or only very little. This kind of data displays a no-change picture. Another way of looking at the implications of the reform is to look at the aggregate social spending on national as against earnings-related pensions (ERP). Then it is revealed that the maturing ERP gradually crowds out the income-tested national pensions (see table 1), which confirms the above argument of a system shift that has indeed taken place.

Earnings-related pensions take the stage

The Finnish earnings- (or employment)-related pension system has been a hybrid combining some elements of the Swedish model (or what Korpi and Palme (1998) call the "encompassing model") and the Central-European "corporatist model". As in Sweden, the Finnish pension system provides basic security for all with earnings-related benefits on top for those with an employment record. The corporatist orientation stems from the decentralized nature of the pensions system. The main employment-related pension

Small System-shifting Changes

Figure 1

Coordination of national pensions (NP) and other legislated pensions in
Finland in 1990 and 2000

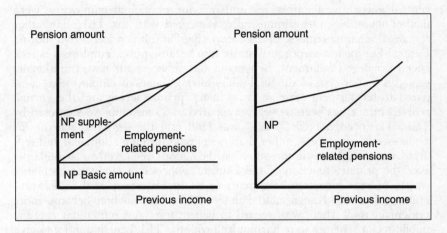

Table 1

Shares of different pension schemes as percentage of total pension expenditure in
Finland, 1950–2000

Year	National pensions	Employment-related pensions			Voluntary pensions (supplement)
		Private sector	State sector	Municipal sector	
1950	28.6	0	69.0	1.5	2.4
1955	49.7	0	47.1	2.0	2.6
1960	69.2	0	27.0	3.0	5.3
1965	66.5	2.9	24.2	5.7	5.7
1970	56.9	11.5	22.4	8.2	5.0
1975	51.6	19.6	19.5	8.1	4.4
1980	42.1	29.3	18.5	8.7	4.5
1985	40.9	32.6	16.4	8.7	4.4
1990	32.4	39.2	16.9	10.0	4.1
1995	27.2	43.1	17.3	11.5	3.3
2000	19.6	48.8	18.8	14.8	2.5

Sources: KELA (2001: 38–9); KELA (1985: 28–9). Since some minor pension schemes (as church pensions, Åland Islands pensions, and seamen's pensions are missing, the percentages do not sum up to 100 per cent.

scheme for private-sector employees (TEL) was established in 1961. Employees on short-term contracts (1961), farmers (1974) and other self-employed people (1974) got their own separate programmes.

The already-existing pension programmes for public employees (one for central government employees and one for municipal employees) were neither financially nor administratively merged with the TEL, but rather remained separate entities. In this respect the Finnish pension design showed Central-European "corporatist" traits, also because public employees experienced privileged treatment. Benefits in the public sector have traditionally replaced 66 per cent of the final salary after 30 years of employment, compared to 60 per cent after 40 years in the private sector, and the normal retirement age has been 63 years compared to 65 for employees covered by TEL. The occupational "bonus" was built into the legislated scheme for public-sector employees, rather than being paid through additional and separate arrangements as in the other Nordic nations (see Overbye 1996). However, the primary function of the Finnish public-sector employees' schemes was to provide income-related pensions in the same way as the TEL programme (see e.g. Kangas and Palme 1996). This function became more evident in 1998 when, with regard to benefit level and retirement age, the public-sector schemes were harmonized with the TEL benefits, and thus civil servants will lose their privileges (Hinrichs 2000: 363).

In the private sector as well, the occupational bonus was integrated into the statutory TEL scheme. First, in 1961, the existing pension institutes could acquire responsibility for the TEL scheme together with the private insurance companies. Second, these institutes were given the option of guaranteeing additional TEL benefits for those interim cohorts that, due to their age, had no prospect of accumulating entitlements to a full pension. In principle, entry into these schemes was voluntary, but after joining TEL they became completely subject to the legislated rules so that stipulations on portability, target benefit levels or benefit adjustment in occupational schemes were precisely the same as in TEL. However, a full pension (targeted at 60 per cent) could be earned by working less than 40 years. The more the TEL scheme approaches maturity the less relevant become those occupational benefits since there are not many employees left who entered private-sector employment before 1961. Whereas in the mid-1970s about 20 per cent of employees were covered by occupational schemes, in 2000 the share was already below 10 per cent (Kangas and Palme 1996: 223; Suutela 2000: 10). The consequences can be seen from table 1, which shows that the spending share of the various voluntary occupational schemes has declined from nearly 6 per cent in 1965 to 2.5 per cent in 1999, and this trend will continue, since (future) retirees with additional occupational pensions gradually die away.

Figure 1 shows that there is no upper ceiling for statutory earnings-related pensions in Finland (but, as a concomitant, also no ceiling for contribution payments). Among OECD countries and, particularly if compared to Sweden and Norway, this is a very exceptional provision. On the one hand, it has hampered the development of supplementary private pension schemes and, on the other hand, it had positively contributed to the legitimacy of the statutory scheme among high-income earners which is greater among them than with workers in the lower income strata (Forma and Kangas 1999). This fact should, moreover, result from the formula for calculating the pension level. Up to 1996, only earnings of the two median years among the four last years spent in employment were relevant for determining the benefit amount. This mode of benefit calculation was beneficial for employees who could prove a "full career" (40 years of employment) and whose earnings increased with seniority, i.e. particularly white-collar workers with relatively higher earnings. Compared to their counterparts in other Nordic countries, these groups had not much reason to demand additional occupational pension schemes (or to engage themselves in individual provision for old age) in order to compensate for a large difference between statutory pensions and previous earnings.

A reform package based on an agreement between the central labour market organizations and subsequent legislation in October 2002 will further change the benefit formula, and that may, again, gradually shift the relative role of the statutory and the occupational schemes. Previously, each year in employment between 23 and 64 years of age was counted at an accrual rate of 1.5 per cent so that the maximum pension of 60 per cent was attained after 40 years. According to the new pension act for private-sector employees, beginning in 2005, workers can earn pension credits for each year of the employment career. The accrual rate is progressive, i.e. from age 17 up to 52 the rate is 1.5 per cent, in the age range 53 to 62 years the accrual rate is 1.9 per cent of annual wages, and after age 63 it is as high as 4.5 per cent, while the retirement age is flexible between 63 and 68 years of age. The pension amount is calculated on the basis of income over the *whole* working career. That stipulation was heavily criticized by the representatives of the academic occupations, but they accepted the agreement due to the "super" accrual rates valid for older employees that will largely compensate for the abolition of the previous "final salary principle". Apart from obtaining academic employees' acquiescence in the reform, the progressive accrual rate serves two additional goals. First, the lower actual replacement ratio due to taking into account earnings of the whole employment record might have triggered an expansion of supplementary occupational pension schemes. Assigning the final years in employment a rate of 4.5 per cent muffles that demand among those whose earnings increase with age. Second, the higher accrual rates after age 52 create a strong incentive not to terminate employment too early.

In Finland, right from their inception in the early 1960s, truly earnings-related statutory pensions played a more central role than in the other Nordic countries, and the abolition of the universal basic pension further enhanced the employment-relatedness of the Finnish pension arrangement (see figure 1). In a way, it moved towards the Central European type, i.e. it became *"Germanized"* with a strong emphasis on employment-based benefits that, only when they are insufficient, are supplemented by income-tested basic pensions.

Has the Finnish system shifted?

What, then, is the magnitude of the changes described above? If one looks at the *target levels* of the pension schemes, no dramatic shifts happened in

Finland during the deep recession of the 1990s. The adjustments in the programme design do not justify speaking of a system shift in the Finnish pension policy. As mentioned in the introduction, even small, incremental policy changes may eventually, after they have developed their impact over a longer period, amount to a system shift. The argument is that this has exactly been the case in Finland.

A first system shift can be ascertained when the *universal* national pension scheme was introduced in the mid-1950s. It occurred as a shift from a residual pension policy towards a citizenship-based model, guaranteeing a basic livelihood to every senior citizen. The second juncture whose consequences mean a clear system shift was the introduction of the employment-related pension scheme for private-sector employees in 1961 even though it actually materialized in an incremental manner (see table 1). The third breaking point, at least conceptually, is marked by the reforms carried through in the 1990s. The harmonization of pension programmes for private- and public-sector employees established a legal equality between these two categories of employees, but in fact this will occur only in the long run. More important is the abolition of the national pension as a citizenship right. The principle of universalism, a central characteristic of the Nordic welfare states, has given way to selectivism in the form of a benefit that is tested against other pension income. With regard to resources during retirement, the individual's employment and earnings record has become more decisive and that means a convergence with Central European pension schemes based on work merit—particularly after the changes of 2002.

Although the Finnish pension policy sketched above indicates a declining relevance of private occupational pensions, there are several developments going on which, most likely, will reverse this trend. First, among the political elite there seems to be an inclination to promote private solutions in social policy. More often than before, the two-pillar (national pensions and statutory employment-related pensions) approach of Finnish pension policy is being questioned, and increasingly vociferous political demands have been presented to strengthen a third pillar of voluntary, private individual and/or occupational pensions.

Second, younger employees are already acting with their feet. The traditionally marginal role of individual pension provision is rapidly shifting: in 1985 there were fewer than 10,000 Finns who had an individual pension policy. In 2000 there were already more than 200,000. Although the main target group of the financial service industry is employees in the age bracket 35 to 50 years, younger ones are also prepared to take out those policies. About one-fourth of all policies were bought by the younger age groups (Suutela 2000: 77).

Third, the future level of statutory pensions is of central importance for the spread of occupational pensions. Despite an increasing preference for private solutions, at present the major actors in pension policy do not question the replacement level (60 per cent) and the general framework of the existing pension schemes. Hence, for the trade unions and other interest organizations the expansion of occupational pension plans is not an important goal at present. However, the pensions of employees retiring after 2012 will be calculated on the basis of the wages and the accrual rate for each year of their working career. Compared to the presently applied formula, this change will lower the actual replacement, particularly for white-collar workers with long periods of education and an income profile that is increasing with age. They and their organizations may feel forced to seek compensation from occupational pension schemes. Whether this shift in favour of private supplements will happen and actually trigger a multi-pillar design of Finnish retirement income policy, amounting to another system shift, remains to be seen.

Conclusion

Over the last decade a number of studies have been published describing developments of (public) pension policy in OECD countries (see, for example, Hinrichs 2000, referring to various studies), Middle and East European transition countries or Latin America (for example, Gillion *et al.* 2000; Müller *et al.* 1999). Those comparative studies have hardly ever attempted to evaluate whether the outcome of legislated changes which regularly remain in the realm of *incremental* reforms justifies a characterization as "systemic change". Figures on public spending are no suitable yardstick in the area of public pension programmes because present changes in expenditure are, to a large extent, the result of political decisions reached (very) long ago, and today's reforms sometimes alter the expenditure and revenue situation with an extended time-lag. Over and above the effects of phasing-in or -out of provisions, changes in expenditure levels reflect the balance of programme expansions and restrictions in the past as well as current demographic and economic changes, so that a "steady state" will hardly ever be attained since pension reform policy is a "never-ending story".

Another peculiarity of public pensions, inhibiting a proper comparative evaluation, refers to standard replacement ratios as yardsticks of changing generosity. They are decreasingly meaningful indicators as, due to changing employment careers of men and women, the "standard case" less and less corresponds to the representative case. Even more important is, as has been shown in the preceding sections, that the most momentous ("systemic") changes, concerning the level and distribution of (future) benefits, have left the target replacement ratio completely unaffected. Thus, an assessment of the *quality* of political changes requires us to inspect the meaning of reforms for the "architecture" of the respective retirement income system in total, whether and to what extent the interplay between public and private (occupational and personal) components of retirement income has already shifted or will shift. Additionally, one has to look into the interplay between different public schemes, providing different "types" of benefits (basic security, employment-related pensions), and whether responsibilities have changed.

The case studies of Finland and Germany show, first of all, that some convergence in the structure of the public pension schemes has taken place (or will materialize) although those processes are hardly the result of intentional policy transfers. While it is true that, due to the schemes' evolved complexity, a multitude of "adjustment screws" can be moved, there is also a limited repertoire of possible responses to comparable policy problems, furthering parallel development.

Among other things, the allocative structure of the public schemes providing basic security and earnings-related benefits became more similar when in Finland the universal elements of the national pension were abolished completely and Germany introduced a special minimum benefit scheme for pensioners in 2003. In both countries the respective change can be considered a large one although the immediate impacts are negligible: Finland (like Sweden) broke with the typically Scandinavian citizenship principle, and Germany eventually joined the other industrialized nations when it established a two-tier pension system and moderated the traditional (family) subsidiarity principle.

Furthermore, in both employment-related schemes the redistributing elements have been reduced. However, a stricter earnings–benefit link was brought about in different ways: in Finland it was the extension of the years of the working career incorporated in the benefit calculation formula, whereas in Germany the elimination and devaluation of non-contributory periods strengthens individual equity, and in both countries premature retirement becomes more "costly" for the individual worker since it implies considerably lowered benefits. The non-egalitarian effect of the schemes' turn towards individual equity will be intensified by increasing wage inequality during working life and, connected to it, by vertically different options for additional private provision coming about as either individual or occupational pensions.

In its effort to shift the public/private mix of retirement income in favour of the funded, private components and thereby reshaping the role of the unfunded, public earnings-related scheme for status maintenance, Germany is not standing alone. Countries like Sweden, Italy and Austria pursue a similar strategy with, however, different emphasis. In Finland, despite the increase in (new) occupational pension coverage and more (young) employees taking out personal pension policies, obviously the architecture of the retirement income system in total shows more, although not complete, stability. This is due not least to ageing becoming a less pressing problem in Finland than in other European countries; earnings-related pensions being paid without an upper ceiling; and the fact that a relatively high share of pension funding (within the TEL programme) makes the system less exposed to political demands for reconstruction which are less likely to be driven by the messages sent out from the international debate on averting a pension crisis.

After all, our starting question whether seemingly small changes with almost no immediate and visible impacts actually represent *system shifts*, has not been unequivocally answered. However, the question of whether the glass of water is half full or half empty becomes less pressing, when the level was considerably higher before and was lowered in short sips.

Note

1. The data sources used for these calculations can be found at BMAS (2002: 19 and 22); Deutscher Bundestag (1994: 66); Statistisches Bundesamt (2002: 58).

References

Abrahamson, P. (1999), The welfare modelling business, *Social Policy & Administration*, 33, 4: 394−415.

Alber, J. (1998), Der deutsche Sozialstaat im Licht international vergleichender Daten, *Leviathan*, 26, 2: 199−227.

BMAS (Bundesministerium für Arbeit und Sozialordnung) (1997), *Entwurf zum Rentenreformgesetz 1999. Begründung, Gesetzestexte (Auszüge), Erläuterungen*, Bonn: BMAS.

BMAS (Bundesministerium für Arbeit und Sozialordnung) (2002), *Sozialbericht 2001. Materialband*, Bonn: BMAS.

Brooks, S. M. (2002), Social protection and economic integration: the politics of pension reform in an era of capital mobility, *Comparative Political Studies*, 35, 5: 491−523.

Bundesregierung (2000), *Entwurf eines Gesetzes zur Reform der Gesetzlichen Rentenversicherung und zur Förderung eines kapitalgedeckten Altersvorsorgevermögens (Altersvermögensgesetz— AvmG)*, Deutscher Bundestag, 14. Wahlperiode, Drucksache 14/4595 (v. 14.11.2000), Berlin.

Carroll, E. (1999), *Emergence and Structuring of Social Insurance Institutions: Comparative Studies on Social Policy and Unemployment Insurance*, Dissertation Series, no. 38, Stockholm: Swedish Institute for Social Research.

Conrad, C. (1998), Alterssicherung. In H. G. Hockerts (ed.), *Drei Wege deutscher Sozialstaatlichkeit. NS-Diktatur, Bundesrepublik und DDR im Vergleich*, München: Oldenbourg, pp. 101−16.

Deutscher Bundestag (1994), *Zwischenbericht der Enquete-Kommission Demographischer Wandel*, Zur Sache 4/94, Bonn: Deutscher Bundestag—Referat Öffentlichkeitsarbeit.

Döring, D. (2000), Grundlinien der langfristigen Systementwicklung der gesetzlichen Rentenversicherung: Personenkreis, Rentenformel, Finanzierung. In S. Fisch and U. Haerendel (eds), *Geschichte und Gegenwart der Rentenversicherung in Deutschland*, Berlin: Duncker and Humblot, pp. 169−87.

Esping-Andersen, G. (1990), *The Three Worlds of Welfare Capitalism*, Princeton, NJ: Princeton University Press.

Forma, P. and Kangas, O. (1999), Need, citizenship or merit: public opinion on pension policy in Australia, Finland and Poland. In S. Svallfors and P. Taylor-Gooby (eds), *The End of the Welfare State? Responses to State Retrenchment*, London: Routledge, pp. 161−89.

Gillion, C., Turner, J., Bailey, C. and Latulippe, D. (eds) (2000), *Social Security Pensions: Development and Reform*, Geneva: ILO.

Hall, P. A. (1993), Policy paradigms, social learning, and the state: the case of economic policymaking in Britain, *Comparative Politics*, 25, 4: 275−96.

Hinrichs, K. (1998), *Reforming the Public Pension Scheme in Germany: The End of the Traditional Consensus?* Universität Bremen, Zentrum für Sozialpolitik, ZeS-Arbeitspapier Nr. 11/98, Bremen.

Hinrichs, K. (2000), Elephants on the move: patterns of public pension reform in OECD countries, *European Review*, 8, 3: 353−78.

Jäntti, M., Kangas, O. and Ritakallio, V.-M. (1996), From marginalism to institutionalism: distributional consequences of the transformation of the Finnish pension regime, *Journal of Income and Wealth*, 42, 4: 473−91.

Kangas, O. (1988), *Politik och ekonomi i pensionsförsäkringen: Det finska pensionssystemet i ett jämförande perspektiv*. Stockholms Universitet, Institutet för social forskning, Meddelande 5, Stockholm.

Kangas, O. and Palme, J. (1996), The development of occupational pensions in Finland and Sweden: class politics and institutional feedbacks. In M. Shalev (ed.), *The Privatization of Social Policy? Occupational Welfare and the Welfare State in America, Scandinavia and Japan*, Basingstoke: Macmillan, pp. 211−40.

Karl Hinrichs and Olli Kangas

Kautto, M. (2001), Moving closer? Diversity and convergence in financing of welfare states. In M. Kautto *et al.* (eds), *Nordic Welfare States in the European Context*, London: Routledge, pp. 232–61.

KELA (1985), *Statistical Yearbook of the Social Insurance Institution*, Helsinki: Kela.

KELA (2001), *Statistical Yearbook of the Social Insurance Institution*, Helsinki: Kela.

Kersbergen, Kees van (2000), The declining resistance of welfare states to change? In S. Kuhnle (ed.), *Survival of the European Welfare State*, London: Routledge, pp. 19–36.

Korpi, W. and Palme, J. (1998), The paradox of redistribution and strategies of equality: welfare state institutions, inequality, and poverty in the Western countries, *American Sociological Review*, 63, 5: 661–87.

Kortmann, K. and Schatz, C. (2000), *Altersvorsorge in Deutschland 1996 (AVID '96). Lebensverläufe und künftige Einkommen im Alter*, ed. Verband Deutscher Rentenversicherungsträger and Bundesministerium für Arbeit und Sozialordnung, DRV-Schriften Bd. 19, Frankfurt a.M.: VDR.

Müller, K., Ryll, A. and Wagener, H.-J. (eds) (1999), *Transformation of Social Security: Pensions in Central-Eastern Europe*, Heidelberg: Physica.

Overbye, E. (1996), Public and occupational pensions in the Nordic countries. In M. Shalev (ed.), *The Privatization of Social Policy? Occupational Welfare and the Welfare State in America, Scandinavia and Japan*, Basingstoke: Macmillan, pp. 159–86.

Palme, J. (1990), *Pension Rights in Welfare Capitalism: The Development of Old-Age Pensions in 18 OECD Countries 1930 to 1985*, Dissertation Series, no. 14, Stockholm: Swedish Institute for Social Research.

Pierson, P. (1994), *Dismantling the Welfare State? Reagan, Thatcher and the Politics of Retrenchment*, Cambridge: Cambridge University Press.

PROGNOS (1999), *Versorgungslücken in der Alterssicherung: Privater Vorsorgebedarf für den Schutz im Alter, bei Erwerbsminderung und im Hinterbliebenenfall*, Gutachten im Auftrag des Gesamtverbandes der Deutschen Versicherungswirtschaft e.V., Basel: PROGNOS.

Salminen, K. (1993), *Pension Schemes in the Making: A Comparative Study of the Scandinavian Countries*, Studies 1993: 2, Helsinki: Central Pension Security Institute.

Schmähl, W. (1993), The "1992 Reform" of public pensions in Germany: main elements and some effects, *Journal of European Social Policy*, 3, 1: 39–51.

Sinn, H.-W. and Thum, M. (1999), Gesetzliche Rentenversicherung: Prognosen im Vergleich, *Finanzarchiv*, 56, 1: 104–35.

Sozialbeirat (1998), Gutachten des Sozialbeirats. In Bundesregierung, *Rentenversicherungsbericht 1998*, Deutscher Bundestag, Drucksache 13/11290, Bonn, pp. 239–51.

Statistisches Bundesamt (2002), *Statistisches Jahrbuch für die Bundesrepublik Deutschland 2002*, Stuttgart: Metzler-Poeschel.

Suutela, A. (2000), Vapaaehtoinen vakuutus osana Suomen kokonaiseläkejärjestelmää [Voluntary Insurance as a Part of Finnish Pension Policy]. Unpublished Master thesis, University of Turku, Department of Social Policy.

4

Organizational Restructuring in European Health Systems: The Role of Primary Care

Ana Rico, Richard B. Saltman and Wienke G. W. Boerma

1. Introduction

This paper analyses the dynamics of organizational change in European health care systems. Our main goal is to review the strategies developed within Western European systems during the 1990s to improve coordination among health care providers. Inter-organizational coordination has long ranked high on the health care agenda. In practice, efforts in that direction have been rare, and often perceived as falling short of achieving the desired objectives. During the 1990s, in contrast, a series of pro-coordination strategies have been launched in European health care systems.

We pay special attention to primary care (PC), based on the perceived strategic importance of steering-system coordination from this level, partly confirmed by the now robust evidence on the moderating effect that a strong PC sector has on health spending (Gerdtham and Jönsson 2000). Two important moves have been expanding task profiles of PC at the expense of other providers, and increasing the power of PC to steer other levels of care. Both changes imply a shift in broader system-coordination mechanisms. They have apparently been effected in parallel with a shift in resources and control mechanisms, and within a context of mounting societal and financial pressures on health care systems.

The evidence on organizational restructuring in European health care is used to address three theoretical questions. First, is there convergence in pro-coordination policies through Europe? How do the mechanisms adopted differ across European countries? Second, what is the impact of different types of pro-coordination policies? Is there a model of best practice which could work across different health care systems? Third, which are the drivers and barriers of recent pro-coordination reforms in health care? To what extent do they differ across European countries?

In section 2 we sketch the analytical framework. Section 3 describes recent pro-coordination strategies in health care, and reviews the available evidence on their impact, based on a comprehensive review of literature since 1995. Section 4 discusses the analytical issues introduced in section 2 in the light of the evidence described in section 3.

Ana Rico, Richard B. Saltman and Wienke G. W. Boerma

2. Understanding Pro-cooperative Reforms in Europe

2.1. Network coordination as inter-professional cooperation

We depart from a simplified view of organizations as pools of (financial, informational, human and technological) resources steered through a set of governance mechanisms. A further analytical simplification, widely used in economics as in political science (e.g. Ring and Van de Ven 1992; Scharpf 1993), consists of the three generic types of organizational governance: markets, hierarchies and networks. Most organizations combine elements of each. These three ideal-type models differ in the way they address the two main governance functions: coordination, and control (or motivation). The term *coordination* has traditionally been used to designate how the division of labour between different organizational units is re-integrated to achieve specific objectives. In modern organizational theory, its meaning is extended to include also the basic governance function of allocating tasks and decision-making powers among organizational units prior to re-integrating them. A necessary requirement for all coordination systems to operate adequately is that the involved actors comply with their expected courses of action. Compliance might derive from combinations of different control mechanisms: financial compensation, hierarchical power and social control by peers. More generally, all control mechanisms are based upon the allocation of costs, benefits, accountabilities and risks across organizational units and actors

Decentralized contracts and financial compensation have a critical role in *markets*; while *hierarchies* tend to rely on centralized directions, plans and power. Some particularly meaningful constraints on effective market and hierarchical coordination in the health care field are generalized uncertainty and asymmetric information problems. In addition, for market and hierarchical coordination mechanisms to be efficient, the interdependencies among different organizational units should be minimal. That is, units should be able to decide independently from each other most of the time. Otherwise the corresponding generalized externalities will hinder market coordination; or, alternatively, each unit hierarchical coordinator will have incomplete information and power to steer the required cross-unit interactions.

Networks can represent an efficient solution to those coordination barriers. Professions do indeed show some of the classic traits required for cooperative coordination mechanisms to work effectively, such as common socialization processes (training), high salience of reputation and shared value systems (deontology). However, the weakness of spontaneous professional networks prior to the 1990 reforms suggests that most likely they were not self-sustainable, and therefore depended on other supporting conditions which were not in place. A critical fact here is that until very recently, local self-coordination among professionals has largely operated as an informal scheme, with formal coordination powers and budgets being attributed to state authorities or insurers (Goddard *et al.* 2000; Hughes Tuohy 1999; Goddard and Mannion 1998; Sheaff 1999; Mannion and Smith 1997). Other coordination barriers specific of networks are as follows.

Hierarchies and markets mainly rely on unilateral decisions. In contrast, network coordination requires direct cooperation, based on group shared financial risks and decision-making. As a result, networks are costly in terms of decision costs and blockages (Scharpf 1988); and vulnerable to free-riding (Ring and Van de Ven 1992). Actors with better reputations (e.g. hospital vs. PC doctors) and organized interests (e.g. specialist-dominated physician organizations) will enjoy more power, which might not always lead to efficient coordination solutions. Because of the importance of trust, it is difficult to include new actors without an established reputation (e.g. nurses or managers). Finally, self-management makes actors focus on the most salient perceived interdependencies (clinical care), leaving other important strategic issues (e.g. cost, public health) uncoordinated (Scharpf 1993).

2.2. Convergence as hybridization: testing selective path dependence

Understanding organizational change requires not only examination of the organizational systems managing service provision, but also of the dynamics of policy change. The goal of the present paper is to test whether the theoretical model and hypotheses derived from a previous in-depth case study (Rico and Costa 2004) help explain the rates at which different types of European health care systems converge. We depart from a simplified view of the policy process as the dynamic interactions of a number of collective actors (or political organizations) subject to a set of formal rules of the game (formal political institutions). Contrary to other approaches, we concede a critical causal role to the socio-political structure (SPS) *vis-à-vis* institutions as a determinant of policy change.

Several clarifications are required here. We define *institutions* in more restricted terms than other research approaches, as the external rules of the game imposed by the state upon other collective actors. *Regulation* and *legislation* are therefore considered as almost synonymous with institutions. We understand *organizations* both as collective actors (capable of independent action) and ruled arenas (a set of internal "rules of the game"). To simplify terminology, we use the term *organizational governance mechanisms* to refer to the internal rules of the game operating within organizations. These are partly derived from, but not identical to, the external regulation prescribed by public policies. Policies in turn can be aimed at (1) modifying the rules of the game (institutional framework), or (2) allocating and redistributing (financial, knowledge and other) resources among collective actors. Institutional change (1) requires policy change of type (2) to be implemented (to achieve a subsequent transformation of organizational governance mechanisms).

We define the SPS in health care, following Hughes Tuohy (1999), as the distribution of informal political power (IPP) among three collective actors: state authorities, private entrepreneurs (insurers and others), and professionals. There are also three main sources of IPP: ownership and financial resources; knowledge and information resources; and social or political support (i.e. collective action resources). Citizens play a critical role in the latter. Figure 1 summarizes the main relationships between variables. Collective actors endowed with IPP can (a) exert informal pressures upon the

Figure 1

Determinants and dynamics of policy change

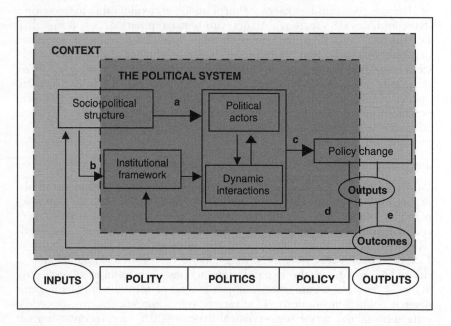

political process (e.g. lobbying by private entrepreneurs and professional associations); and also (b) exercise formal influence mediated by the institutional framework (as in neo-corporatist schemes involving joint decision-making among professionals, insurers and the state). Institutions matter precisely because they translate socio-political actors' IPP into formal political power (FPP).

The SPS can be expected to evolve partly independently of the political system, driven by broader societal changes (such as an expansion of private health care following economic growth). Therefore, as time passes, the correspondence between formal institutions and IPP weakens, and resisting informal pressures for change will be increasingly difficult to resist for actors with FPP. As a result, policy shifts may result (c). There are two main feedback effects. Changed policy (d) prompts institutional change, and (e) modifies the SPS via resource shifts induced by public authorities. Policy-induced changes in the SPS in turn point to the centrality of the political process as an endogenous determinant of social change.

Based on Bouget (see below, this issue), there are three main positions within the debate on policy convergence: (1) all countries converge towards best practice; (2) *clubs* of countries converge towards shared policy solutions; and (3) each country endogenously develops its own policy changes through national trial and error processes. Position (1) argues that policy change is the result of broad external societal pressures which affect all countries. Positions (2) and (3) mainly focus on the role of institutional legacies in each country or group of similar countries as the main determinants of the type of policy change which can be effected.

The implications of our explanatory model for the debate on convergence are as follows. First, the success of societal pressures in bringing about policy convergence is likely to depend on the extent to which the new institutions threaten national IPP structures. Countries with initially compatible SPS will more rapidly and thoroughly adopt international best practice models. Elsewhere, unless parallel shifts in IPP resources are effected via redistributive policies, perceived threats will provoke opposition from socio-political actors; and therefore reduce the likelihood or scope of institutional change. Second, the latter will advance by the lines of least resistance in each country, thereby generating a progressive institutional and organizational hybridization. Accordingly, different patterns of *selective* PD are to be expected across groups of countries, rather than generalized convergence or PD. Third, our model opens the possibility that positions (1), (2) and (3) above, rather than alternative explanations, represent complementary phases of a longer-term convergence process understood as progressive hybridization.

3. Redistributing Powers and Functions across the Interface: Pro-coordination Reforms in European Primary Care

Given our emphasis on system coordination, we classify PC reforms in three categories: (1) reforms that increase the power of PC (as purchaser or coordinator) over other care levels; (2) reforms directed at broadening the sevice portfolio of PC (as provider), often at the expense of other care levels; (3) concurrent changes in PC organizational resources and control systems. Strategies (1) and (2) imply a change in broader system coordination mechanisms, and therefore constitute our main focus of empirical analysis in this section. We conceptualize reforms included within strategy (3) as organizational requisites for the success of pro-coordination reforms, and discuss them in section 4 below.

3.1. Increasing the coordination power of PC over other care levels

Market mechanisms: delegating coordination power to PC purchasers. Delegation of purchasing power to gate-keeping GPs constitutes an ambitious attempt to strengthen the role of the PC sector in system coordination through market-like mechanisms. The United Kingdom has successfully implemented different schemes and pilots in this direction since 1991. In particular, standard fundholding, by which individual GPs were entitled to purchase about 40 per cent of the specialist care, was extended to 40 per cent of the PC providers between 1991 and 1996 (1,500 PC groups), with more than 50 per cent of the population covered by the scheme (Bloor *et al.* 2000). Interestingly, in other NHS-type countries, purchasing powers were delegated to local authorities or agencies rather than GPs. Similar, but much smaller-scale, reforms, also targeting GPs (e.g. an experiment in Berlin, and a pilot experiment in Leningrad), have been piloted with little success in other Bismarck and Semashko countries (see section 4.2 for a description of different European health care systems).

Systematic reviews of the available evidence point to relatively encouraging results: giving GPs purchasing powers seems to have a positive impact on efficiency (by lower prices for hospital services and shorter waiting periods); on responsiveness to patient needs and preferences; and, after initial opposition, also on the professional status and satisfaction of fundholding GPs. Evidence about the impact of the scheme on equality and quality of care remains inconclusive (Mays *et al.* 2000; Bloor *et al.* 2000; Goodwin 1998; Whynes *et al.* 1999).

Cooperative arrangements across the interface. There is also evidence that the best-performing fundholding GPs spontaneously developed cooperative, network-like arrangements. Based on those bottom-up experiments, the British government launched two subsequent large-scale waves of pro-cooperative, network-like reforms from 1996 onwards. In 1996–7, some 83 Total Purchasing Pilots (TPPs) involved a complete delegation of the purchasing function to GP group practices (Baxter *et al.* 2000). In April 1999, some 481 PC Groups were created which involved compulsory membership of GPs, community and specialist nurses, and local health social services authorities in shared decision-making on service coordination.

The official evaluation of TPPs suggests that there are coordination/control trade-offs linked to organizational size. In bigger PC group practices, cooperation and shared decision-making are more difficult to obtain (due to higher decision costs and incentives for free-riding), but an equitable and cost-efficient allocation of clinical and financial risks across GPs and patient groups is easier to achieve due to bigger reference populations. In smaller practices, the higher prevalence of joint decision-making observed is linked to a greater reduction in referrals, but also might involve higher management and financial costs (Baxter *et al.* 2000). PC groups have also been studied since their creation (Audit Commission 1999; Wilkin *et al.* 2000). Evidence on the impact on delivery and outcomes is still lacking.

Experiments with network coordination mechanisms operating within public sector hierarchies were also launched in the Scandinavian countries, in which PC steers collective decision-making across care levels. The pioneering country was Denmark, where practising GPs started to be contracted by hospitals as part-time advisors and coordinators from the mid-1990s. The scheme, which spontaneously developed at the local level as a result of professional initiative, soon covered all Danish hospitals. At this stage, the national GP union negotiated salary complements to compensate GPs for their new tasks as coordinators; regional authorities, by agreement with the College of GPs, started to steer the process. In contrast with the British case, no market-based instruments were used to promote the scheme. By 1997, some 10 per cent of GPs worked as part-time coordinators, initially for hospitals, and latterly also for community purchasing boards led by local health authorities. There is some evidence that in the late 1990s other Scandinavian countries had started to introduce similar types of networks (Olesen *et al.* 1998).

Gatekeeping as a hierarchical coordination mechanism. Mechanisms through which hierarchical coordination power over other levels of care is delegated to GPs were introduced in European NHS-type health care systems starting in the 1960s. The most important example is the delegation of a gatekeeping function to GPs, establishing a monopoly over patient entry flows into specialist and community care. Until the advent of the 1990 pro-coordination reforms, administrative rules dominated the referral process, leaving little margin for choice of alternative providers. This is consistent with the fact that communication between GPs and other specialists was as weak in gatekeeping countries as in non-gatekeeping ones (e.g. Grundmeijer 1996; Vehvilainen *et al.* 1996; Gérvas *et al.* 2001). In spite of that, there is fairly robust evidence that gatekeeping curbs health expenditure, especially if operated by a resourceful PC sector (Gerdtham and Jönsson 2000).

Since the mid-1990s, some social health insurance (SHI) countries (e.g. France, Israel, Germany), and most countries of Central and Eastern Europe (CEE) launched reforms aimed at promoting gate-keeping. A recent study on the French experience shows that the planned introduction of the scheme was aborted due to the strong opposition of most professional associations, which ended up weakening the initial support of some PC associations (Polton 2004). The available evidence on the pioneering Dutch case points to additional problems in implementing the scheme under a SHI context characterized by patient choice of provider: the role of gatekeeper is apparently unpopular; and wealthier patients seem prepared to pay to go directly to a specialist (Kulu-Glasgow *et al.* 1998). Recent research findings concerning this theme are as follows. Countries where PC has gatekeeping functions include greater rationing of specialized care, mainly expressed through longer waiting lists; it is this second problem, and not the role as gatekeeper itself, that generates dissatisfaction (Grumbach *et al.* 1999). Finally, research in Israel emphasizes that attitudes towards gatekeeping vary across social classes and political parties, with the lower and middle classes in favour of it (Gross *et al.* 2000; Tabenkin and Gross 2000).

3.2. Pro-coordination reforms expanding the service portfolio of PC provision

Antecedents: The first wave of reforms. During the 1970s and 1980s, the service portfolio of PC in most European countries was being extended. New preventive and PC services were covered. In SHI countries, it developed as one response to market-like competition between independent GPs and medical specialists. In Beveridge countries with predominant public provision, it was affected by state regulation expanding task profiles at the PC level, and/or via hierarchical integration of several individual GP practices and other first-contact professionals within multidisciplinary PC teams.

In the Beveridge countries where GPs are independent contractors, PC teams were formed by more network-like arrangements, like professional partnerships, long-term rent contracts, etc. GPs were free to decide whether to integrate or not and whom to integrate with, as well as to contract support staff autonomously. Accordingly, the constitution of multidisciplinary teams proceeded at a slow rhythm, and single-handed practices subsisted, co-existing with group ones (Gérvas *et al.* 1994; Starfield 1991; Boerma *et al.* 1997).

Ana Rico, Richard B. Saltman and Wienke G. W. Boerma

In SHI countries, expanded task-profiles via competition has led to duplication of services (Boerma *et al.* 1997). Available research concerning the impact of multidisciplinary groups in Beveridge countries also suggests that inter-professional collaboration is difficult to attain via hierarchical mechanisms only. Frequently the groups do not work together, with each professional working in a relatively isolated manner (Sergison *et al.* 1997). Without collaboration, task profiles expanded by decree are not easy to implement either. However, when there is shared decision-making and management of patients, results improve (Halliwell *et al.* 1999).

The 1990s pro-coordination reforms. During the 1990s, extension of services provided at this level took on a new rhythm in Western Europe. Preventive care (routine checks, health promotion clinics), community care (home, palliative and mental care), together with substitution of some hospital care (e.g. minor surgery, diagnostics, and rehabilitation) constituted the main objectives of reforms (Broadbent 1998; Florin 1999; Pritchard and Hughes 1995; Walzer *et al.* 1999; Halliwell *et al.* 1999). Three successive waves of reform were launched in Europe aimed at modifying the service portfolio of PC and other care levels, based respectively on market-based, network-like and hierarchical mechanisms, which in some countries overlapped in time.

In some Beveridge countries, and most notably in Great Britain, the unexpected outcome of market-based incentives to expand PC tasks was again the spontaneous development by PC professionals of network cooperation with other PC colleagues and across the interface. As a result, a series of cooperative arrangements developed, closely linked to expanded PC task profiles, but also derived from the new powers of GPs as active coordinators of other care levels. Some examples of this type of experiment are as follows:

* outreach clinics that contract part-time specialists to attend consultations with the GPs in health centres
* integration of nurses specialized in community services (geriatrics, mental care, public health) into PC groups, but maintaining their contractual ties with their original level of care
* PC teams in charge of part-time provision and coordination of hospital accidents and emergencies departments
* GP cooperatives for the joint management and provision of out-of-hours care
* schemes of in-house referral to other GPs within group practices for specially complex or expensive cases

Evaluation of the results and characteristics of these experiences has begun. Most of the available literature concentrates on the relative cost-effectiveness of having PC deliver these services as compared to other providers (Bentur 2001; Bond *et al.* 2000; Somerset *et al.* 1999; Walker *et al.* 1999; Roland and Shapiro 1998; Williams *et al.* 1997; Dale *et al.* 1996; Scott 1996). PHC-based specialist care seems to be generally able to obtain similar health outcomes at less cost than other specialist consultants in the case of frequent conditions, which allows them to see enough patients annually to acquire the necessary skills directly. For less prevalent interventions, which rely more heavily on inter-professional collaboration, either hospitals or other specialist community providers (such as home care organizations or specialist nurses) apparently deliver more cost-effective care.

One problem is that existing assessments have not yet been in place long enough to permit evaluation of the long-term dynamics of substitution policies, which are likely to give a different picture than short-run investigations (due, for instance, to learning economies and slowly developing trust relationships between the actors involved). Moreover, they often do not include all the costs and benefits accruing to patients and GPs. In the few cases for which there is evidence, patient and GP satisfaction usually increased as a result of the assumption of new tasks by PC at the expense of other levels. This was due to the reduced travel time costs for patients, the improved opportunities for expanding knowledge and skills for GPs, and the enhanced continuity and comprehensiveness of care guaranteed by the new schemes.

In SHI countries, the expansion of tasks through pro-cooperation mechanism has been mainly stimulated by targeted economic incentives, in the form of public grants for spontaneously developed professional networks providing integrated care and disease management programmes for the chronically ill. The Netherlands pioneered "transmural" care reforms, which were launched in 1994. By 1999 there were 504 transmural networks in operation, involving almost all hospitals and home care providers in the country. GPs participated in 45 per cent of them and GP practices in 20 per cent (Van der Linden *et al.* 2001). France started similar reforms in 1996, but implementation was retarded by the slow collective decision-making process which led to the exclusion of the schemes of insurer-run managed care plans competing for public funds (Polton 2004). Germany followed in the late 1990s (Busse 2000).

4. Towards Convergence? Drivers and Barriers of Pro-coordination Reforms across Europe

4.1. Shared context and policy feedback: cooperation as a competitive strategy

Few advances in inter-professional and inter-organizational collaboration were made prior to the 1990s. From then on, a series of transformations in the broader societal context, as well as some shared feedback effects, drove improvements in this field. Two types of policy feedback started to operate across European countries. Collaborative arrangements have indirectly (and mostly unexpectedly) resulted from broader reform measures aimed at fostering cost-containment and market competition. Improvements in PC financing, training and technology have significantly, although only slowly, reduced the structural obstacles to coordination.

As for the social context, a development overlooked in the previous literature is the impact of the increasing prevalence of chronic illnesses on the need for coordination between care services (since these patients are frequent users of all levels simultaneously). The resulting inter-organizational interdependencies pose critical problems for both market and hierarchical coordination. There are two main solutions to this problem (Scharpf 1993):

(1) coordination power can be transferred to front-line professionals; and (2) organizational units can be expanded or merged, in order to internalize previous inter-unit interactions. These two strategies correspond well with the process of organizational restructuring in PC.

4.2. Institutional and socio-political power legacies: the dynamics of hybridization and selective PD across Europe

The common trend towards experimentation with pro-coordination reforms in Europe during the 1990s points to policy convergence across Europe. However, both the rhythm of reforms, and the fate of the different institutional and organizational mechanisms embodied within them, vary across groups of countries, suggesting differential selective PD patterns. Great Britain, Denmark, and to a lesser extent, the Netherlands, can be considered examples of best practice for the design of pro-cooperation reforms; and they have successfully implemented the attempted transfer of powers and tasks to PC. Comprehensive, strong inter-organizational networks emerged as a result. In SHI countries, additional public funds were made available to new, virtually integrated, hospital-centred networks. PC played a very minor role, and the initial attempts at expanding its powers and scale in France and Germany failed. In CEE and Southern Europe, the few pro-coordination experiments that were launched did not lead to institutional reform. Ex-communist countries, however, experimented with radical transformation of their health care systems towards the SHI model, including the privatization and disintegration of PC providers. Since the late 1990s they have started to incorporate some traditional Beveridge-type tools to strengthen PC. Serious financial difficulties, however, resulted in implementation gaps and a contraction of their health care systems.

Institutional legacies and PC organization. Next we examine the potential effects of the inherited institutional framework and socio-political structure (SPS) in explaining reform pathways across Europe. At the start of the 1990s, there were three main types of European health care systems, and four main models of PC organization. As for political institutions, the main actors with formal political power (FPP) in Beveridge or NHS-type countries (Nordic, Great Britain, and Southern Europe) were state authorities. This is also generally true for CEE countries during the early 1990s, when the transition to the SHI model was launched and implemented. From then on, political institutions in CEE countries started to move towards the neo-corporatist (network-like) schemes typical of SHI countries, based on joint decision-making by the state, insurers and professionals.

Organizationally, the map was as follows. In the countries which pioneered pro-cooperation reforms in Europe, most PC providers are independent partnerships under a long-term contract with the public sector, a type of network-like organizational arrangement (model 1, M1). They also share a relatively strong position of PC within system coordination (i.e. monopoly of first contact, multidisciplinary groups with expanded task profiles). In SHI countries, which developed weaker, hospital-centred coordination networks,

PC professionals were also independent entrepreneurs, but most worked as individuals in competition with ambulatory specialists for first contact (model 2: M2). Publicly operated Beveridge countries (M3) share with M1 countries the strong coordination role of PC professionals; but these as state officials enjoy less autonomy (and other resources) than their private counterparts. The institutional position of PC in the CEE countries still retaining a Soviet model (M4) is considerably weaker than in Beveridge or Bismarck countries, with the partial exception of the ex-Yugoslavian countries (Boerma *et al.* 2004).

Differences in political institutions can explain some of the different trajectories of reform across European countries. For instance: (1) in two of the three vanguard countries of Western Europe the state had monopoly FPP rights; and (2) a radical privatization of insurance and PC provision was rapidly implemented under the centralized rule of state authorities in CEE countries. They cannot explain (3) the pioneering role of The Netherlands, or (4) the fact that the 1990s pro-coordination reforms progressed more rapidly in SHI countries than in publicly operated Beveridge countries or CEE countries. Differences in PC organization and strength across Europe might explain the reform paths (1) and (3), but do not match well with developments (2) and (4). They do not explain either (5) why few advances in coordination across the interface were achieved before the 1990s in M1 countries.

Accounting for selective PD and hybridization: socio-political structures, redistributive policies and the centrality of the political process. In section 2, we defined the SPS as the distribution of informal political power (IPP) resources (ownership, knowledge and social support) among the three major socio-political actors in health care (the state, insurers and professionals). For PC-based pro-coordination policies, the relative IPP of PC professionals versus other specialists can also be expected to play a critical role. We also developed two main hypotheses about the causal role of the SPS: (H1) that it is a major determinant of the political process, and, therefore, of the likelihood of policy change; and (H2) that changes in the SPS result from the interaction between wide societal pressures and specific policy feedback processes (with redistributive policies expected to have a prominent role). Both hypotheses apparently fit the available evidence well.

(*H1*) In the three vanguard M1 countries as well as in SHI M2 countries PC professionals are private entrepreneurs; they therefore share ownership-based IPP with the state (who often own most hospitals). This also increases their professional status *vis-à-vis* their salaried hospital colleagues. However, in all SHI countries the monopsonic power of the state in financing is shared with insurance companies and ambulatory care is largely privately owned and operated; in addition, and with the exception of the Netherlands, PC shares its market power with ambulatory specialists, who control more than 50 per cent of the first contact care market (Boerma *et al.* 1997). This in turn points to lower patient support for PC professionals *vis-à-vis* specialists in M2 than in M1 countries. In M1 countries, relatively autonomous PC group practices provide more opportunities to expand the knowledge-based

IPP, and to assume new functions. In contrast, in most M3 and M4 countries, PC doctors do not enjoy ownership-based IPP; and as in M2 countries, they are frequently skipped by the upper social classes (private specialist care), and consequently enjoy less market power and support from them. CEE M4 countries mainly differ from WE M3 countries in that the support for the private sector also extended during the 1990s to the middle and lower classes, following the financial and political breakdown of the ex-Soviet Union.

These differences in the SPS structure across countries, and its effects on the political process, go a great way to explain the differential reform patterns numbered as (1)–(5) in the subsection above. They imply that PC professionals are powerful lay actors within the political process in M1 countries; a weaker presence in SHI countries, where insurers and ambulatory specialists are their direct competitors; and a nearly irrelevant role in M3 and M4 countries. In fact, there is evidence that strong PC associations, the natural coalition parties of state authorities in PC-based pro-coordination reforms, helped design and ended up supporting the reform schemes both in Denmark and Great Britain (Olesen *et al.* 1998; Whynes *et al.* 1999), thereby facilitating policy change and granting implementation. There is also evidence that the fierce informal opposition of powerful professional (specialist-dominated) associations divided PC professionals, initially favourable, and ended up blocking PC-based pro-coordination reforms in France (Polton 2004).

(*H2*) The predominant role of the SPS as a determinant of the likelihood of policy change does not however imply that the differential patterns of selective PD are immutable. The best-performing countries in Europe in terms of pro-coordination policies are also the ones which have effected a major redistribution of financial and human resources towards and within the PC level (Halliwell *et al.* 1999; Bloor *et al.* 2000; Jenkins-Clarke *et al.* 1997). This helps explain a critical fact so far unaccounted for, namely the final support of PC professionals and citizens after their initial frontal opposition in most countries. Generally speaking, state authorities in SHI played a more hands-off, reactive role by comparison with the pro-active, targeted interventions in the pioneering Beveridge countries. Redistributive policies (e.g. improvements in training) usually take more time to obtain the expected results than regulatory policies. Recent reform experiences in CEE countries, carefully tailored to effect a shift of resources towards PC, also suggest that other redistributive policies (like financial or manpower transfers) can attain more rapid effects (McKee 2004).

5. Summary and Policy Implications

During the 1990s, a series of parallel pro-coordination reforms involving a broader organizational restructuring in health care were launched and implemented across Europe. New sophisticated virtual integration strategies were tailor-made to promote cooperation and redistribute functions and resources across the interface. Virtual integration allows for simultaneous enjoyment of the advantages of autonomy and of organizational integration. The countries in which PC was strong, and closer to the network model prior to the 1990s (mainly Great Britain, Denmark and the Netherlands), are examples of best practice also in the latest generation of PC-based pro-cooperation policies and supporting mechanisms. In these countries, powerful PC associations ended up supporting state-induced reforms, facilitating policy change. While there is inconclusive evidence on the impact of these changes, existing research points to substantial cost-effectiveness and satisfaction improvements. In European SHI countries, PC-based pro-coordination experiments have been blocked by powerful professional (specialist-dominated) groups and insurers' associations, faced with relatively weak PC associations groups and hesitant state authorities; and more limited and weaker professional virtual networks resulted therefore from more acute contextual pressures. Elsewhere there was only limited experimentation with pro-cooperation reforms by health care professionals, which were often not given the necessary state support.

Cooperative networks hold considerable promise of achieving system coordination in health care, but they are not self-sustaining, and require demanding supporting conditions to be effective. Some market mechanisms, like decentralization of purchasing power to PC groups, seem to induce cooperation. Others, like competition, can inhibit it. The public sector can play an important role in removing the obstacles for networks to effect cost-efficient system coordination, by regulating network participants, financial mechanisms, and decision-making rules; and by providing supporting services (information and research, juridical and financial advice, etc.). More generally, inter-organizational coordination involves tasks not previously performed in health care systems. Consequently, in spite of its potential long-term cost-reducing effect, an initial increase in resources is needed. In fact a basic policy implication of our research findings is that the transfers of powers and tasks should be tightly coupled with parallel shifts in accountability and resources to be successful.

Acknowledgement

Based on the preliminary work done for the book "Primary care in the driver's seat? Organizational reform of primary care in Europe", jointly funded by the European Observatory on Health Care Systems and the Nuffield Trust. The authors are also grateful to the EU Network COST A15, which supported the group discussion of previous versions of the paper.

References

Audit Commission (1999), *PCGs: An Early View of Primary Care Groups in England*, London: Stationery Office.

Bartlett, W. (1996), The regulation of general practice in the UK, *International Journal of Health Planning and Management*, 11: 3–18.

Baxter, K., Bachmann, M. and Bevan, G. (2000), PC groups: trade-offs in managing budgets and risk, *Public Money and Management*, 20, 1: 53–61.

Bentur, N. (2001), Hospital at home: what is its place in the health system? *Health Policy*, 55: 71–9.

Ana Rico, Richard B. Saltman and Wienke G. W. Boerma

Bloor, K., Maynard, A. and Street, A. (1992), *How Much Is a Doctor Worth?* Discussion paper no. 98, Centre for Health Economics, University of York.

Bloor, K., Maynard, A. and Street, A. (2000), The cornerstone of Labour's *New NHS: Reforming PC*. In P. Smith (ed.), *Reforming Markets in Health Care*, Buckingham: Open University Press.

Boerma, W., Dubois, C. A., Rico, A. and Saltman, R. (2004), Mapping PC organization in Europe. In R. Saltman, A. Rico and W. Boerma (eds), *Primary Care in the Driving Seat? Organizational Reforms in European Health Care*, Buckingham: Open University Press (in preparation).

Boerma, W., Van der Zee, J. and Fleming, D. M. (1997), Service profiles of GPs in Europe, *British Journal of General Practice*, 47: 481–6.

Bond, M., Bowling, A., Abery, A., McClay, M. and Dickinson, E. (2000), Evaluation of outreach clinics held by specialists in general practice in England, *British Medical Journal*, 54: 149–56.

Broadbent, J. (1998), Practice nurses and the effects of the new GP contract in the British NHS: the advent of a professional project? *Social Science and Medicine*, 47: 497–506.

Buckley, G. (1999), Revalidation is the answer to one question—but many more remain, *British Medical Journal*, 319: 1145–6.

Busse, R. (2000), *Health Care Systems in Transition: Germany*, Copenhagen: European Observatory on Health Care Systems.

Callaghan, G., Exworthy, M., Hudson, B. and Peckham, S. (2000), Prospects for collaboration in PC: relationships between social services and the PCGs, *Journal of Inter-professional Care*, 14: 19–26.

Dale, J., Lang, H., Roberts, J., Green, J. and Glucksman, E. (1996), Cost effectiveness of treating PC patients in A & E departments, *British Medical Journal*, 312: 1340–4.

Florin, D. (1999), Scientific uncertainty and the role of expert advice: the case of health checks for coronary heart disease prevention by GPs in the UK, *Social Science and Medicine*, 49: 1269–83.

Gerdtham, U.-G. and Jönsson, B. (2000), International comparisons of health expenditure: theory, data and econometric analysis. In A. J. Culyer and J. P. Newhouse (eds), *Handbook of Health Economics*, vol 1, Amsterdam: Elsevier.

Gérvas, J., Palomo, L., Pastor-Sánchez, R., Pérez-Fernández, M. and Rubio, C. (2001), Problemas acuciantes en atención primaria [Pressing problems in PC], *Atención Primaria*, 28, 7: 472–7.

Gérvas, J., Pérez-Fernández, M. and Starfield, B. H. (1994), PC, financing and gate-keeping in western Europe, *Family Practice*, 11: 307–17.

Goddard, M. and Mannion, R. (1998), From competition to cooperation: new economic relationships in the National Health Service, *Health Economics*, 7: 105–19.

Goddard, M., Mannion, R. and Smith, P. (2000), Enhancing performance in health care: a theoretical perspective on agency and the role of information, *Health Economics*, 9: 95–107.

Goodwin, N. (1998), GP fundholding. In J. Le Grand, N. Mays and J. Mulligan (eds), *Learning from the NHS Internal Market: a Review of the Evidence*, London: King's Fund.

Grielen, S. J., Boerma, W. G. W. and Groenewegen, P. (2000), Unity or diversity? Task profiles of GPs in Central and Eastern Europe, *European Journal of Public Health*, 10: 249–54.

Gross, R., Tabenkin, H. and Bramli-Greenberg, S. (2000), Who needs a gatekeeper? Patients' views of the role of the PC physician, *Family Practice*, 17, 3: 222–9.

Grumbach, K., Selby, J., Damberg, C., Bindman, A., Quesenberry, C., Truman, A. and Uratsu, C. (1999), Resolving the gatekeeper conundrum: what patients value in PC and referral to specialists, *Journal of the American Medical Association*, 282, 3: 261–6.

Grundmeijer, H. (1996), GP and specialist: why do they communicate so badly? *European Journal of General Practice*, 2: 53–5.

Halliwell, S., Sibbald, B. and Rose, S. (1999), *A Bibliography of Skill-mix in Primary Care: The Sequel*, NCRPC working paper, University of Manchester.

Harrison, M. and Calltorp, J. (2000), The reorientation of market-oriented reforms in Swedish health care, *Health Policy*, 50: 219–40.

Harrison, S. (2001), Structural interests in health care: *reforming* the UK medical profession. In M. Bovens, P. t'Hart and G. Peters (eds), *Success and Failure in Government. A Comparative Analysis*, Aldershot: Edward Elgar.

Hughes Tuohy, C. (1999), Dynamics of a changing health sphere: the United States, Britain, and Canada, *Health Affairs*, 18, 3: 114–34.

Hunter, D. (2000), Disease management: has it a future? *British Medical Journal*, 320: 530.

Jenkins-Clarke, S., Carr-Hill, R., Dixon, P. and Pringle, M. (1997), *Skill Mix in Primary Care—A Study of the Interface between the GP and Other Members of the Primary Health Care Team*, Occasional paper no. 29, York: Centre for Health Economics.

Kulu-Glasgow, I., Delnoij, D. and de Bakker, D. (1998), Self-referral in a gatekeeping system: patients' reasons for skipping the GP, *Health Policy*, 45: 221–38.

Landau, J. (2001), Organizing GPs into group practices in Italy. Paper presented to the 2001 Conference of the EHMA, Granada: 24–5 June.

McKee, M., Maclehose, L. and Rico, A. (2004), Health care needs and reform trends. In M. McKee, L. Maclehose and R. Busse (eds), *Health Care Reforms in Pre-accession Countries*, Buckingham: Open University Press (in press).

Mannion, R. and Smith, P. (1997), Trust and reputation in community care: theory and evidence. In P. Anand and A. McGuire (eds), *Changes in Health Care: Reflection on the NHS Internal Market*, London: Macmillan.

Mays, N., Mulligan, J. and Goodwin, N. (2000), The British quasi-market in health care: a balance sheet of the evidence, *Journal of Health Services and Research Policy*, 5: 49–58.

Mays, P. G., Halverson, P. K. and Kaluzny, A. D. (1998), Collaboration to improve community health, *Journal on Quality Improvement*, 24: 518–40.

Olesen, F., Jensen, P. B., Grinsted, P. and Henriksen, J. S. (1998), GPs as advisers and coordinators in hospitals, *Quality in Health Care*, 7: 42–7.

Polton, D. (2004), The French experience. Unpublished case study prepared for R. Saltman, A. Rico and W. Boerma, *Primary Care in the Driving Seat? Organizational Reforms in European Health Care*, Buckingham: Open University Press (in preparation).

Pritchard, P. and Hughes, J. (1995), *Shared Care: the Future Imperative?* London: Royal Society of Medicine Press.

Rico, A. and Costa, J. (2004), Power rather than path? The dynamics of health policy under health care federalism, *Journal of Health Politics, Policy and Law* (forthcoming).

Ring, S. P. and Van de Ven, A. H. (1992), Structuring cooperative relationships between organizations, *Strategic Management Journal*, 13: 483–98.

Roberts, E. and Mays, N. (1998), Can PC and community-based models of emergency care substitute for the hospital A & E department? *Health Policy*, 44: 191–214.

Roland, E. M. and Shapiro, J. (1998), Specialist outreach clinics in general practice, *British Medical Journal*, 316: 1028.

Saffran, D. G., Rogers, W. H., Tarlov, A. R., Inui, T., Taira, D. A., Montgomery, J. E., Ware, J. E. and Slavin, C. P. (2000), Organizational and financial characteristics of health plans. Are they related to PC performance? *Archives of Family Medicine*, 160: 69–76.

Salisbury, C., Trivella, M. and Bruster, S. (2000), Demand for and supply of out of hours care from GPs in England and Scotland, *British Medical Journal*, 320: 618–21.

Scharpf, F. (1993), Coordination in hierarchies and networks. In F. Scharpf (ed.), *Games in Hierarchies and Networks*, Frankfurt: Campus Verlag.

Ana Rico, Richard B. Saltman and Wienke G. W. Boerma

Scharpf, F. (1988), The joint-decision making trap, *Public Policy and Administration*, 66: 239–78.

Scott, A. (1996), Primary or secondary care? What can economics contribute to evaluation at the interface? *Journal of Public Health Medicine*, 18: 19–26.

Sergison, M., Sibbald, B. and Rose, S. (1997), *Skill Mix in PC: A Bibliography*, NCRPC working paper, Manchester: University of Manchester.

Sheaff, R. (1999), The development of English primary care group governance: a scenario analysis, *International Journal of Health Planning and Management*, 14: 257–68.

Somerset, M., Faulkner, A. and Shaw, A. (1999), Obstacles on the path to a primary-care led National Health Service: complexities of outpatient care, *Social Science and Medicine*, 48: 213–25.

Starfield, B. (1991), PC and health. A cross-national comparison, *Journal of the American Medical Association*, 266: 2268–71.

Tabenkin, H. and Gross, R. (2000), The role of the PC physician in the Israeli health care system as a gatekeeper—the viewpoint of health care policy makers, *Health Policy*, 52: 73–85.

Van der Linden, B., Spreeuwenberg, C. and Schrijvers, A. J. (2001), Integration of care in the Netherlands: the development of transmural care since 1994, *Health Policy*, 55: 111–20.

Vehvilainen, A. T., Kumpusalo, A. and Takala, J. K. (1996), Feedback information from specialists to general practitioners in Finland, *European Journal of General Practice*, 2: 55–7.

Walker, Z., McKinnon, M. and Townsend, J. (1999), Shared care for high-dependency patients: a review, *Health Services Management Centre*, 12: 205–11.

Webb, A. (1991), Coordination: a problem in public sector management, *Policy and Politics*, 19: 229–41.

Whynes, D. K., Ennew, C. T. and Feighan, T. (1999), Entrepreneurial attitudes of primary health care physicians in the United Kingdom, *Journal of Economic Behaviour and Organization*, 38: 331–47.

Wilkin, D., Gillam, S. and Leese, B. (2000), *The National Tracker Survey of PC Groups and Trusts. Progress and challenges, 1999/2000*, London: Kings Fund.

Williams, G., Flynn, R. and Pickard, S. (1997), Paradoxes of GP fundholding: contracting for community health services in the British NHS, *Social Science and Medicine*, 45: 1669–78.

5

The Uncertain Convergence of Disability Policies in Western Europe

Björn Hvinden

Introduction

This paper asks whether we are witnessing a trend towards greater similarity —*convergence*—between Western European countries in the area of disability policy. Generally speaking, "convergence" means a movement towards the same point. But the term is used about quite different aspects of social policy. For instance, it has been used to refer to a greater similarity of

1. *constraints and conditions* for policy-making (and more generally for the functioning of welfare states);
2. *policy objectives*;
3. *policy instruments* (means, measures, approaches to realize these objectives);
4. *outputs* (e.g. the number of beneficiaries of a particular provision, the level of spending); and/or
5. *outcomes* (e.g. the employment situation, economic well-being or social integration of a population group in question, for instance disabled people).

In organization theory a distinction has been drawn between general objectives and operational goals. According to March and Simon (1993: 61) the operationality of goals refers to "the extent to which it is possible to observe and test how well goals are being achieved". General objectives—for instance in disability policy—have to be translated into more concrete and specific operational goals. Objectives that are not operationalized remain statements of good intentions and their main significance may be of symbolic nature. Operational goals and policy instruments are closely related, blurring the distinction between objectives and the means to reach them. The process of operationalizing general objectives implies that one is not only specifying desirable outcomes but also limiting the relevant instruments to reach these. Operational goals are in one sense themselves means to achieve the general goal. Thus a convergence of general objectives is more abstract and "thin" than convergence of operational goals and policy instruments. An important issue is therefore whether there is scope for convergence of operational goals

and approaches in Western European disability policy, and not only convergence in terms of general objectives.

A number of studies have demonstrated that there is much cross-national
divergence in the objectives and instruments of disability policy of Western
European countries (EC 2001, 1998a; van Oorschot and Hvinden 2001;
SSA 1999; Thornton and Lunt 1997; Machado and de Lorenzo 1997; Aarts
and de Jong 1996; Aarts *et al.* 1996; Aarts *et al.* 1998, 1999; Wilson 1996; Prins
and Bloch 2001; Prinz 2003; OECD 2003). If so, are there any reasons to
expect that these aspects of policy are becoming more similar? First, one may
claim that most countries of Western Europe are to an increasing extent
faced with similar challenges, e.g. ageing populations, more fluid and changing families, growing pressure on public budgets, more open and competitive
markets for goods and services, and so on. Second, one may point to the
international exchange of policy ideas and the possible policy learning resulting from this sort of exchange. More specifically, supranational bodies like
the UN, ILO, EU and OECD seek to promote common perceptions of con-
tingencies and problems, perhaps leading to what has been called "epistemic
communities" among experts and policy-makers (Deacon 1999). Third, one
may refer to the emergence of a fairly strong transnational network of disabled
people's organizations, putting pressure on supranational bodies for the
acceptance of stronger rights and protection against discrimination (Newman
1997; Geyer 2000). Arguably we may on the basis of this expect some force
towards more similar general objectives—and possibly the adoption of more
similar instruments in disability policy—between Western European countries.

The main thesis of this paper is, however, that a cross-national examination of recent developments does *not* suggest any clear trend towards policy
convergence in the overall disability protection systems of member states.
Hence it may be fruitful to formulate more specific assumptions in relation
to different parts of these systems. The underlying idea here is that some
areas of disability policy are more "crowded" by established objectives, rules,
measures and instruments, than others. Areas filled up with long-existing
policies, power balances or vested interests are—*ceteris paribus*—more likely to
remain resilient and resistant to substantial change than more "vacant" areas.
In other words, there will be stronger path-dependency in crowded areas. As
defined by Levi (1997: 28) path dependency means "that once a country or
region has started down a track, the costs of reversal are very high. There
will be other choice points, but the entrenchment of institutional arrangements obstructs an easy reversal of the initial choice." Conversely, we may
assume there will be greater potential scope for adopting similar problem
definitions, objectives and instruments across countries, that is, a trend
toward convergence, in vacant areas.

In order to clarify this thesis I will draw a line between two aspects of the
ongoing public discussion or "discourse" about the disability protection
system in Western Europe. This distinction is partly analytical but sufficiently
real to illustrate that those parts of the protection system that receive the
greatest attention from policy-makers at national and transnational levels are
not necessarily those with the greatest potential for convergence. The two
contrasting discourses are here rendered in a simplified, "ideal-type" fashion.

The discourse of societal costs of disability takes as its point of departure the high levels of expenditure on income maintenance for disabled people—often called "passive benefits"—and the substantial proportion of the adult population receiving such benefits. This is mainly seen as representing a problem for society, for public finances, economic efficiency and the functioning of the labour market. There is concern about disincentive effects resulting from the level of benefits or replacement compared to minimum or average wages, leading too many people to claim these benefits. A related but slightly different concern is that not all possibilities for using the (residual) work capacity of disabled people are pursued, for instance by assisting them to acquire alternative vocational qualifications. As a consequence of these failures, excessive pressure on public budgets is created, the level of taxes becomes too high and/or the possibilities to introduce other improvements of public provision become restricted (opportunity costs). These concerns may be expressed even more strongly in countries where the design of the public income maintenance system means that disabled people who have previous earnings are granted substantial income-related supplements to a general basic pension. The persistence of fairly high levels of unemployment in some countries implies that the unused labour power, capacities and qualifications of people receiving disability benefits have not necessarily been missed so far. Still the long-term effects of low entry into or high exit from the labour market on the part of disabled people may still be seen as detrimental. In many European countries as well as within the EU and the OECD there is a concern for the impact of ongoing demographic changes, especially the ageing of populations. These changes result in a worsened balance between the number of people of working age and the number of people below and over this age, that is, a worsened dependency rate, creating a shortage of labour. If a substantial minority of the working-age population is permanently excluded from the labour market for disability-related reasons, this will obviously cause additional difficulties.

The discourse of equal rights and opportunities takes as its point of departure the overall situation, experiences and perspectives of disabled people. Here the focus is on the objectives of promoting self-determination, independent living, equal treatment and opportunities for disabled people. Participation in the labour market is also here seen as important but more as a right than an obligation, and clearly not at the price of reduced living standards and diminished economic security for the disabled person. From this perspective, the relationships between the different aspects of the disabled person's life situation are stressed. Benefits and services that facilitate independent living in one's own home, mobility and transport, participation in social and cultural life, are regarded as important in themselves, as conditions for the enjoyment of full citizenship of disabled people, and not only as possible conditions for their participation in gainful employment. Moreover, many of the obstacles, barriers and difficulties faced by disabled people are seen as the result of ways in which society (including working life) is organized and physically designed, and not as caused by the person's impairment as such. This view suggests that disabled people are institutionally discriminated against and that action that makes such discrimination illegal and raises people's awareness about these issues is required.

As indicated by this outline the two sets of considerations may partly be overlapping in some of their concerns and the proposals for reform that they inspire. Still, they are parts of two broader policy contexts or discourses and they will not necessarily be interlinked or coordinated with each other. Broadly speaking, the first set of considerations has emerged within the Jobs Strategy and Disability Study of the OECD (1999a, 2003) and the Employment Strategy of the EU with its machinery of guidelines and yearly national employment plans responding to these. These reform programmes have encompassed concerns for the level of labour market participation of disabled people and proposals for ways to improve their labour market prospects. Similar concerns have been expressed with the EU's current efforts at modernizing the social protection systems of member states, in order to make these more sustainable and employment-friendly. The second set of considerations has to a great extent been codified through the emerging disability strategy of the EU. Similar differences in focus and concerns relating to disability can be refound in national policy contexts.

Methodological Limitations: Some Cautions

Disability is a *gendered* policy field, in the sense that protection systems tend to work differently in systematic ways and provide dissimilar entitlements as well as outcomes for women and men. Unfortunately, it is still rare that the routine statistics collected by transnational bodies present figures for expenditure and beneficiaries for women and men separately. Similarly, there are notable differences in the use of disability provisions by *age*. Hence it would be helpful if statistics on the numbers of beneficiaries and expenditure as a matter of routine were broken down on *age*, at least to make it possible to distinguish between people under, in and over working age (16–64 years). Finally, we are faced with the problem of *substitution effects*. For instance, there are reasons to believe that disability benefit schemes in some countries have served to conceal problems of structural unemployment, especially in relation to older sections of the labour force. The existence of substitution effects implies that one effect of changes in eligibility rules may be that some people are moved from one benefit scheme to another, and thus administratively reclassified, with limited consequences for the overall level of public expenditure or the total number of beneficiaries. Such substitution effects are illustrated by the OECD (1999b: 60), van Oorschot and Boos (2001), de Vroom and Guillemard (2002) and Judge (2001: 83).

What Kind of Picture of the Development in Disability Protection Emerges within the Discourse of Societal Costs?

In this presentation of recent trends in the outputs of disability policy, I adopt the division between four geo-social European families of countries developed by Ferrera (1998). This division is based on an overall summary of four characteristics of the countries' social protection systems; rules of access (eligibility) benefit formulae, financing regulations, and organizational-managerial arrangements. Thus one can distinguish between the following groups of countries:

- *Nordic countries*: Denmark, Finland, Norway and Sweden
- *Continental countries*: Austria, Belgium, France, Germany, Luxembourg and the Netherlands
- *Southern countries*: Greece, Italy, Portugal and Spain
- *Western countries*: Ireland and the United Kingdom

Developments in the number of beneficiaries

Western European countries have strongly dissimilar social protection systems covering the disabled section of the population. In some countries the relevant benefit schemes are more strongly integrated and coordinated, while in other countries they are more differentiated and fragmented. Similarly, schemes meant to cover the needs of disabled people may be parts of broad mainstream programmes, making it difficult to identify the exact number of disabled beneficiaries. For these reasons international bodies like the OECD and the EU have until recently been reluctant to present comparative statistics for the number of recipients. Two exceptions to this (OECD 1999b, table 2.9; OECD 2003, chart 3.13) present the number of beneficiaries of the main income maintenance system for disabled people. Thus these figures are likely to be most reliable for countries with fairly unified and disability-specific systems of income protection. Taking these limitations into consideration we can make some tentative observations. First, the proportion of the adult populations in receipt of these cash benefits varied considerably between Western European countries, ranging from 1 to 9 per cent. Second, there were different trends in the last 20 years: the Nordic countries, Luxembourg and the Netherlands had the highest proportion of beneficiaries during this period. The same countries also experienced an upward trend in the proportion receiving income maintenance benefits for disabled people, while this also seemed to be the case with Austria and the United Kingdom. In the other countries the proportion was stable or fluctuating. If we allow ourselves to simplify, the Continental and Nordic groups of countries continued to have higher proportions of beneficiaries than the Southern group and the United Kingdom (here representing the Western group). At the same time there were notable intra-group variations within both the Continental and Southern groups. In all, there emerged no overall trend towards more similar rates of the population in receipt of income maintenance benefits for disabled people; on the contrary the pattern of dispersion appeared fairly stable.

Labour market participation of older women and men

Generally speaking, the proportion of disability beneficiaries tends to be higher in the somewhat older sections of the population of working age (see, for example, the findings summarized by OECD 1999b: 59, 2003: 25). Thus it is informative to look at the changes in labour market participation in these sections of the populations. OECD (2001a) presents figures for the trends in the labour market participation of men and women 55–64 years separately from 1984 to 1999. First, these figures indicate that there was a marked decline in the labour market participation of older *men* in Western Europe in the first part of this period. Eight of the sixteen countries studied increased their labour market participation of older men in the second half of the 1990s. These countries were all in the Nordic and Continental groups. Most remarkable was the increase in the Netherlands. These increases were probably related to generally improved labour market conditions. However, goal-directed efforts to switch from passive to active measures, through vocational rehabilitation and other employment provisions, may also have played some role. Second, the labour market participation of older *women* remained fairly stable until the end of the period under study and then it increased markedly. Again there were some striking and fairly stable inter-group differences: the Continental group of countries had a remarkably lower level of labour market participation for older men than the Nordic, Southern and Western groups of countries. Finland was an exception to this overall pattern, being closer to France and the Netherlands than to its Nordic neighbours. The particular situation of the Continental countries (and Finland) was likely to be the result of a combination of several factors. These included structural characteristics of labour markets, lower formal retirement ages, extensive use of early retirement schemes and/or (as in the cases of Luxembourg and the Netherlands until recently) relatively accessible disability benefit schemes. The Continental group of countries also had a low level of labour market participation for older women, fairly similar to the Southern group (with the exception of Portugal) and Ireland. Again Finland represented an exception in the Nordic group, and more so at the end of the period of study. More detailed studies are called for to establish to what extent somewhat older women in these countries were eligible for and receiving disability or other income replacement benefits or maintained by their spouse/partner. In the case of Finland we may also see a particular impact of the exceptionally severe problems of recession and high unemployment rates in the 1990s.

The implications of the trends summarized here were substantially different for men and women. For *men* increasing disability rates in older age were part of a broader trend towards decreasing labour market participation and earlier exit. For *women*, an increased level of labour market participation meant that more women qualified for disability benefits schemes, to the extent that eligibility depends on the amount of previous employment and the person's own earnings records (Drøpping *et al.* 2000; de Vroom and Guillemard 2002). Women's labour market participation was still lower than men's at the end of the period. But to the extent that more women were now employed for longer periods of adult life, an increasing proportion of them was able to—and probably did—claim disability benefits. Moreover, increased female labour market participation was likely to be associated with a diminishing role for family-based and unpaid care for disabled persons and a growing provision of paid care services (where the workers also tend to be women).

Generally, we would expect that the proportions of women and men claiming disability-related benefits would become more equal in the period in question. This is even more likely to be the case, as there is no reason to suppose that the prevalence of problems related to impairment was substantially lower among women than among men in the Western Europe of the 1990s. According to the findings of the European Community Household Panel (ECHP) between 2 and 8 per cent of both men and women of working age reported that they were severely hampered in their daily activities (Eurostat 2001b, chart 2). The inter-country differences tended to be greater than the differences between women and men. It is difficult, however, to judge whether the variation between countries reflected real differences in degree of disablement, different average age of respondents or differences in the wording and meaning of the questions used in each country.

Developments in expenditure on disability protection in general

Cross-national data on public spending related to disability protection are somewhat more complete and up-to-date than data about the number of beneficiaries. Here Eurostat (2001a, table C 1.3.2) has presented figures for expenditure on disability protection in general as a percentage of the country's Gross Domestic Product (GDP) covering the last 20 years. With some caution it is possible to relate these figures to the figures referred to previously on the number of disability income beneficiaries, and to suggest the following patterns and trends. The Nordic group continued to have high numbers of beneficiaries as well as high levels of spending, while the Southern group continued to have comparatively low numbers of beneficiaries and levels of spending, with the Continental group (as a whole) in an intermediate position in both respects. The United Kingdom appeared to have had an upward trend both in numbers of recipients and expenditure. Luxembourg and the Netherlands, however, stood out as countries that seemed to have growing or fairly stable numbers of recipients while experiencing a downward trend in total expenditure. Moreover, the differences in levels of expenditure between the four groups of countries appeared stable, that is, there was no clear sign of increased similarity, i.e. a trend towards convergence, in the period covered by these data.

A shift towards activation in the social protection system for disabled people?

If governments see the number of beneficiaries and the expenditure related to disability protection as a problem, they have obviously different options. Two major options are: (1) to tighten up the various schemes under this system; and (2) to assist beneficiaries to become less in need of these schemes, for instance by improving their possibilities for self-sufficiency through gainful employment (cf. Drøpping *et al.* 1999). Obviously, these options may also be combined in various ways (cf. Hvinden *et al.* 2001; Kuptsch and Zeiter 2001).

Attempts to tighten up benefit schemes may take the usual forms: making eligibility rules stricter, lowering replacement levels and/or limiting the period of receipt. More specifically, rules regarding what kind of alternative jobs to take into consideration, when assessing degree of diminished work or earning capacity, may be widened, making it more difficult to be deemed unable to work. There are a number of reports of attempts to undertake this sort of tightening from single countries or smaller groups of countries (e.g. Drøpping *et al.* 2000; van Oorschot and Hvinden 2001; OECD 1999b: 60; Visser and Hemerijck 1977). It will be of considerable interest to have more systematic comparative assessments of such attempts, based on longitudinal data and with a larger number of countries.

So far we have only few and incomplete data about the introduction and implementation of strengthened efforts to assist disabled people to become self-supporting through gainful employment. A rough indicator of such attempts is the amount of resources spent on special labour market programmes for disabled people (OECD 1994, 1998, 2001a). As defined by the OECD (1994: 53) such programmes encompass "(a) vocational rehabilitation. Ability testing, work adjustment measures and training other than ordinary labour market training, (b) work for the disabled. Sheltered work and subsidies to regular employment". The OECD secretariat emphasizes that these two categories do not cover the total policy effort in support of disabled people. That is, many disabled people may also benefit from participation in other, less specific and "mainstream" labour market measures, such as general labour market training or youth measures. Even with these limitations it is interesting to note that the overall pattern of expenditure of special labour market programmes for disabled people is largely as one would expect on the basis of the number of income maintenance beneficiaries and overall expenditure on social protection for disabled people. *Ceteris paribus*, it seems reasonable that countries with comparatively high numbers and high expenditure were more concerned to adopt active measures (either alone or in combination with a tightening of the income maintenance system), than countries with comparatively low figures for recipients and expenditure:

- The Nordic countries (with the exception of Finland) and the Netherlands tended to be high spenders both on income maintenance and active measures to assist disabled people into work. As a country with a moderate increase in income maintenance, Germany also had a moderate level of active expenditure.
- Conversely, the Southern group of countries tended to be low spenders both in relation to income maintenance and active measures.
- Finland and the United Kingdom stood out as somewhat striking exceptions. Given their relatively high or increasing levels of spending on income maintenance for the disabled, one would also have assumed that they would have adopted stronger policy efforts on the active side in the period up to 1999. If such efforts were made in Finland and the United Kingdom, they found other expressions than in increased public spending on special labour market measures for disabled people, for instance through regulative steps to make employers take greater responsibility for their disabled employees, and/or efforts to tighten benefit schemes, or they started more recently. The recent attempts to strengthen "welfare to work" measures

aimed at disabled people, under the heading of "The New Deal for Disabled People" (Floyd and Curtis 2001) might be an example of this.

Again, it is worth noting that there is hardly any indication of decreasing differences between the countries included, that is, towards convergence, in the proportion of GDP spent on special labour market programmes for disabled people. Throughout the 1990s we witnessed some fluctuations in the level of spending in each single country, but the relative differences between the countries and groups of countries remained strikingly stable.

Summary of trends according to data collected within the societal costs discourse

All in all we have found few—if any—clear indications of a trend towards a reduction in diversity of outputs from the systems of disability protection in Western Europe until the end of the 1990s, when using the kind of quantitative indicators available within the context of the societal costs discourse. While there were examples of downward trends in numbers or spending in some countries these did not amount to a more general "cooling-down" convergence. Conversely, there were cases of upward trends in countries starting from a low level, but they did not add up to any clear "catch-up" convergence. First of all, the data discussed here suggest a high degree of stable divergence of outputs between countries and groups of countries. The lack of convergence in outputs is probably the result of interplay between (i) partly divergent constraints and conditions for policy-making, and (ii) long-existing differences in operational goals and policy instruments adopted in these countries.

An Alternative Discourse on Disability Protection in Western Europe: Equal Rights and Opportunities for Disabled People

It is significant that the political agenda in relation to disability has recently moved in the direction of the second policy discourse outlined above, not least within the European Union. This does not suggest that the governments in member states (or the EU) are not any longer concerned about the number of recipients or level of expenditure on disability protection. Rather, the point is that to an increasing extent we find another and largely alternative public discourse, more or less in parallel to or independent of the former. It may be that the potential for a convergence of disability policies between Western European countries will be greater on the basis of this second and emerging discourse. Before discussing these prospects in greater detail I will briefly describe the recent changes in the EU's disability strategy, as this is likely to have considerable impact on how issues of social protection for disabled people will be framed in Europe in the years to come.

The Emerging European Union Disability Strategy

The European Union's engagement in the disability field has changed substantially in the course of the last 20 years (Contreras and Riego 1997; Geyer 2000; Hantrais 2000). For a long time this engagement was constrained by

Björn Hvinden

the EU's lack of legal competence in social policy in general and disability policy in particular. From the early 1980s until the mid-1990s the EU was primarily involved in disability issues through three successive action programmes. These encouraged the exchange of experience, dissemination of innovations, ideas and information to promote good practice in the member states. In this period the EU had a relatively cautious and non-directive role in this policy area. It was not in a position to influence established policy aims and practice of member states to any great extent. Indicative of this is that the Council's policy statement from 1986 on the employment possibilities for disabled people had the form of a Recommendation (CEU 1986).

Since the mid-1990s the EU has developed a new, broader disability strategy, together with a stronger ambition to influence the policies and practice of member states. This shift was signalled by a Communication from the Commission in 1996 (EC 1996). The aims and principles of this policy document were endorsed by the Council of Ministers at the end of the same year in the form of a Resolution (CEU 1996). Key elements in these statements were the notions of equal opportunities for disabled people, non-discrimination, mainstreaming, the rights-based approach, inclusion, full participation, and identifying and removing barriers to equal opportunities and full participation. Later policy papers from the Commission have elaborated these aims and instruments and discussed to what extent they are adopted and implemented in the member states (EC 1998b, 1999, 2000).

The Amsterdam Treaty of 1997 furnished the EU with a new basis for its policy development and engagement in relation to disability issues. Article 13 of the Treaty opened the way for Community action to combat discrimination on grounds of sex, racial or ethnic origin, religion or belief, disability, age or sexual orientation. A significant next step in providing the EU with legal competence in this area was made by the Council Directive of November 2000 establishing a general framework for equal treatment in employment and occupation (CEU 2000a). According to Articles 1 and 2 of the Directive there shall be no direct or indirect discrimination on the grounds of religion or belief, disability, age or sexual orientation in this area. When judging whether a disabled person is discriminated against, it shall be taken into account whether the employer has provided "reasonable accommodation", that is, taken appropriate measures to enable a person with disability to have access to, participate in, advance in employment or undergo training, unless this would imply a disproportionate burden for the employer (Article 5). Responsibility for implementing the new anti-discrimination policy will rest principally with the member states. They are to adopt the laws, regulations and administrative provisions necessary to comply with the Directive by December 2003 (Article 18). In order to take into account particular traditions, member states may be given an additional period of three years from December 2003, that is, a total of six years from November 2000, to implement the provisions relating to disability discrimination (Article 18). Thus to the extent that the Directive will promote a more similar disability policy in member states, we are mainly talking about a possible *future* development, after 2003 or even after 2006.

The Commission appears to encourage and mobilize the efforts of stakeholders—affected and interested actors—within the member states, for instance by contributing to improved knowledge, strengthening the capacity of these actors and raising awareness. Arguably the Directive opens up new opportunity structures for disabled people in Europe. However, whether this potential will be realized will largely depend on the degree of self-activity and mobilization of disabled EU citizens themselves. Important here will be the amount of information and awareness-raising campaigns, practical and financial support from self-organized groups, as well as the initiatives of individuals who see themselves as discriminated against, for instance through law suits.

The Commission has provided financial support to a working group of legal experts to follow the process of transposing the Directive against employment discrimination into national legislation. This work of this may have significance in increasing awareness and harmonizing understandings of the aims and provisions of the Directive at the level of central government in member states. Still, it is more open to question how close the links between the legal experts and the key policy-makers in the member states are, that is, "inside" governments. Pressure, campaigning and lobbying from disabled people's organizations and their supporters from the outside may therefore be essential for how far-reaching changes in national provisions will be adopted, as seemed to have happened in countries that have already introduced anti-discrimination legislation in relation to disability.

Majone (1993) has clarified the distinction between social policy understood as *redistribution* of public resources and as *regulation*, in particular of the market and the behaviour of non-governmental actors. Most EU policy provisions have been of the regulation type, with the common agricultural policy and the structural funds, for instance the European Social Fund (ESF), as important exceptions. The emphasis on regulation rather than redistribution has first of all been related to the dominant focus of removing restrictions on market exchange and the free movement of capital, labour, goods and services, within the history of the European Communities. Secondly, there has been strong resistance from member states to letting the Union take over policy provisions that have traditionally been under the control of national or even sub-national levels of governance (Newman 1977: 77–108). It has been argued that these provisions include tasks that most appropriately are taken care of at these lower levels, and that it is neither necessary nor desirable to move the responsibility for them up to a higher level (the "subsidiarity" principle). In combination, this implies that income maintenance, employment and care provisions aimed at disabled people—as they exist in member states—make up a fairly crowded area where a development towards a joint EU system is less likely to take place in the foreseeable future.

The EU has redistributed quite substantial funds to disabled people in member states through temporary projects under the previous Action Programmes (e.g. HELIOS I and II) and the ESF. But the emphasis of the Disability Strategy that the Commission developed from the mid-1990s and that so far has found its clearest expressions in Article 13 of the Amsterdam Treaty, the Directive and the new Community Action programme, has mainly been on regulation. For the time being, regulatory provisions from the EU are likely to be more acceptable to the member states than redistributive ones would be. But even the legitimacy of a Disability Strategy based on a regulatory approach has been questioned by some member states.

In November 2000 the Council also agreed on an ambitious Community Action programme to combat a wider range of discrimination (CEU 2000b). This programme covers treatment by public agencies and services (e.g. police, judicial systems, health, social security, and education), the media, participation in decision-making, and access to goods and services (including housing, transport, culture, leisure and sport). Thus the programme points towards regulative measures that are more collective in form. The Commission is committed to following up these objectives in the further development of the single market, for instance, in future EU regulations of transport systems, communication and information technologies, and public procurement of goods and services from private producers. In other words, much will depend on the ability of the EU to "mainstream" the principle of non-discrimination and equal opportunity horizontally in the areas of the other Directorates-General than the one directly responsible for employment and social affairs.

Are these diverse and largely future processes likely to contribute to a more similar approach to the social protection of disabled people in the member states? As already indicated there are many "ifs" and uncertainties here that make it difficult to formulate firm assumptions about what the results eventually will be. For instance, it is not evident how member states seek to adjust the transposition of the Directive to what has existed already in the way of special employment provisions, e.g. legal rules about employment protection, organizational modification or technical adaptation in the workplace for disabled employees (cf. "reasonable accommodation"). Neither is it clear to what extent the European Court of Justice in its future decisions under the anti-discrimination Directive will challenge the existing—and highly variable—systems of industrial relations in member states.

Concluding Discussion

On the basis of the analysis presented here we do not see strong reasons to expect a general convergence in the systems of disability protection in Western Europe. We may observe signs of a trend toward greater similarity in terms of general goals and policy principles, for instance expressed in official support for aims like promoting equal opportunities, fuller participation in economic and social life, economic self-sufficiency, independent living, and combating discrimination, poverty and exclusion. So far it is not possible to demonstrate that this has led to a convergence at the level of outputs. On the level of policy instruments the prospects appear mixed and uncertain:

- Within the terrain of traditional social policy understood as *redistribution*— social security, employment and care provisions benefiting disabled people —a substantial change towards less diversity does not seem likely in the foreseeable future.
  Within the area of *regulation* the potential scope for adopting similar operational goals and approaches appears to be greater, for two reasons. First,

there may generally be fewer pre-existing provisions here, that is, established and competing arrangements for taking into account or accommodating the requirements of disabled people. Second, efforts from the EU to introduce new measures of regulation to promote more equal treatment and opportunities for the disabled may be seen as more legitimate and more in line with what the governments of member states think the EU should engage in.

- Yet, even within the area of regulation policy some fields may be more crowded than others, at least in some member states. Industrial relations, systems of collective bargaining and employment protection legislation may be one of these relatively more crowded subfields of regulation. Thus some national governments may initially seek to interpret the Directive and future regulation in a conservative or restrictive way. On the other hand, increased public debate, awareness and attention around the issues of exclusion and discrimination against disabled people may encourage European governments to greater boldness in this area. Similarly, it may also be that the future decisions of the European Court of Justice will stimulate a more expansionist and far-reaching interpretation of the Directive and other legal provisions in member states, as has happened in other areas previously.

Acknowledgements

The author would like to thank Denis Bouget, Jane Lewis, Ann Lavan, Christopher Prinz, Peter Taylor-Gooby, Jelle Visser and Richard Whittle for helpful and challenging comments to earlier versions of this paper. The article uses quantitative indicators collected by the Eurostat and the OECD. While the author appreciates the possibility to draw on this material he emphasizes that the responsibility for the way in which the material is used and interpreted is his solely.

References

Aarts, L. J. M. and de Jong, P. R. (1996), European experiences with disability policy. In J. Mashaw, V. Reno, R. Burkhauser and M. Berkowitz (eds), *Disability, Work and Cash Benefits*, Kalamazoo, MI: W. E. Upjohn Institute of Employment Research.

Aarts, L. J. M., Burkhauser, R. V. and de Jong, P. R. (eds) (1996), *Curing the Dutch Disease: An International Perspective on Disability Policy Reform*, Aldershot: Avebury.

Aarts, L. J. M., Burkhauser, R. V. and de Jong, P. R. (1998), A cross-national comparison of disability policies: Germany, Sweden, and the Netherlands vs. the United States. In S. Klosse, S. den Uijl, T. Bahlman and J. Shippers (eds), *Rehabilitation of Partially Disabled People*, Amsterdam: Thesis Publishers.

Aarts, L. J. M., Burkhauser, R. V. and de Jong, P. R. (1999), Convergence: a comparison of European and United States disability policy. In T. Thomason, J. F. Burton and D. Hyatt (eds), *New Approaches to Disability in the Workplace*, Ithaca, NY: Cornell University Press.

CEU (1986), 86/379/EEC: Council Recommendation of 24 July 1986 on the employment of disabled people in the Community, *Official Journal* No. L 225, 12/08/1986: 0043–0047.

CEU (1996), Resolution of the Council and the Representatives of the Governments of the Member States meeting within the Council of 20 December 1996 on equality

Björn Hvinden

of opportunities for people with disabilities, *Official Journal* C 012, 13/01/1997: 0001–0002.

CEU (1999), Council Resolution of 17 June 1999 on equal employment opportunities for people with disabilities, *Official Journal* C 186, 02/07/1999: 0003–0004.

CEU (2000a), Council Directive 2000/78/EC of 27 November 2000 establishing a general framework for equal treatment in employment and occupation, *Official Journal* L 303, 02/12/2000: 0016.

CEU (2000b), Council Decision 2000/750/EC of 27 November 2000 establishing a Community action programme to combat discrimination (2001 to 2006), *Official Journal of the European Communities*, L 303: 23–8.

Contreras, M. L. and Riego, J. (1997), Introduction [to European Union disability law]. In Machado and de Lorenzo (1997).

Deacon, B. (1999), Social policy in a global context. In A. Hurrell and N. Woods (eds), *Inequality, Globalization and World Politics*, Oxford: Oxford University Press.

De Vroom, B. and Guillemard, A. M. (2002), From externalisation to integration of older workers: institutional changes at the end of the worklife. In J. G. Andersen and P. H. Jensen (eds), *Changing Labour Markets, Welfare Policies and Citizenship*, Bristol: Policy Press.

Drøpping, J. A., Hvinden, B. and Vik, K. (1999), Activation policies in the Nordic countries. In M. Kautto, M. Heikkilä, S. Marklund and N. Ploug (eds), *Nordic Social Policy: Changing Welfare States*, London and New York: Routledge.

Drøpping, J. A., Hvinden, B. and van Oorschot, W. (2000), Reconstruction and reorientation: changing disability policies in the Netherlands and Norway, *European Journal of Social Security*, 2, 1: 35–48.

EC (1996), *Communication of the Commission on Equality of Opportunity for People with Disabilities*, COM (96) 406, final of 30 July 1996.

EC (1998a), *Employment and People with Disabilities*. Report of the special meeting of the High-Level Group on Disability, Brussels, 15 October, Luxembourg: Office for Official Publications of the European Communities.

EC (1998b), *Raising Employment Levels of People with Disabilities: The Common Challenge*, Commission Staff Working Paper, SEC (1998) 1550.

EC (1999), *Mainstreaming Disability within EU Employment and Social Policy*, DG V services working paper.

EC (2000), *Towards a Barrier Free Europe for People with Disabilities*, Communication from the Commission to the Council, the European Parliament, the Economic and Social Committee and the Committee of the Regions, Com (2000), 284 final of 12 May 2000.

EC (2001), *MISSOC: Mutual Information System on Social Protection. Social protection in the EU member states and the European Economic Area. Situation on 1 January 2001*, European Commission, Directorate-General for Employment and Social Affairs, Luxembourg: Office for Official Publications of the European Communities.

EU (1997), Consolidated version of the treaty establishing the European Community. In *Consolidated Treaties*, Luxembourg: Office for Official Publications of the European Communities.

Eurostat (2001a), *European Social Statistics: Social Protection Expenditure and Receipts 1980–1999*, Luxembourg: Office for Official Publications of the European Communities.

Eurostat (2001b), *Disability and Social Participation in Europe*, Luxembourg: Office for Official Publications of the European Communities.

Ferrera, M. (1998), The four "Social Europes": between universalism and selectivity. In M. Rhodes and Y. Meny (eds), *The Future of European Welfare*, Basingstoke: Macmillan.

Floyd, M. and Curtis, J. (2001), An examination of changes in disability and employment policy in the United Kingdom. In van Oorschot and Hvinden (2001).

Geyer, R. R. (2000), *Exploring European Social Policy*, Cambridge: Polity Press.

Hantrais, L. (2000), *Social Policy in the European Union*, 2nd edn, Basingstoke: Macmillan.

Hvinden, B., Heikkilä, M. and Kankare, I. (2001), Towards activation: the changing relationship between social protection and employment in Western Europe. In M. Kautto, J. Fritzell, B. Hvinden, J. Kvist and H. Uusitalo (eds), *Nordic Welfare States in the European Context*, London and New York: Routledge.

Judge, K. (2001), Targeting social provisions in Britain: who benefits from allocation formulae? In N. Gilbert (ed.), *Targeting Social Benefits. International Perspectives and Trends*, New Brunswick and London: Transaction.

Kuptsch, C. and Zeitzer, I. R. (2001), Public disability programs under complex pressures. In D. D. Hoskins, D. Dobbernack and C. Kuptsch (eds), *Social Security at the Dawn of the 21st Century*, New Brunswick and London: Transaction.

Levi, M. (1997), A model, a method, and a map: rational choice in comparative and historical analysis. In M. I. Lichbach and A. S. Zuckerman (eds), *Comparative Politics*, Cambridge: Cambridge University Press.

Machado, S. M. and de Lorenzo, R. (eds) (1997), *European Disability Law*, Madrid: Escuela Libre Editorial.

Majone, G. (1993), The European Community: between social policy and social regulation, *Journal of Common Market Studies*, 31, 2: 153–69.

March, J. G. and Simon, H. A. (1993), *Organizations*, 2nd edn, Oxford: Blackwell Business.

Newman, M. (1997), *Democracy, Sovereignty and the European Union*, London: Hurst and Company.

OECD (1994), *OECD Employment Outlook*, Paris: Organization for Economic Cooperation and Development (OECD).

OECD (1998), *OECD Employment Outlook*, Paris: OECD.

OECD (1999a), *Implementing the OECD Jobs Strategy: Assessing Performance and Policy*, Paris: OECD.

OECD (1999b), *A Caring World: The Social Policy Agenda*, Paris: OECD.

OECD (2001a), *Labour Force Statistics 1980–2000*, Paris: OECD.

OECD (2001b), *OECD Employment Outlook*, Paris: OECD.

OECD (2003), *Transforming Disability into Ability*, Paris: OECD.

Prins, R. and Bloch, F. S. (2001), Social security, work incapacity and reintegration. In F. S. Bloch and R. S. Prins (eds), *Who Returns to Work and Why? A Six-country Study on Work Incapacity and Reintegration*, New Brunswick, NJ: Transaction.

Prinz, C. (ed.) (2003), *European Disability Pension Policies*, Aldershot: Ashgate.

SSA (1999), *Social Security Programs Throughout the World*, Washington DC: US Social Security Administration (http://www.ssa.gov/statistics/ssptw/1999/English/index.html).

Thornton, P. and Lunt, N. (1997), *Employment Policies for Disabled People in Eighteen Countries: A Review*, York: Social Policy Research Unit, University of York.

Van Oorschot, W. and Boos, K. (2001), The battle against numbers: disability policies in the Netherlands. In van Oorschot and Hvinden (2001).

Van Oorschot, W. and Hvinden, B. (eds) (2001), *Disability Policies in European Countries*, The Hague: Kluwer Law International.

Visser, J. and Hemerijck, A. (1997), *A Dutch Miracle? Job Growth, Welfare Reform and Corporativism in the Netherlands*, Amsterdam: Amsterdam University Press.

Wilson, V. (1996), People with disabilities. In B. Munday and P. Ely (eds), *Social Care in Europe*, London: Prentice-Hall and Harvester Wheatsheaf.

6

Adaptation to Labour Market Change in France and the UK: Convergent or Parallel Tracks?

Anne Daguerre and Peter Taylor-Gooby

Adaptation to Labour Market Change in France and the UK: Convergent or Parallel Tracks?

European welfare states are under pressure from labour market, family and household change, population ageing and globalization. One question is whether broadly similar pressures are now causing welfare systems that developed on different lines during the postwar golden age to converge. We examine changes in childcare and unemployment policy in France and the UK in response to shifts in the labour market. The transition to a post-industrial, service-oriented economy coupled with technological change and increased international competition led to the emergence of new social risks from the late 1970s onwards—most markedly, lack of relevant skills and long-term unemployment on the one hand, and the lack of adequate childcare on the other. Long-term unemployment is now addressed by activation policies which provide specific programmes to help the most vulnerable to return to paid employment. The notion of activation can refer to a range of different approaches (Hvinden *et al.* 2001). The EU strategy stresses positive activation, understood as a policy emphasis on labour market integration through better access to training and employment opportunities, coupled with "making work pay" strategies, that increase the incomes available to lower-paid workers in comparison with benefits. Family-friendly policies figure relatively prominently on the EU agenda, especially since 1995. The Council of Ministers and the EC have continuously stressed the importance of good and affordable childcare policies in the promotion of the European Employment Strategy. The problem of long-term unemployment and lack of adequate childcare are thus addressed by employment and family policies with increasing links between these two policy areas.

We contrast the UK, typically seen as an adaptive and innovative but relatively weak market-centred welfare system, with France, which has higher spending, stronger provision and more intervention, but is often seen as conservative and slow to change. Unemployment and childcare policies are chosen because they relate closely to adaptation to the labour market shifts that are at the heart of welfare state policy reform. The paper thus examines responses to labour market change in two contrasting cases separated by 25 kilometres of water: a limited, liberal-leaning, individualist but potentially adaptive, and a substantial, conservative, collectivist but traditionally sluggish welfare state. The question is whether pressures for convergence can overcome the different traditions of two very different EU partners.

The Context: Labour Market Change and Family Change

Employment and family policies are at the forefront of the debate on the future of the welfare state in contemporary Europe. The founding fathers of the welfare state were committed to a full-employment society. Social welfare was designed to protect individuals against interruptions to labour market income from such factors as sickness, old age and unemployment, while social care for a dependant, such as a child or a frail elderly person was provided through the unwaged labour of women in the family (Esping-Andersen 1999). The four types of welfare regimes identified by Esping-Andersen and Ferrera (Esping-Andersen 1990; Ferrera 1996)—Continental, Southern Europe, Scandinavian and Liberal—covered the average male production worker against such risks.

The stable labour market of the so-called postwar golden age no longer exists in contemporary Europe. The impact on different social groups varies according to the structure of the national labour market and benefit system, less flexible labour markets and conservative social insurance benefit systems being in general most likely to produce strong insider/outsider divisions (Ferrera and Rhodes 2000). Low-skilled workers are more exposed to the risk of long-term unemployment and social exclusion than others. Women's skills are increasingly needed to face the challenges posed by the long-term shrinkage in the population of working age and the shift to a service economy. Women, especially married women, are moving into the labour market in increasing numbers in those countries where female employment has traditionally been low. This contributes to an expansion in the workforce and is typically seen as implying a need for active childcare policies, assuming that women workers will continue to take chief responsibility for family care (OECD 2001). Single-parent families tend to have high poverty rates—their living standards average 23 per cent below that of all households with children (Chambaz 2001)—and are increasing in number. Thus labour market change requires a more skilled and adaptable workforce at the same time as the need to tackle poverty among unemployed people and among single-parent families implies greater engagement in paid work for the groups who face the most severe barriers to employment. The need to address long-term unemployment coupled with the wish to address the persisting adverse effect of maternity on women's participation in the labour market, especially for low-income and/or single mothers, has been at the forefront of the policy debate at the European level.

Employment policies developed at the European Union (EU) level attempted to address those concerns in the 1990s. First, this period witnessed the emergence of an international policy paradigm that analyses unemployment as the result of inadequate supply-side policies. The 1993 White Paper (EU 1993) identified unemployment as "the major challenge which confronts us all" and analysed the problem in terms of cyclical, structural and technological unemployment. The solution thus included both greater flexibility in labour markets (to combat structural rigidities) and investment in infrastructure—especially transport and ICT—and training (to provide alternatives for those whose jobs are lost through technological change and to foster countercyclical trends). The Luxembourg summit initiated a process which included national action plans and benchmarking, embodied in a series of "Employment Strategy" papers (EC 1997 onwards). This approach directly influenced European efforts to modernize the social protection systems of member states (EC 1999). The Lisbon summit in 2000 reviewed progress and endorsed plans which included the main features of the programme set out in the White Paper, but also specifically endorsed "making work pay" strategies (keeping benefits below wages to promote work-incentives—EC 2000a).

The issue of reconciling work and family life had been on the agenda since the 1980s, but gained momentum in recent years. In 1998, the European Commission adopted the report regarding the Council 1992 Recommendation on childcare. The 1998 guidelines for employment policies also called for adequate provision to be made for the care of children and other dependants (EFILWC 2002).

During the past decade various reforms have been implemented on three main fronts by European welfare states:

- modification of many aspects of the *old* welfare state programmes, especially to unemployment benefits (availability, duration and replacement rates);
- promotion of *new* welfare schemes and policies promoting job creation and "availability" for work as well as the "employability" of workers (training, employment subsidies, *in-work* benefits, new forms of contract, etc.);
- introduction of women-friendly policies, to remove barriers to paid employment for mothers with dependent children.

Some countries have moved faster than others. In particular, continental countries have found the modification of social insurance benefits a considerable challenge given the character of "acquired rights" assumed by such benefits and the role of the social partners in the formation and management of these schemes. By contrast, liberal countries, where the interests of labour are less well entrenched, have restructured unemployment protection. However, family-friendly policies—especially the expansion of childcare places—remain a crucial challenge for market-based welfare systems. In more collectivist countries, family-friendly policies have been more responsive to changes in the labour market. France and the UK differ substantially in national traditions and in policy-making mechanisms and thus represent contrasting cases for examining developments in labour market and childcare policies from the early 1980s onwards.

Convergence between France and the UK is limited. In relation to unemployment policies, France's capacity to implement rapid changes has been affected by the social partners' reluctance to accept significant cuts in unemployment benefits and welfare-to-work schemes. Instead, French policy-makers have developed social assistance benefits and work-related programmes with limited success owing to the selectivity of the labour market. In the UK, such resistance is slight, since central government has long-established control over benefits. The British welfare state performs much better than its French counterpart in terms of employment rates, due to the relatively high flexibility of the labour market. By contrast, its record on the removal of barriers to paid work for low-income mothers remains weak, due to the virtuous combination of public childcare and early state intervention in family life which supports the model of the French working mother (Fagnani 2001). The British welfare state traditionally considered childcare a private issue (Hantrais and Letablier 1996).

Labour Market Policy and Unemployment

Table 1 shows three things: French male unemployment exceeded the UK's in the mid-1990s and remains higher; women's unemployment is higher than men's in France, but not in the UK; and in both countries (especially France) there are exceptionally high rates among young people.

The two countries differ markedly in terms of policy-making mechanisms. The strong social insurance basis of the French system offers good protection to male production workers (breadwinner "insiders"), but low protection to "outsiders"—young people, women and the long-term unemployed. Social partners have a strong role and reform is necessarily slow. The state provides social assistance to those not included in insurance. The UK has lower benefits and relies extensively on targeted social assistance (chief support for 81 per cent of unemployed people—DWP 2001a, table 1.1). National insurance benefits have been drawn together with assistance as the Jobseeker's Allowance. Social partners are ineffective. Reform is more rapid, due to the greater authority of government over policy-making.

France

The French labour market is characterized by a sharp divide between insiders (job-ready people with good employment records) and the others, such as the young, the low-skilled and the long-term unemployed, who are most at risk of social exclusion (Daguerre and Palier 2001). In the late 1990s French labour market policies gradually moved away from passive employment measures—defined as income-maintenance policies designed to protect job-seekers against job loss—towards active measures for all categories of job-seekers.

The brutal rise in unemployment from the 1970s took public authorities by surprise. Their first response was to reduce the labour supply by removing older and younger people from the labour market through early retirement and education/training schemes and creating subsidized jobs (Bichot 1997). The jobs were often linked to the "reinsertion dimension" of the guaranteed minimum income—the RMI (*Revenue Minimum d'Insertion*)—established in 1989. At the same time, eligibility for insurance benefits was tightened. The "social treatment of unemployment" was a short-term, reactive policy, which

Anne Daguerre and Peter Taylor-Gooby

Table 1

Employment and unemployment in France and the UK: 1991–2002

	1991		1995		2000		2002	
	France	UK	France	UK	France	UK	France	UK
Women								
Unemployment								
rate: 15–64	12	8	14	7	12	5	11	4
15–24	25	12	31	13	22	12	22	10
Employment								
rate: 15–64	51	61	52	62	55	65	n/a	65*
15–24	29	59	23	54	26	54	n/a	n/a
Men								
Unemployment								
rate: 15–64	7	10	10	10	8	6	8	6
15–24	18	17	24	18	18	14	20	13
Employment								
rate: 15–64	70	78	67	75	69	78	n/a	72*
15–24	35	63	29	59	32	58	n/a	n/a

* 2001
Source: EC (2001, 2002).

could not address the growing problems of massive unemployment and social exclusion.

Financial pressures were brought home to the government in the early 1990s, in the period preceding the introduction of the Maastricht Treaty rules. The main political parties of right and left (the *Parti Socialiste* and the *Rassemblement pour la République*) concurred in the famous slogan "We can no longer afford it". Early retirement was cut back and insurance benefits were brought together as the *Allocation Unique Dégressive* (AUD). This benefit decreased every four months and expired after 30 months, after which unemployed people must use the tax-financed assistance benefits, producing savings in insurance benefits and an expansion of the means-tested RMI; there were 3 million RMI recipients in 1999. The new benefit regime was introduced in the context of an expansion of subsidies for lower-paid work and reductions in employers' insurance contribution to encourage job creation.

The Socialist Party, returned to government under Jospin in 1997, rehabilitated full employment as a feasible policy goal in the context of increasing public dissatisfaction about levels of unemployment. This commitment marked a turning point in government's thinking, since previous "welfare without work" policies were based on the tacit acceptation of jobless growth. The socialist administration promoted labour market integration through the development of activation policies in three phases:

- New activation policies for the most vulnerable sections of the labour force (young people, long-term unemployed)—*emplois jeunes* (minimum-wage public-sector jobs for young people)—with a substantial impact on youth unemployment (see table 1).
- The 35-hour week in 1998 and 2000, which also provided incentives for employers to invest in productivity and encouraged the renegotiation of local agreements about wage freezes, productivity, parental leave and such matters.
- The replacement of selective activation policies with universal activation and "making work pay" programmes. Personal assistance with job search was the core objective of the *Plan d'aide et de retour à l'emploi* (PARE) in 2001, available to all job-seekers. This ends the persisting division between insured job-seekers and more vulnerable sections of the labour force covered by social assistance schemes. It consisted of improved services with job placement and job retention for unemployed people. In the new system, the Employment Service (*Agence Nationale pour l'Emploi* [ANPE]) invites the job-seekers for an assessment interview every six months. Those who fail to attend are deregistered, which leads to benefits cuts (*Le Monde*, 28 January 2003). In 2002, this new provision led to the deregistration of 350,000 job-seekers. Although the signature of the PARE is theoretically not a condition for benefit receipt, in practice this scheme has enabled the ANPE to sanction job-seekers for non-compliance with new programme requirements.

The trajectory of French policy has been conditioned by a number of factors. Governments initially implemented incremental, piecemeal changes in order to tackle the problem of structural unemployment. They sought to manage threats within the existing framework by increasing expenditure with minor reforms during the 1980s. As it became obvious that this was no longer possible in the 1990s, interventionist and directive policies emerged. From 1992 to 1997 the emphasis was on market incentives through the successive decreases in AUD payments, with additional job-creation schemes for the most vulnerable groups. This changed radically in 1997 with the rehabilitation of full-employment objectives. However, the Jospin government's thinking regarding activation policies remained torn between conflicting universal and selective objectives: the socialist administration was constantly hesitating between the need to create universal activation policies regardless of the status of job-seekers and the necessity to design specific programmes for low-income, socially excluded groups. The persisting divide between state-run programmes for non-insured job-seekers and programmes run by the UNEDIC (an unemployment insurance scheme) reflected these contradictory policy goals.

In 2002, following the re-election of the right-wing President Jacques Chirac, Jean-Pierre Raffarin replaced Lionel Jospin as prime minister. The new government has already reversed some of the main employment policies of its predecessor, especially in relation to the working hours and youth programmes. For instance, the current government is recycling previous measures (subsidized jobs in the private sector) to address the persisting problem of youth unemployment. In brief, there is no consistent French activation policy as programmes are particularly vulnerable to party politics and ideological U-turns.

The UK

In contrast to France, UK governments enjoy considerable autonomy over policy formulation, owing to the relative lack of veto points and institutional constraints. While the Conservatives (1979–97) stressed workfare[1] as the central element of their policies, New Labour (1997 to the present) placed much more emphasis on positive activation and social exclusion, and developed an ambitious "make work pay" strategy, based on minimum wage and tax credits for workers.

Conservative policy during the 1980s was essentially concerned to tackle unemployment by freeing the labour market, cutting benefits, tightening eligibility and work requirements. The UK scored zero on a 6-point OECD index of labour market protection standards against six for France and Germany in 1993 (OECD 1994: 154). National insurance unemployment benefit was replaced by Jobseeker's Allowance in 1996, time-limited for 6 months (renewable once) and conditional on approved job-seeking activities.

New Labour, from 1997, stressed activation as the centrepiece of its unemployment policy: "work for those who can, security for those who cannot" (DSS 1998: 23). This approach formed the basis for the five New Deal programmes for various vulnerable groups of workless people, establishing compulsory training and work placement in return for benefits (effectively a workfare/trainfare scheme) for young people and over-25s unemployed for more than two years. Thus Labour retained some Conservative policies, but also stressed positive activation programmes, to improve skills and incentives. Throughout the period UK policy was dominated by market principles and a concern with flexibility, but the approach was essentially passive under the Conservatives, while, after 1997, policy-makers sought to "lead the market" and expand individual opportunities within it. Poverty risks among those who remain unemployed are relatively high (see table 2).

Table 2

Social exclusion in France and the UK, selected groups 1995

	France	UK	EU13
Employed	41	31	46
Unemployed	313	421	293
Single parent	199	509	305
Couple + 1 child	55	50	63
Couple + 2 children	62	82	81
Couple + 3 children	138	177	169

Note: Statistics represent the relative risk of falling below 60 per cent of median income expressed as an index on which the population score is 100. EU13 omits Finland and Sweden.
Source: EU (2000b).

Unemployment protection systems in both countries have converged owing to similar financial pressures since the mid-1990s. However, the workfare approach is explicitly much more developed in the UK than in France. In the 1990s, both systems witnessed the erosion of contributory-based protection of the economic risk of unemployment. In the UK, New Labour's welfare-to-work strategy intensified the erosion of insurance principles. In France, a comparable trend has emerged with the introduction of a less generous unemployment benefit in 1992. Moreover, the reduction in the level of benefits has been even stronger for means-tested benefits than for insurance benefits (Bonoli and Palier 2000). This being said, France and the UK continue to differ in terms of the level of benefits, delivery mechanism and work requirements.

First, the UK lags behind France in terms of replacement rates of unemployment benefits. Average out-of-work benefit in the UK ranks among the lowest in the EU, below 30 per cent of per capita GDP, while France is at 40 per cent (EC 2001: 26). Second, the French system of benefit administration and delivery is much more fragmented than its British counterpart. Third, the French system remains formally much less coercive than the British system despite the introduction of PARE in 2001. In the French context, workfare is seen as an erosion of basic social rights, damaging to social solidarity. Thus RMI recipients are not obliged to accept job offers or to participate in training programmes. In fact, French legislators carefully avoid any assimilation to Anglo-Saxon activation policies, although the introduction of the PARE has in practice rendered the unemployment protection system much more workfare-oriented than is officially implied.

We go on to examine how female participation in the labour market in the context of rising unemployment and single-parenthood has been supported by social policy.

Childcare and Women's Participation in Paid Work

The long-term trend in both countries is for an increase in women's activity rates while those for men are tending to decline (EC 2001, table 18). A slightly lower proportion of women than of men participate in the labour market (table 1). The most striking differences between France and the UK are in the impact of childrearing on paid work by mothers, especially among single parents, and in the risk of poverty among single parents. In 1997, participation rates for women aged 25 to 49 with no children below 15 were broadly similar—just over 80 per cent in France and just over 85 per cent in the UK. Of these just under two-fifths work part-time in France and just over two-fifths in the UK. For women with at least one child below 5, participation falls to just under 70 per cent in France and under 60 per cent in the UK. However, in the UK, those mothers who work are much more likely to work part-time. In France about a third of women with a child under 15 work part-time, but in the UK, the proportion is close to two-thirds (EC 2000b, tables 11–15).

The UK has the highest proportion of single-parent families in the EU—25 per cent of children grow up in such families, as against 12 per cent for the EU as a whole and 11 per cent in France (Chambaz 2001). Some 47 per cent of single parents are in work in the UK, compared with 59 per cent in

Anne Daguerre and Peter Taylor-Gooby

the EU and 76 per cent in France. Their standard of living averages 76 per cent of that of all families with children in France compared to a corresponding figure of 62 per cent for the UK (Chambaz 2001). The risk of poverty is dramatically greater in the UK, at over five times that for the average citizen, compared to twice in France (table 2).

Policies to support women in paid work have been high on the policy agenda in both countries, but approaches differ (Hantrais and Letablier 1996; Lewis 1998). Each nation has addressed the childcare challenge in different ways depending on the nature of the post-welfare consensus. In the UK, the post-welfare consensus on the privacy of the family and childcare, the notion of the sanctity of the bond between mother and child, proved extremely resilient to change and was at the roots of governments' reluctance to invest in day nurseries. This eventually collapsed in the mid-1990s. New Labour implemented a National Childcare Strategy (NCS) when it came to office in 1997 but remained reluctant to create a universal, publicly funded network of childcare facilities. The debate has focused on the poverty of a minority of mothers in low-income families, especially single parents, and the importance of work for this group, both to tackle their obvious needs and to reduce social security costs. By contrast, France has developed an explicit family policy owing to the predominance of the model of the *working mother*, which explains the relatively strong pattern of state intervention in childcare policy. The concern is now primarily with maintaining policies to support flexible women's employment in order to permit the development of a more efficient labour market. This led to a shift from strong state support in the 1970s–1980s to a policy mix which includes more paid parental leave and caregiver allowances in the 1990s (Martin et al. 1998; Jenson and Sineau 2001).

France

French family policies were first designed to support large families but have increasingly favoured women's participation in the labour market since the early 1970s (Fagnani 2001). The vast majority of women (nearly 80 per cent by 1990; Bonnet and Labbé 1999) are in paid employment, and the proportion of single mothers in work (76 per cent) is only slightly lower than that for all mothers (Chambaz 2001). French family policies drew on the pro-natalist tradition established in the nineteenth century, in response to demographic concerns.

Recent policy development falls into three phases. In the first (1981–6) President Mitterrand expanded the provision of public childcare through nurseries for children under 3 (Martin et al. 1998). The objective was to promote gender equality in access to employment and also to encourage women's labour force participation to aid the productivity of the French economy. The strong state support for family services was in sharp contrast with the British childcare model where the main care responsibility was left to the women or the market. From the mid-1980s onwards the public model of childcare services, based on the notion of equity (between men and women but also between social classes) gradually gave way to the rhetoric of free choice

Adaptation to Labour Market Change

in relation to childcare arrangements. The new benefit, *Allocation Parentale d'Education* (APE), a cash payment to those responsible for the care of initially a third and then a second child, was created in 1986 to manipulate the supply of female labour.

The second phase of policy-making occupied the early and mid-1990s. More flexible childcare was needed to accommodate the needs of the employers in relation to a more flexible labour force. The newly elected right-wing government emphasized a freer choice between work and childcare for parents, involving new benefits and tax reliefs to support private childcare costs, and tending to benefit middle-class people.

In the third phase, the socialist Jospin government announced in 1997 that childcare would be consciously redistributive and designed to reduce the gender gap in access to employment. The childcare benefits were tapered for higher earners, and proposals were brought forward to introduce means-tested benefits to target help on lower-income groups. Universal child benefits are virtually sacrosanct and the government was forced to withdraw this proposal in the face of concerted opposition from right-wing parties, conservative trade unions and the powerful family lobby represented by the National Union of Family Associations. In 2001, the government also introduced a new benefit to pay childcare costs for women returning to work, and announced a programme to expand the numbers of public childcare places. Policy debates have centred on state support for childcare and the question of whether it should be provided through public nurseries or benefits to help people pay private carers. The result is that current policies tend to favour dual-earner households to the detriment of lower-income households, who are less able to afford private childcare and use the new benefits. There are gaps in provision for young children: childcare is only available for about a third of children under 3 (ILO 2002). In 2003, the French childcare model was significantly altered by the introduction of private provision and the expansion of childcare allowances but both main political parties of the right and the left agree that policies should support mothers in paid employment. The universal model of childcare has been replaced by a policy mix which is only slightly closer to the Anglo-American model of a childcare market.

The UK

Britain has long been characterized as a country with no explicit family policy, where children are mainly seen as a private responsibility. The main benefit for families has been child benefit, established in 1946 and paid as a universal family allowance. The limitations on benefits and childcare provisions have resulted in acute poverty among single parents, who are highly likely to be below the poverty line, dependent on benefits rather than in paid work (see table 2). State help with childcare costs is therefore targeted at deprived areas and special-need groups; the dominant model is of a private approach (Strategy Unit 2002). Of the 634,000 childcare places officially registered in 2000, 55 per cent were provided through private childminders and 41 per cent through private nurseries (ONS 2002). Payment for private childcare is thus a major issue which bears most heavily on lower-paid workers.

As a result, the likelihood of mothers being in full-time paid employment is closely related to the age and care needs of younger children.

Conservative family policy between 1979 and 1997 was limited to the development of Family Credit (a means-tested wage supplement paid to low-waged workers, with a small contribution towards childcare costs), a child benefit supplement for single parents and experiments with nursery vouchers. However, the Conservatives never questioned the hegemony of the market or the family in childcare provision.

New Labour adopted an innovative family policy based on the need to facilitate paid employment for single mothers and low-paid families as the best way out of poverty (Driver and Martell 2002). This emphasis on employment led Labour to establish the NCS, delivered through a range of programmes, including nurseries, after-school care and "Sure Start", which provided flexible funding for a variety of schemes for children in disadvantaged areas, mainly to stimulate private and community provision. These schemes contributed to the shift in care provision from childminders to day nurseries by 2000 (ONS 2002), and to an overall expansion in the number of places. The number of places with registered childminders fell from 402,000 to 369,000 between 1997 and 1999, whereas private day nursery places increased from 206,000 to 262,000 (ONS 2001, table 8.23). These trends continue. The government has provided targeted support for a number of measures to address areas of market failure, including support for the creation of over 250,000 childcare places by March 2006 (Strategy Unit 2002).

The problems of the current approach have been the limited impact on poverty and the high cost of childcare. The average Childcare Tax Credit payment of £37.30 a week is less than a third of the cost of a full-time nursery place. Low-income parents who receive the benefit are unable to afford such provision and pay on average just over 30 per cent of childcare costs. This compares with an average of 20 per cent across Europe (Daycare Trust 2002). In its general commentary on the UK employment strategy, the European Commission noticed that the UK "has the lowest labour force participation rates for single parents in the EU" (EU 2000a). The Council of Ministers set a target of 70 per cent of single parents to be in work by 2010, a very substantial increase (NAP 2001).

Recent policies for childcare and the balance between family life and paid work represent a shift in state engagement. The government's vision is "a childcare market where every parent can access affordable, good quality childcare" (Strategy Unit 2002). In this respect the UK is moving closer to a more pan-European model of childcare provision. Childcare is no longer seen as simply a private matter, in which the state should intervene only for specific need groups, but as a matter of policy which demands a national strategy. However, the mechanism of intervention follows that of other New Labour policies. Direct state benefits and interventions are targeted specifically on low-income groups, such as children in the deprived neighbourhoods involved in Sure Start or the single parents out of work. The policies for the mass of parents are designed to "lead the market" by providing subsidies and benefits for private provision and incentives to work, and the majority of the population is still expected to pursue private solutions.

Conclusion

The emerging consensus on labour market policy at the European level is that national governments need to promote higher skill levels, higher levels of workforce participation and greater labour market flexibility, in order to enhance economic competitiveness and tackle problems of poverty and social exclusion (Esping-Andersen 2002). These arguments feed through into policies to activate unemployed people and encourage mothers to take paid work. The practical implications are different in different national contexts.

This paper shows that France and the UK continue to display strong patterns of path-dependency: corporatist/conservative/family-oriented France is seeking to erode the rigidities associated with social insurance protection against unemployment risks, which lead to an entrenched labour-market division between insiders and outsiders, with limited success. The employment rate for young people remains among the lowest in the EU. By contrast, the historical commitment to a high level of public childcare provision coupled with acceptance that mothers should work has strongly favoured female participation (including single parents) in the labour market.

The privatized/individualist/market-oriented UK regime has pursued a highly flexible labour market strategy, despite the adoption of a minimum wage at a relatively low level in 1999. As a result the UK "provides a large pool of easily accessible first-entry jobs. This helps to integrate youth, women and immigrants into the labour market" (Esping-Andersen 1996: 17). The associated features of the Anglo-American model—notably the reliance on families and the market for childcare—has had adverse effects on female paid employment, especially for single mothers, with implications for child poverty.

Both countries acknowledge similar pressures. There are obvious differences in the direction of reforms to meet them. In employment, France has moved to voluntary training contracts (although now with pressure to attend six-monthly interviews) while the UK has instituted a system close to trainfare/workfare. In childcare, France has maintained a high level of state support but has made provision more flexible, while the UK relies mainly on cash/tax credit benefits to facilitate individual private purchase of services. The essential contrast between liberal and conservative regime remains. Even under the pressures of the silver age of the welfare state, welfare state types do not appear to exhibit strong tendencies to convergence, at least so far as the major policy area of labour market reform goes.

Notes

1. Workfare is a contraction of the expression *welfare to work*. In American English, workfare refers to compulsory schemes for the unemployed. Workfare means that receipt of benefits is conditional on participation in work-related activities. Negative activation thus combines carrots (cash benefits) and sanctions (reduction, later abolition of benefits in case of non-compliance with programme requirements).

References

Bichot, J. (1997), *Les politiques sociales en France au 20ème siècle*, Paris: Armand Colin.

Bonnet, C. and Labbé, M. (1999), L'activité des femmes après la naissance du premier et deuxième enfant, l'impact de l'APE, *Collection études et statistiques*, no. 10, Paris: Ministère de l'Emploi et de la Solidarité.

Bonoli, G. and Palier, B. (2000), How do welfare states change? Institutions and their impact on the politics of welfare state reform, *European Review*, 8, 2: 333–5.

Chambaz, C. (2001), Single parent families in Europe, *Social Policy & Administration*, 35, 6: 658–71.

Clasen, J. (2001), *Managing the Economic Risk of Unemployment*, working paper, Florence: EUI.

Daguerre, A. and Palier, B. (2001), *Welfare system and the management of unemployment, the French case*, working paper, Florence: EUI.

Daycare Trust (2002), *National Childcare Survey*, London: Daycare Trust.

Driver, S. and Martell, L. (2002), New Labour, work and the family, *Social Policy & Administration*, 36, 1: 46–61.

DSS (1998), *A New Contract for Welfare*, Cm 3805, London: HMSO.

DWP (2000), *Opportunity for All: Second Annual Report*, Cm 4865, London: HMSO.

DWP (2001a), *Jobseekers' Allowance, quarterly statistical enquiry—November*, London: ONS.

DWP (2001b), *Low-income Families in Britain*, Report 138, London: DWP webpages.

DWP (2002), *Households Below Average Income Statistics 1994/5–2000/1*, First Release (http://www.dss.gov.uk/asd/hbai/hbai2001/pdfs/FirstRelease.pdf).

EC (1997), *1998 Guidelines For Member States Employment Policies*, Brussels: EC Commission.

EC (1999), *A Concerted Strategy for Modernising Social Protection*, document drawn up on the basis of COM (99) 347, Brussels: EC Commission.

EC (2000a), *Joint Employment Report 2000*, COM (2000) 551, Brussels: EC Commission.

EC (2000b), *Social Protection in Europe 1999*, DG for Employment and Social Affairs, Brussels: EC Commission.

EC (2001), *Employment in Europe, 2001*, DG for Employment and Social Affairs, Brussels: EC Commission.

EC (2002), *Euro-zone Unemployment Stable*, News Release 53/02, Brussels: Eurostat.

EFILWC (European Foundation for the Improvement of Living and Working Conditions) (2002), *Reconciliation of Work and Family Life and Collective Bargaining*, European Industrial Relations Observatory (www.eirofound.eu.int).

Encarta Dictionary (2002) (http://dictionary.msn.com/).

Esping-Andersen, G. (1990), *The Three Worlds of Welfare Capitalism*, Princeton, NJ: Princeton University Press.

Esping-Andersen, G. (ed.) (1996), *Welfare States in Transition*, London: Sage.

Esping-Andersen, G. (1999), *Social Foundations of Post-industrial Economies*, Oxford: Oxford University Press.

Esping-Andersen, G. et al. (2002), *Why We Need a New Welfare State*, Oxford: Oxford University Press.

EU (1993), *Growth, Competitiveness, and Employment*, COM (93) 700, Brussels: EC Commission.

EU (2000a), *Joint Report on Employment Policies in the EU and in the Member States*, Brussels: EU.

EU (2000b), *Statistics in Focus, Population and Social Conditions*, no. 14, Brussels: Eurostat.

Fagnani, J. (2001), Les Françaises font toujours plus d'enfants que les Allemandes de L'Ouest, *Recherches et Prévisions*, 64: 49–63.

Ferrera, M. (1996), The southern model of welfare in social Europe, *Journal of European Social Policy*, 6, 1: 17–37.

Ferrera, M. and Rhodes, M. (2000), Recasting European welfare states, and building a sustainable welfare state, *West European Politics*, 23, 2: 1–10, 257–82.

Hantrais, L. and Letablier, M. T. (1996), *Families and Family Policies in Europe*, Harlow: Longman.

Hvinden, B., with M. Heikkilä and I. Kankare (2001), Towards activation? In M. Kautto, J. Fritzell, B. Hvinden, J. Kvist and H. Uusitalo (eds), *Nordic Welfare States in the European Context*, London: Routledge.

ILO (2002), *Equal Opportunity for Men and Women, National Statistics*, ILO: webpages.

Jenson, J. and Sineau, M. (2001), *Who Cares? Women's Work, Childcare, and Welfare State Redesign*, Toronto: University of Toronto Press.

Kuhnle, S. (ed.) (2000), *The Survival of the European Welfare State*, London: Routledge.

Lewis, J. (ed.) (1998), *Lone Mothers in European Welfare Regimes*, London: Jessica Kingsley.

Martin, C., Math, C. and Renaudat, E. (1998), Caring for very young children and dependent elderly people in France. In J. Lewis (ed.), *Lone Mothers in European Welfare Regimes*, London: Jessica Kingsley.

NAP (2001), *UK Employment Action Plan*, London: NAP.

National Audit Office (2002), *The New Deal for Young People*, HCP 639 2001–2 (http://www.nao.gov.uk/pn/01-02/0102639.htm).

OECD (1994), *The Jobs Strategy*, vol. 2, Paris: OECD.

OECD (2001), *Employment Outlook*, Paris: OECD.

ONS (1997, 2000, 2002), *Social Trends* (annual), nos 27, 30, 32, London: HMSO.

Pierson, P. (1994), *Dismantling the Welfare State?* Cambridge: Cambridge University Press.

Pierson, P. (ed.) (2001), *The New Politics of the Welfare State*, Oxford: Oxford University Press.

Savage, S., Atkinson, R. and Robbins, L. (1994), *Public Policy in Britain*, London: Macmillan.

Scharpf, F. and Schmidt, V. (2000), *Welfare and Work in the Open Economy*, vols 1 and 2, Oxford: Oxford University Press.

Strategy Unit (2002), Delivering for families and children (http://www.cabinet-office.gov.uk/innovation/2002/childcare/report/index.htm).

Taylor-Gooby, P. (ed.) (2001), *Welfare States under Pressure*, London: Sage.

Taylor-Gooby, P. (2002), The silver age of the welfare state, *Journal of Social Policy*, 31, 3.

Treasury (2001), *Budget Report 2001*, chapter A (http://www.hm-treasury.gov.uk/budget/budget_2001/budget_report/bud_budo1_repchapa.cfm).

Tuchszirer, C. (2002), Réforme de l'assurance chômage du PAP au PAP/ND—le programme d'action Personnalisée pour un nouveau départ, *Revue de l'IRES*, 38, 1.

Visser, J. and Hemerijck, A. (2000), *A Dutch Miracle*, Amsterdam: Amsterdam University Press.

Werner, E. and Smith, R. (1989), *Vulnerable but Invincible*, New York: Adams, Bannister and Cox.

7

Mending Nets in the South: Anti-poverty Policies in Greece, Italy, Portugal and Spain

Manos Matsaganis, Maurizio Ferrera, Luís Capucha and Luis Moreno

Introduction

The reform of the welfare state, one of the most successful and resilient institutions of the last century, continues to be a bitterly contested issue. As the debate on the future of the "European social model" gathers pace, attention is focused on pensions and other core programmes. In contrast, social assistance—the focus of this paper—remains a relatively neglected topic by policy-makers and analysts, despite a recent emphasis on fighting poverty and exclusion. Yet the powerful forces that drive welfare reform (namely, the slow transition from one type of labour market, family and social protection configurations to another) also work to increase the relative importance of social assistance within the welfare state as a whole.

The arguments are well rehearsed. The foundations of the "golden age of welfare capitalism" in the postwar era can no longer be relied upon. In particular, the end of "Fordism" and the rise of the "new economy" have dealt a heavy blow to the labour market underpinnings of the welfare state (Esping-Andersen et al. 2002). Social protection systems rested on the assumption that the (labour) market provided steady incomes to most workers, so that the (welfare) state could limit itself to protecting those too old or too young to join the labour market, or those unable to do so because of illness or disability. However, the generalized expectation of lifelong employment, often with the same employer, has been replaced by rising insecurity, frequent job change, long unemployment spells and widespread precariousness (Taylor-Gooby 2001). Where the bulk of social protection remains linked to occupational status, labour market instability often translates into poverty and exclusion (Ferrera et al. 2000).

While economic change undermined the labour market foundations of the "male-breadwinner model", social change made less prevalent the domestic arrangements rendering it possible. Higher age at marriage, fewer children per couple, increased marital instability and the other manifestations of the "crisis of the family" have undermined the traditional assumption of a working husband supporting a housewife and their two or more children. Traditional families often acted as a redistributive mechanism (pooling resources in favour of members in need), and as a provider of social services (directing female unpaid work to the care of children, the old, the sick). As modern families become less able (and, perhaps, less willing) to perform such functions, the pressure on formal systems of social protection intensifies (Lewis 2001). Needless to add, demographic change compounds such pressure in the form of higher demands on pension, health and social care systems.

The rise of atypical careers and of non-standard household forms puts in question the capacity of current arrangements to support low incomes and to prevent poverty. This is because conventional systems of social protection rested on the occupational attachment of workers and the family attachment of dependants. As these cease to be the norm, effective and well-designed social safety nets become the key to a successful strategy against poverty and exclusion. In the light of these trends, social assistance—the component of the welfare state best suited to poverty relief—is expected to rise in prominence (Saraceno 2002).

Social assistance in southern Europe has often been described as "rudimentary" (Gough 1996; Leibfried 1993). This is not entirely unjustified: after all, social safety nets there clearly lack the pedigree of their counterparts in northern Europe. Nevertheless, recent developments suggest that a more complex analysis may be due.

This paper aims to contribute to such an analysis by critically examining the experience of anti-poverty policies in Greece, Italy, Portugal and Spain. Its structure is as follows. The next section reviews constraints on creating effective social safety nets in southern Europe. The third section offers a brief account of policy innovations in the four countries. The paper concludes with a discussion of unresolved issues and their implications for future policy.

Policy Constraints

The issue of strengthening social safety nets has particular resonance in southern Europe. The marginal role of social assistance, identified as a key characteristic of southern European welfare states (Ferrera 1996; Rhodes 1996), leaves their anti-poverty armour vulnerable. "Social benefits other than pensions" reduce poverty by a mere 1 and 3 percentage points in Greece and Italy respectively, though their effect is stronger—but still below the European average—in Spain and Portugal (see table 1).

Poor anti-poverty performance is partly linked to the limited reach to those in poverty: in Greece and Italy, where the problem is most serious, only 31 per cent of persons in the lowest income quintile received such benefits (Marlier and Cohen-Solal 2000). As this figure implies, many poor households are ineligible for social assistance because they fail to fulfil the narrow categorical conditions of the various programmes. Those affected include the long-term unemployed (whose eligibility to benefit has been exhausted), new entrants to the labour market (ineligible for unemployment insurance because

Manos Matsaganis, Maurizio Ferrera, Luís Capucha and Luis Moreno

Table 1

Selected social indicators

	Year	Greece	Italy	Portugal	Spain	EU-15
GDP per capita (€ thousand)	2001	12.0	21.0	11.9	16.2	23.2
Social expenditure (% GDP)	1999	25.5	25.3	22.9	20.0	27.6
Poverty *before* social transfers[a]	1998	23	23	27	25	26
Poverty *after* social transfers	1998	22	20	20	19	18
Distribution of income (S80/S20)[b]	1998	6.5	5.9	7.2	6.8	5.4
People in jobless households	2000	4.2	5.0	1.2	5.1	4.5
Unemployment rate	2000	11.1	10.5	4.1	14.1	8.2
Youth unemployment rate	2000	29.6	30.8	8.9	26.2	16.2
Female employment rate	2000	41.2	39.6	60.3	40.3	54.0

Notes:
[a] Social transfers other than pensions.
[b] Ratio of income shares earned by the top and bottom quintiles.
Source: CEC (2002).

never employed), the precariously employed (with no social entitlements to draw upon in the event of temporary loss of earnings) and others.

Descending into poverty through holes in the safety net is a common experience among immigrant workers and their families. Though registered foreign workers theoretically enjoy full social rights, illegal ones have nowhere to turn except to the emergency services provided by charitable organizations and/or by informal support networks run by their own communities (Baldwin-Edwards and Arango 1998). Among other factors, the "lesser eligibility" of immigrant workers is the inevitable effect of a social protection regime that continues to rely on formal employment, the insurance principle and the extended family. Seen in this light, the creation of an effective, universal safety net assumes additional importance, as it becomes instrumental for the enfranchisement of "outsiders" and the maintenance of social cohesion.

However, it is important to acknowledge that the "patchiness" of social safety nets in southern Europe is no mere symptom of a more general underdevelopment of welfare institutions. On the contrary, the relative neglect of a comprehensive anti-poverty dimension has often coincided with the steady growth of total social spending. If anything, certain social programmes (for example pensions in Italy or Greece) are *over*developed, to the point of crowding out investment in other policy areas. Therefore, it is elsewhere that the causes of the low profile of social assistance in southern Europe must be sought: in the unique set of constraints that inhibit its development. The two most relevant of these are the role of the family and the "softness" of state institutions.

South European families historically functioned as an effective (though informal) safety net: a "social shock absorber" active across a whole range of policy areas such as childcare, unemployment assistance, care for the elderly, housing or social assistance. There is evidence that resource pooling has intensified over recent years (Fernández Cordón 1997). None the less, as the family itself comes under stress, its endurance as a provider of home-made welfare becomes uncertain (Moreno 2002). In any case, "familialism" is known to rely on unpaid female work: often caring for children or older relatives is only possible at the expense of erratic careers or full withdrawal from the labour market. Low rates of female employment, especially in Spain, Italy and Greece, clearly indicate the high social costs of the southern model of welfare (Saraceno 2000).

On the other hand, the delivery of targeted benefits requires a degree of administrative capacity that is often simply unavailable in southern Europe. Specifically, administrative systems suffer from low implementation capabil-ities, caused in part by a paucity of resources available to street-level admin-istrators. Moreover, the low level of political autonomy of the administrative system in some parts of southern Europe may make it difficult for officers in charge of benefit delivery to stand up to external pressures. As a result, the relationship between benefit administrators and beneficiaries is in some parts of southern Europe mediated by "brokerage" structures. To these, one must add the poor integration of social assistance, which has left a structure allowing eligibility overlaps and coverage gaps (Ferrera 1996).

Since social assistance benefits are typically granted on the basis of a means test, the ability of administrators to assess "need" with some degree of accuracy is an absolute requirement. In this sense, southern Europe presents a real challenge to social policy: a variety of factors such as extended households, high rates of self-employment, large informal economies and endemic tax evasion combine to create a peculiar situation. As a result of that, administrators may be unable to judge the material circumstances of applicants and thus their "real" eligibility for benefits (Atkinson 1998).

As the above implies, the construction of social safety nets in a context characterized by complex socio-economic patterns, low administrative capacity and persistent tax evasion faces specifically "southern" dilemmas (Addis 1999; Aguilar et al. 1995). As a result of these, a straight transfer of policy know-how from more highly developed systems of social assistance in the North would fail to offer satisfactory answers to such questions. In effect, policy-makers in southern Europe are left with no alternative but to search for original solutions.

To a rather considerable extent, this is precisely what has happened in recent years. The renewed emphasis on anti-poverty policies led to a range of policy innovations in southern European social assistance in spite of the structural difficulties mentioned above. This policy shift is typified by the spread of minimum income schemes, the absence of which was thought to be a defining feature of the "southern model of welfare" (Gough 1996). The successful launch of *Revenue Minimum d'Insertion* (RMI) in France in 1988 set in motion developments that led to the adoption of similar schemes throughout southern Europe. Variations of RMI were adopted in the Basque Country in 1988, in Catalonia in 1990 and in other Spanish regions later. A national pilot scheme was introduced in Portugal in 1996 and became fully operational in 1997, while in Italy a formal experiment was started in 1998 and extended further in 2000. Only in Greece has this trend so far been resisted, though the issue of tightening the safety net is gaining in visibility even there. These national policy trajectories are put in context and briefly reviewed below.

National Profiles

Greece

The restoration of democracy in 1974 ushered in a period of welfare state expansion, accelerated after the socialist landslide in the 1981 general election. The unprecedented growth in social spending was a response to the expectations nurtured by large sections of society over decades of politically motivated discrimination. Greece's accession to the European Community in 1980, widely considered to be a guarantee of political stability, legitimized aspirations for levels of income and social protection comparable to those enjoyed by other Europeans (Guillén and Matsaganis 2000).

Today, a high level of social spending, rapidly approaching the EU average, is combined with a weak performance in terms of poverty reduction. This apparent contradiction can be explained by the predominance of social insurance, which fits well the "Fordist" norms of long and uninterrupted careers, but not those precariously and atypically employed who become "social insurance outsiders".

Conversely, social services remain at an early stage of development, while a marginal role is reserved for social assistance. Benefits are poorly integrated, administered as they are by different agencies and subject to different rules. Their interaction leaves in place not a coherent whole, but an uneven structure that combines eligibility overlaps with coverage gaps. Given that non-contributory transfers are more naturally suited to the pursuit of anti-poverty objectives, their relative underdevelopment leaves plenty of holes in the social safety net, through which individuals and their families can slip into poverty. Poor households are ineligible for existing benefits if they do not fit to the "identikit" imagined by legislators, failing to fulfil their narrow categorical requirements.

For instance, the safety net in old age is patchy. Those with sufficient contributions may be entitled to a minimum pension plus an income-tested supplement. Lower non-contributory pensions are paid to farmers and the non-insured. No universal minimum guarantee is available. Partly as a result, Greece features a unique combination of high pension spending *and* widespread old-age poverty (Matsaganis 2002).

Fragmentation and incomplete coverage are evident in all other areas of social security. Unemployment benefit is contributory and of limited duration (12 months), so that only 44 per cent of the registered unemployed claimed benefit in 1999. Income transfers to families are targeted on those with three children or more, so that poor children in smaller families receive little or no assistance. Disability benefits vary by condition and recipient status (10 categories and 22 subcategories of benefit). Housing assistance is contributory and favourable to owner occupation, i.e. beyond the reach of the poor.

Overall, non-contributory benefits accounted for 16.3 per cent of all spending on social security in 2001, and income-tested benefits for a mere 4.7 per cent. The gradual phasing-out of basic farmer's pensions since 1998 and the abolition of the income test on "many-children benefits" in 2002 (9.3 per cent and 1.9 per cent respectively of all expenditure on social security) will further reduce the space reserved for these two types of benefits within Greece's social protection system.

Yet, selectivity has been a fashionable idea since 1996, when the socialist government under a new leadership declared EMU membership an overriding aim, while pledging its commitment to a "cohesive society". Indeed, the concept of selectivity was hit upon as the obvious way to square the circle. The strategy yielded some early results, but soon ran out of steam, presumably for lack of obvious targets in a social protection system still dominated by contributory benefits.

The 2001 National Action Plan implicitly ruled out the option of minimum income, while simultaneously reiterating a commitment to selectivity. Three new measures, taking effect from 2002, were announced. The most promising was unemployment assistance for older workers, paid for 12 months to long-term unemployed persons aged 45–65 in low-income families. Nevertheless, ten months after the scheme's launch only 711 of the 35,000 unemployed workers officially expected to claim had actually done so. Very low take-up beset another high-profile scheme, the social contribution rebate for minimum-wage earners introduced in 2000.

On the whole, the "danger that some groups experiencing poverty may not be eligible for income support" (CEC 2001) remains largely undiminished despite improvements. The absence of a last-resort benefit targeted in nature but universal in scope, remains a crucial missing link in the social safety net. Resistance to minimum income renders the anti-poverty armour of the social protection system vulnerable. The administrative difficulties involved in implementing such a scheme must not be underestimated. Still, the financial requirement could be modest: a simulation exercise calculated the cost of minimum income transfers in 2000 at €269 million or 0.23 per cent of GDP (Matsaganis et al. 2001).

Italy

Poverty and social exclusion, marginal in the national debate and policy agenda in Italy before the 1990s, has gained increasing salience more recently. A standard diagnosis of the historical failings of *assistenza* has emerged, widely shared by political actors and social partners: high fragmentation, policy overlaps, a bias towards transfers (against services), marked territorial differentiation, the absence of a safety net of last resort.

In 1977 responsibility for social assistance was devolved to regional and local tiers of government. Guiding principles and general standards were left for consideration by a national framework law regulating social assistance, which was only issued in 2000. Various regions allowed wide discretion at city level. Local minimum income schemes were the product of municipal initiative. Turin in 1978, Ancona in 1981, Catania in 1983 and Milan in

1989 introduced a non-categorical means-tested benefit known as *minimo vitale*, even though other cities (such as Bari or Rome) did not.

At the national level, social assistance caters for specific categories such as the disabled and the elderly, but its role is marginal (6.4 per cent of total social expenditure in 2000). Social assistance measures include civil invalidity pensions (*pensione di inabilità civile, assegno di assistenza*) and the social pension (*pensione sociale*), gradually to be replaced, since the 1995 pension reform, by *assegno sociale*. Care allowance (*indennità di accompagnamento*), aimed at those in need of continuous help because unable to care for themselves but irrespective of income, has over the years gained ground as a source of support to the frail elderly.

Moreover, low-income groups may be eligible for a number of social insurance benefits. Family allowance (*assegno per il nucleo familiare*) is a means-tested transfer paid to active or retired employees with family burdens. Benefit rates are directly related to family size and inversely related to family income. Income-tested pension supplements (*integrazioni al minimo*) are paid to those with a contributory record of at least 15 years and a pension below the statutory minimum (post-1995 entrants may be entitled to the new social allowance instead). Invalidity pensions (*pensione di inabilità*) require a contributory record of at least five years. Until 1984, when medical criteria were tightened and periodic reassessments began, invalidity pensions functioned as *de facto* minimum incomes, particularly in the South, a hard currency for clientelist exchanges between politicians and voters (Ferrera 1996).

As the concentration of resources on categorical, contributory benefits left protection gaps at the bottom of the income scale, expert commissions since the mid-1990s started to recommend remedial action. In particular, the Onofri Report (1997) provided a blueprint on which subsequent reforms were eventually based. The report emphasized the need to enact national legislation on social assistance and to introduce a national, non-categorical minimum income scheme. It also recommended phasing out some of the current social assistance programmes and establishing a new mechanism to determine the financial situation of claimants.

Significant innovations followed. *Indicatore della situazione economica* (ISE), a new set of rules to assess the material circumstances of potential claimants, was devised in 1998. ISE specifies how incomes and assets may be taken into account when assessing claims for means-tested benefits. The decision to take into account wealth as well as income rested mainly on practical considerations, as a correction for the unfairness caused by tax evasion on the part of some categories of potential claimants (Baldini *et al.* 2002). ISE applies to two benefits introduced in 1998: *large family benefit* (targeted at families with three or more children) and *maternity allowance* (aimed at mothers ineligible for contributory maternity benefit). Moreover, in 2000 a new framework law reformed the institutional setting of Italian social assistance, according to principles of decentralization and subsidiarity within national guidelines and performance standards.

The minimum income experiment began life in 1998. *Reddito minimo di inserimento* (RMI) consists of a monetary and an "activation" component: entitlement to cash assistance is conditional on participation in insertion programmes. Cash assistance amounts to the difference between the income guarantee adjusted for family size and the resources available to beneficiaries (disregarding family benefits, medical expenses, 25 per cent of earnings and part of rent). Most beneficiaries (93 per cent) lived in the South, where some municipalities devised ingenious methods of coping with the implications of the underground economy for income assessment. Overall, the first phase of the experiment (1998–2000) involved 34,700 families in 39 municipalities. The 2001 budget law extended the experiment for another two years and raised the number of eligible municipalities to 306.

The independent evaluation report on the first phase of the experiment (IRS, Fondazione Zancan and CLES 2001) threw light on various aspects. On the positive side, RMI—the missing pillar of Italian social assistance—breaks with a long tradition of categorical, discretionary income support to the poor that had proved ineffective as anti-poverty policy. Prior to 1998 residents in some participating municipalities were ineligible for any form of cash assistance even when in acute economic need. On this evidence, the generalization of RMI throughout Italy (foreseen, though not in an automatic way, by the 2000 framework law on social assistance reform) may be considered as the logical next step. The same report estimated the cost of RMI at a national scale from €2,200 million to €2,950 million (0.18 to 0.24 per cent of GDP) in 2001—a significant but not excessive figure compared to other welfare programmes.

Two serious obstacles block the road to a full implementation of the minimum income scheme: the weak institutional capabilities of local administrations and the socio-economic environment of the Italian South. Like similar schemes, RMI is demanding in terms of administrative and managerial skills, while it also risks a functional overload: rather than a programme of last resort, RMI tends to become "the only game in town".

In view of the above, a substantial improvement of organizational capabilities at both the macro and the micro levels has to be combined with a further effort to rebalance the existing menu of labour market and family/social policies. The proper institutional location of RMI is at the base of a system of cash transfers to the unemployed and to families with children or other dependants. Equally, the correct functioning of its insertion component rests on an articulated system of active labour market policies and family-supporting social services. Some echoes of this diagnosis can be found in the 2001 National Action Plan, though the plan falls short of spelling out policy implications, let alone precise commitments.

The new centre-right government seems disinclined to proceed to a generalization of RMI. It has so far left the matter to the regions, refraining from either setting national standards or committing financial resources. The opposition has voiced its protest. But the trade unions (especially CISL and UIL) do not seem willing to fight a battle on this front: they are definitely more interested in defending the entitlement status quo for employed workers. As a consequence, recent moves towards implementing a minimum income programme in Italy are likely to remain incomplete for some time to come.

Portugal

Portugal joined the European Community in 1986, ending the long cycle of backwardness begun 58 years earlier with the conservative-corporatist dictatorship of the *Estado Novo*. Until then, neither universal social protection nor a public health system existed (Viegas and Costa 2000). During the dictatorship, that 40 per cent of the population lived in poverty was not a policy concern. The democratic revolution of 1974 introduced a set of social rights and institutions formally defining a modern welfare state. However, the adverse conditions in the ensuing period limited the financial and institutional resources needed to put the newly created social policies into practice. Measures to fight poverty remained scarce and social assistance fragmented.

In 1984 social protection was reorganized. A framework law defined the basis of social security as foreseen in the Constitution, setting out a three-level structure. The general regime provided contributory benefits to workers and their dependants, while the non-contributory regime and social assistance catered for interventions not allowed for under the general regime. Anti-poverty policies received a boost from Portuguese participation in the 1986 II European poverty programme that favoured action-research projects targeted to specific groups. Its stress on participation made it adaptable to the local development methodology used at that time. From then on, anti-poverty policy relied on a territorial integrated approach and partnerships at national and local level (Almeida *et al.* 1994).

By 2000, when social security legislation was next revised, the level and composition of social expenditure approached the European average. The new law aimed at raising benefits and ensuring the sustainability of social security by reinforcing the public pension fund and by ascribing responsibility for social assistance to the national budget. The reform was supported by an agreement with all social partners except the Industrial Employers Federation CIP. The law built on a new generation of social policies, launched in 1995, intended to "activate" individuals but also institutions, through an individualized approach to citizens' needs and conditions.

The minimum income scheme *Rendimento Mínimo Garantido* (RMG) was undoubtedly the flagship of these new policies (Capucha 1998). In the run-up to the 1995 general election, a high-profile debate on Council Recommendation 92/441 on sufficient resources (issued during the Portuguese presidency of the EU) put poverty at the centre of the political agenda. The incoming socialist government introduced RMG on an experimental basis in 1996 and extended it nationwide on 1 July 1997.

RMG can be thought of as a contract: it provides income support in exchange for a commitment to participate in social integration activities. These involve integration into the labour market, return to school, vocational training, access to health services, housing interventions, etc. Income support is through a differential cash allowance, calculated to bring a household's net income to the guaranteed minimum. The latter is linked to the social pension: the first two adults in the household receive a full amount each, other adults 70 per cent and children 50 per cent of a social pension respectively. The household's net income excludes family allowances, student grants and 20 per cent of earnings (raised to 50 per cent in the first year).

The programme is open to all legal residents if at least 18 years old, except for younger parents or pregnant women or carers of older people with disabilities. As RMG is subsidiary to other social benefits, participants are required to claim first any other benefit they may be eligible to. Benefit is initially awarded for a year, with the possibility of automatic renewal if beneficiaries continue to meet the requirements. Social workers from local social services access the material circumstances of claimants. Substantial discrepancies between actual and reported incomes lead to adjustment or even termination of benefit.

The social worker in charge of each claimant produces an individual report, which must include a description of the problems faced by the household and propose a "integration plan". This takes the form of an agreement signed by the social worker on behalf of the local monitoring committee and the members of the household. The agreement specifies the tasks to be accomplished by beneficiaries and the support offered by local institutions. The agreement may be renegotiated with the beneficiary if it is unsuitable or needs to be amended. Access to benefit is conditional on participation in integration plans and the whole process is legally binding.

By December 2001, some 752,000 persons (7.5 per cent of total population) had at some time participated in the programme, of which 354,000 (3.6 per cent of population) were still in receipt of benefit. A significant number of beneficiaries seem to have been reintegrated into society after a period of receiving minimum income assistance: of the 398,000 persons who left the programme, 258,000 did so because they were no longer in a situation of acute need. Total expenditure on minimum income benefits reached a peak of €284 million (0.25 per cent of GDP) in 2000 and fell back to €235 million (0.19 per cent of GDP) in 2001.

Two difficulties have been identified: the first concerns the ability to control fraud, the other activation for labour market participation (including the quality of insertion plans provided by institutions). Evidence shows fraud to be insignificant, in spite of the hype surrounding the few cases actually detected. Work disincentives are also limited, since benefit values are low and activation measures act as an effective screening device. On the other hand, the scheme faces a shortage of human resources, as the individualized approach and the need to monitor the complex process of reinsertion places a heavy burden on a limited number of social workers.

RMG became once again the subject of a political debate in the course of the 2002 election campaign. Although abolishing RMG was not on any political agenda, the need to cut public expenditure and the risk of a poverty trap were used to argue in favour of changes in the scheme. As a matter of fact, the centre-right coalition that had severely criticized the minimum income programme emerged victorious from that campaign. Significantly, the new government accepted the principle of a universal right to minimum income. Some minor changes to the scheme were nevertheless put forward. First, the scheme was renamed Social Insertion Income (RSI) to stress "activation". It is also expected that eligibility criteria will be tightened and new mechanisms to limit fraud will be introduced. The Constitutional Court has judged some proposals to tighten criteria as unconstitutional. On the whole, the essential traces of the scheme's design are likely to remain unaltered for the time being. Future challenges could derive from budget constraints depriving the scheme of vital human resources.

Spain

Social assistance under the Franco dictatorship was meagre. Church and family were the main providers of welfare to the needy. The democratic Constitution of 1978 inaugurated a period of institutionalization of social services and assistance. The *Carta Magna* left basic legislation and social security in the domain of central government, but social assistance became an "exclusive" competence of the 17 *Comunidades Autónomas* (regions). These immediately claimed several functions with respect to social assistance in their constitutional charter. In 1982–93 regional parliamentary acts established social services open to all citizens.

In 1987, an agreement between central, regional and local governments resulted in the approval of the "concerted plan for the development of basic provision of social services by the local authorities", promoting administrative cooperation between the three tiers of government. In 1988 (taking effect from 1990), old age and disability pensions were universalized. Non-contributory benefits became available to the elderly, the disabled and to low-income families with dependent children on a means-tested basis. Earlier, unemployment assistance was introduced in 1984 in response to mounting joblessness.

In April 1995, a report on the "analysis of the structural problems of the social security system and of the main reforms required", undersigned by all main political parties and trade unions as the "Toledo Pact", was ratified by the Congress of Deputies and became law. Its provisions included a clearer separation of contributory and non-contributory benefits, as a result of which universal health and social services and means-tested social assistance became fully financed through general taxation, while a reserve fund was created within the contributory regime to strengthen its future viability. Recent reforms favoured the "activation" of claimants, the adoption of stricter criteria of access to unemployment assistance and the establishment of a personal and family minimum allowance in the form of a refundable tax credit. The main forms of cash assistance currently available to low-income citizens are briefly described below.

Income-tested pension supplements (*complementos de mínimos de pensiones de la seguridad social*) raise contributory pensions to a legally established minimum. The supplements apply to over 30 per cent of all contributory pensions (paid to 2.4 million people in 2000). Unemployment assistance (*subsidios de desempleo, subsidio de desempleo agrario* and, more recently, *renta activa de inserción laboral*) is provided on a means-tested basis to about 600,000 jobless workers, no longer eligible for contributory unemployment insurance. Non-contributory pensions for old age and disability (*pensiones no contributivas de la seguridad social, pensiones asistenciales* and *subsidio de garantía de mínimos*) can be claimed by low-income individuals with inadequate contributions. In 2000, over 620,000 people received one of these pensions. Family benefits (*prestaciones familiares de la seguridad social*) are available to those with dependent children. Benefit amounts were increased in 2000 and new benefits were introduced (birth grants for the third or successive children and in the event of multiple births), but their impact remains rather limited. Finally, minimum income programmes (*rentas mínimas de inserción*) are operated at regional level as a safety net of last resort. Approximately 80,000 families with 200,000 members (0.5 per cent of the population) claimed minimum incomes in 2000.

Regional minimum-income programmes differ in benefit adequacy and the nature of "insertion" required of beneficiaries. Only the Basque scheme can be considered a genuine minimum-income programme. Well-developed schemes also operate in Madrid and Catalonia. At the other extreme, some regions provide minimum-income programmes of limited coverage at a low level, or merely offer temporary employment in "socially useful" projects (see Aguilar *et al.* 1995).

In 2000, the basic monthly rate (for beneficiaries living alone) varied from €239 in the Canary Islands to €305 in the Basque Country and €319 in Extremadura and Navarre. Adjustments for family size are made according to flat equivalence scales (the presence of an additional member may increase the allowance granted to the household by up to 30 per cent of the basic rate), while total benefit amounts are subject to a maximum limit. Total expenditure on minimum income benefits reached €210 million (0.03 per cent of GDP) in 2000. At the regional level, expenditure varied from €337,000 in La Rioja (this is below 0.1 per cent of the regional budget), reaching €53 million in the Basque Country (over 1 per cent of the regional budget). Catalonia, Andalusia and Madrid spent between them €89 million (Arriba and Moreno 2002).

Future prospects for minimum-income programmes are uncertain. Their implementation contributed to the legitimacy of the new *Comunidades Autónomas* and was favoured by fiscal federalism: from 3 per cent in 1981, regional spending accounted for as much as 33 per cent of all public expenditure in 2001. Regions have been able to integrate social services and social assistance into common local networks of provision, but most programmes are seriously underfunded. Moreover, even if top-down harmonization can hardly be regarded as a viable option in a federalized country like Spain, their decentralized nature risks exacerbating regional disparities in welfare provision (Moreno 2003). Still, in a not-too-distant future, regions could face the dilemma of either requesting co-funding from central government or limiting the scope of existing programmes.

The 2001 National Action Plan was an important occasion for intergovernmental coordination, providing the first synthetic overview of the fight against social exclusion in Spain. It remains to be seen whether the next rounds of this process will be a source of fresh ideas (and, possibly, funds) to sustain the efforts of all stakeholders involved.

Conclusion

As the preceding discussion illustrates, southern European countries differ both in terms of the design of anti-poverty policy and the institutional

Table 2

Low-income benefits (2002)

	Greece	Italy	Portugal	Spain
Unemployment insurance (minimum rate)	265[a]	[g]	390	442[a]
Unemployment assistance	150[b]	n/a	312[d]	332[a]
Contributory minimum pension (aged 70)	474[ac]	516[h]	190	386[ad]
Non-contributory social pension (aged 70)	156[ad]	516[h]	138	259[d]
Family allowance (1 child aged 7)	n/a[e]	n/a[e]	26	24
Family allowance (3 children aged 10, 7 and 4)	141[f]	110[i]	92	73

Notes: Monthly benefit in € for low-income worker or family, paid 12 times a year unless otherwise indicated.
[a] Paid 14 times a year.
[b] Only available to workers aged over 45.
[c] Pensioner solidarity supplement included.
[d] Rate for beneficiaries with no dependants.
[e] No general scheme. Contributory allowances available to families of dependent workers.
[f] Only available to families with a third child aged below 6.
[g] Ordinary unemployment benefit paid at 40 per cent of reference earnings (no minimum rate).
[h] Paid 13 times a year.
[i] Large-family benefit only. Contributory allowance not included.
Source: MISSOC (2002); FIPOSC final report.

configuration in which such policy operates (see table 2). Yet they continue to form a distinct cluster as they all face a similar set of challenges, pointing to a common social policy agenda.

In contrast to the stagnation of previous decades, the 1990s have definitely witnessed significant and promising policy innovations in the field of poverty and social exclusion in southern Europe. The new targeted benefits and services, introduced in all four countries, moved in the right direction: they filled some—often the most macroscopic—of the traditional gaps in coverage, going some way towards the necessary reallocation of social expenditure towards the most needy.

Without doubt, EU initiatives played a significant role in prompting such recalibration. The influence of Council Recommendation 92/441 has already been noted, while Article 2 of the Maastricht Treaty specifically referred to the need to integrate persons excluded from the labour market. Recently, the 2001 National Action Plans for Social Inclusion were in all four countries the occasion for the first serious attempt at formulating a comprehensive diagnosis of current challenges and existing policies. Greater attention towards "social minima" and the safety net has been encouraged by the EU discourse of cohesion, inclusion and guaranteeing sufficient resources (Ferrera *et al.* 2002).

The drive to establish effective minimum-income guarantees moved at different speeds and along different paths in the four countries (see table 3).

Table 3

Minimum income programmes (2000)

	Greece[a]	Italy	Portugal	Spain
Income guarantee (€ per month), single person	*148.0*	268.0	125.0	286.0[e]
Income guarantee, couple + 2 children	*444.0*	660.0	374.0	386.0[e]
Number of beneficiaries (thousand)	*700.0*	86.0[b]	418.0	202.0
Number of beneficiaries (% population)	*6.4*	3.6[b]	4.2	0.5
Cost of minimum income scheme (€ million)	*269.0*	220.0[c]	284.0	210.0
Cost of minimum income scheme (% GDP)	*0.23*	*0.21*[d]	0.25	0.03

Notes:
[a] There is no minimum income programme in Greece. The figures cited derive from a simulation of the effects of such programme as reported in Matsaganis et al. (2001). The version of minimum income simulated was linked to the social pension (€1775 p.a. in 2000), with a Portuguese RMG equivalence scale (1.0 for each of the first two adults, 0.7 for each additional adult and 0.5 for each child under 18), and a 20 per cent earnings disregard.
[b] Number of beneficiaries (and percentage of local population) in the 39 municipalities participating in the first wave of the RMI experiment.
[c] Cost of RMI in the 39 municipalities over the two-year period ending 31 December 2000.
[d] Mid-point estimate of total cost in 2001 if RMI were generalized throughout Italy.
[e] Value of minimum income benefit in Catalonia.
Source: FIPOSC final report.

Portugal successfully implemented a national rights-based scheme. Spain followed a decentralized approach: in some regions minimum income is a legal right, but others have adopted a more cautious, discretionary approach within limited resources. The Italian pilot scheme was launched with a view to subsequently establishing a national guarantee: the experiment still goes on, though the destination seems more uncertain. Greece, on the other hand, seems so far unable to go beyond the level of policy debates: the option of introducing some form of minimum income guarantee is still considered too contentious.

Strengthening the social safety net raises the question of the most appropriate level for action. This is especially relevant in Spain and Italy, where the issue is intertwined with the wider debate on subsidiarity and decentralization. While this undeniably opens up new opportunities for innovation and virtuous experimentation at the regional level, it also raises the risk of perpetuating, even reinforcing, traditional gaps and disparities. On balance, the Spanish experience leans towards the former, whereas Italy's emerging scenario points to the latter.

On the whole, the verdict must remain open: in spite of positive developments in the 1990s, southern European safety nets still remain rather frail— in terms of institutional design as well as political support and legitimacy. This weakness should be a cause for concern: as the traditional capacity of families to respond to social needs declines, the pressure on formal social protection will inevitably intensify. Meeting this challenge will certainly require a substantial effort to upgrade administrative capabilities, but the fiscal cost of strengthening safety nets is likely to remain modest.

The future of anti-poverty policies and, in particular, minimum income programmes will ultimately rest on political considerations. These programmes are vulnerable because so are their beneficiaries. Sustaining the momentum for reform depends on the ability and strength of transversal coalitions in their favour. At this moment, it can only be hoped that the efforts of recent years to weave and mend social safety nets in the South are not discontinued: social protection outsiders are still too many and still too poor.

Acknowledgements

This paper draws on the project "Fighting poverty and social exclusion in southern Europe: dilemmas of organization and implementation", funded by the European Commission (HPSE-CT-2001-60020). Thanks are due to Ana Arriba, Francesca Bastagli, Teresa Bomba, Teresa Buil, Rita Fernandes, Giselas Matos and Stefano Sacchi for their contribution to the country reports, and to participants in the FIPOSC seminar (Milan 23–24 May 2002) for feedback. The authors are finally grateful to Peter Taylor-Gooby and an anonymous referee for comments and suggestions on an earlier draft of this paper.

References

Addis, E. (1999), Gender in the reform of the Italian welfare state, *South European Society and Politics*, 4, 2: 122–50.

Aguilar, M., Laparra, M. and Gaviria, M. (1995), La caña y el pez: el salario social en las comunidades autónomas 1989–1994, Madrid: Foessa.

Almeida, J. F., Capucha, L., Costa, A. F., Machado, F. L., Nicolau, I. and Reis, E. (1994), Exclusão social, factores e tipos de pobreza em Portugal, Oeiras: Celta Editora.

Arriba, A. and Moreno, L. (2002), *Poverty, social exclusion and "safety nets"*. UPC Working Paper 02–10, Madrid (www.iesam.csic.es/doctrab).

Atkinson, A. (1998), *Poverty in Europe*, Oxford: Blackwell.

Baldini, M., Bosi, P. and Toso, S. (2002), Targeting welfare in Italy: old problems and perspectives on reform, *Fiscal Studies*, 23, 1: 51–75.

Baldwin-Edwards, M. and Arango, J. (eds) (1998), Immigrants and the informal economy in southern Europe, *South European Society and Politics*, 3, 3.

Capucha, L. (1998), *Rendimento Mínimo Garantido: avaliação da fase experimental*, Lisboa: CIES/MTS.

CEC (2001), *Draft joint report on social inclusion*, Communication from the Commission, COM (2001) 565 final.

CEC (2002), *The Social Situation in the European Union*, Luxembourg: Office for Official Publications of the European Communities.

Esping-Andersen, G., Gallie, D., Hemerijck, A. and Myles, J. (2002), *Why We Need a New Welfare State*, Oxford: Oxford University Press.

Fernández Cordón, J. A. (1997), Youth residential independence and autonomy: a comparative study, *Journal of Family Issues*, 6: 576–607.

Ferrera, M. (1996), The "southern model" of welfare in social Europe, *Journal of European Social Policy*, 6, 1: 17–37.

Ferrera, M., Hemerijck, A. and Rhodes, M. (2000), *The Future of Social Europe: Recasting Work and Welfare in the New Economy*, Oeiras: Celta Editora.

Ferrera, M., Matsaganis, M. and Sacchi, S. (2002), Open co-ordination against poverty: the new EU "social inclusion process", *Journal of European Social Policy*, 12, 3: 227–39.

Gough, I. (1996), Social assistance in Southern Europe, *Southern European Society and Politics*, 1, 1: 1–13.

Guillén, A. and Matsaganis, M. (2000), Testing the "social dumping" hypothesis in southern Europe: welfare policies in Greece and Spain during the last 20 years, *Journal of European Social Policy*, 10, 2: 120–45.

IRS, Fondazione Zancan and CLES (2001), *Valutazione della sperimentazione del Reddito Minimo di Inserimento*, Rome: Presidenza del Consiglio dei Ministri.

Leibfried, S. (1993), Towards a European welfare state? In C. Jones (ed.), *New Perspectives on the Welfare State in Europe*, London: Routledge.

Lewis, J. (2001), The decline of the male breadwinner model: the implications for work and care, *Social Politics*, 8, 2: 152–70.

Marlier, E. and Cohen-Solal, M. (2000), *Social benefits and their redistributive effect in the EU*, Statistics in Focus (Theme 3 9/2000), Luxembourg: Eurostat.

Matsaganis, M. (2002), Yet another piece of pension reform in Greece, *South European Society and Politics*, 7, 3: 109–22.

Matsaganis, M., Papadopoulos, F. and Tsakloglou, P. (2001), Eliminating extreme poverty in Greece, *Journal of Income Distribution*, 10, 1–2: 40–57.

MISSOC (2002), Social protection in the EU member states and the European Economic Area (http://www.europa.eu.int/comm/employment_social/missoc).

Moreno, L. (2002), *Mediterranean welfare and "superwomen"*, UPC Working Paper 02–02, Madrid (www.iesam.csic.es/doctrab).

Moreno, L. (2003), Europeanisation, mesogovernments and safety nets, *European Journal of Political Research*, 42, 2: 185–99.

Onofri Report (1997), *Commissione per l'analisi delle compatibilità macroeconomiche della spesa sociale (Relazione Finale)*, Rome: Presidenza del Consiglio dei Ministri.

Rhodes, M. (1996), Southern European welfare states: identity, problems and prospects for reform, *South European Society and Politics*, 1, 3: 1–22.

Saraceno, C. (2000), Italian families under economic stress: the impact of social policies, *Labour*, 14, 1: 161–83.

Saraceno, C. (2002), *Social Assistance Dynamics: National and Local Poverty Regimes*, Bristol: Policy Press.

Taylor-Gooby, P. (ed.) (2001), *Welfare States under Pressure*, London: Sage.

Viegas, J. and Costa, A. F. (2000), *Crossroads to Modernity: Contemporary Portuguese Society*, Oeiras: Celta Editora.

8
The Trajectory of Post-communist Welfare State Development: The Cases of Bulgaria and Romania

Dimitri A. Sotiropoulos, Ileana Neamtu and Maya Stoyanova

Introduction: The Transition Dilemma

Transitions to democracy and to the market system are accompanied by some hard policy choices. In the postwar period West European governments could view state intervention in the economy, on the one hand, and economic efficiency, on the other, as mutually compatible goals. In the last quarter of the twentieth century, this view was changed: state intervention was understood to hamper efficiency and growth. In that historical period, two successive sets of transitions took place, the first in Southern Europe (transition from authoritarian rule to democracy) and the second in Eastern and South-eastern Europe (transition from communist rule to democracy and the market). The first set of these transitions was accompanied by what Jose-Maria Maravall has called the "Southern European Syndrome". The South-European governments

> faced a declining competitiveness of their economies in an international context that was changing very rapidly; ... not only their economies were weaker [than those of Western Europe], but the effect of economic inefficiency on political legitimacy was a more delicate problem ... Attachment to parties was also low, and political participation was comparatively limited ... From the beginning of the transition, demands on the state were very strong ... extended social demands contrasted with comparatively underdeveloped welfare in the new democracies. (Maravall 1992: 6–8)

In other words, the syndrome, which was also a difficult dilemma, was the following: neglecting the welfare state in order to promote economic competitiveness would probably affect adversely the political legitimacy of new-born democracies. This is because people often tend to associate new democratic regimes with higher living standards. Regime change is often linked with high hopes for a better life; otherwise people may tend to downgrade democratic achievements and be less enthusiastic about political democracy itself. Some of these hopes for a better life may be fulfilled by a generous welfare state. During the 1970s and the 1980s, the expansion of the welfare state in Greece, Portugal and Spain has probably contributed to the political legitimacy of the new South European democratic regimes. However, owing to welfare generosity, such expansion has to some extent damaged the already ailing national economies (particularly those of Greece and Portugal in the post-transition period).

One could argue that the above short description of the transition period in Southern Europe between the mid-1970s and the mid-1980s to a certain extent bore some similarities with the situation in Eastern and South-eastern Europe in the 1990s. Throughout post-communist Europe, expectations from the new democratic regimes were high. However, after the initial break-through from communism, political participation faded away, and the economy performed less well than expected. The crisis was acute particularly in the countries of South-eastern Europe. South European governments of the late 1970s and East and South-east European transition governments faced a similar policy dilemma: how to respond to demands for better welfare services without endangering the competitiveness of their national economies. Compared to Greece, Portugal and Spain in the transition period, the countries of South-eastern Europe entered their transition period equipped with more comprehensive welfare services, which they had inherited from the communist regimes. Such services, however, were of low quality and used to hide many inequalities based on political criteria (for example, communist party members versus the rest, men versus women; Deacon 1992b). In fact, in the case of South-eastern Europe the policy constraints were even harder, since in the Western Balkans the wars linked to the disintegration of Yugoslavia were taking place at the same time, in the first half of the 1990s, destabilizing the Balkan region as a whole.

How did the governments of Greece, Portugal and Spain solve the policy dilemma sketched above? With the benefit of hindsight and following Jose-Maria Maravall, we can argue that South European governments opted for a two-step solution. First, they preferred welfare expansion in order to consolidate the democratic regimes and then, earlier in the case of Spain and Portugal (in the 1980s) and much later in the case of Greece (in the 1990s), they made an about-turn and resorted to measures of economic austerity, in order to rescue their economies and meet the requirements of European integration. How have East and South-east European governments and par-ticularly the governments of Bulgaria and Romania, on which we would like to focus, responded to the same dilemma? A possible answer is that it is too early to say and that there are many different answers, depending on the policy sector in question. If one may wish to detect a single visible pattern in these two countries, this would be the following: the Bulgarian and Romanian governments seemed to prefer first keeping the welfare state intact, then rolling it back, in order to promote macro-economic efficiency and growth, and later (that is, very recently) taking measures to meet the rising social costs of transition to the market system. We go on to review social policy develop-ments in these countries in general and in particular services, before drawing conclusions about the impact of economic and political factors on the trajectory of reform.

The Development of the Bulgarian and Romanian Welfare States during the Transition

In terms of economic development, under communism South-east European countries traditionally lagged behind other East European countries. Industrialization and urbanization were less extended in the former than in the latter countries. Since the onset of transition, such underdevelopment was compounded by additional problems, which set the countries of post-communist South-eastern Europe apart from the rest of Eastern Europe. The particular problems were related to the following characteristics of South-east European countries in the early 1990s: relatively low GDP per capita (averaging less than $US 2,000 per year), a low level of industrialization and low-skilled service industries, a relatively large agricultural sector, weak institutions (including the lack of rule of law), and export structures which were characteristic of economic dependency (raw materials, agricultural products, some light industrial goods; East-Western Institute 2000: 6). These characteristics were reflected in the large pockets of poverty and unemployment as well as extended income inequality visible in South-eastern Europe throughout the 1990s.

We have chosen to study Bulgaria and Romania because cases of countries of South-eastern Europe are less well known than those of Central-Eastern Europe and because some trends in welfare systems visible in the 1990s in Eastern Europe as a whole have acquired more acute forms in South-eastern Europe. In this particular region, in terms of access to data it seems more difficult to study the Western areas (mostly consisting of countries emerging from the disintegration of Yugoslavia) than the Eastern areas (i.e., Bulgaria and Romania).

Comparative data on Eastern Europe confirm that Bulgaria and Romania are similar cases in many respects, while they also have some differences. In 1998 the GNP per capita of Bulgaria was $1,220 while that of Romania was $1,360. However, the share of the population who lived on less than $4.30 a day was 18.2 per cent in Bulgaria (in 1995) while that of Romania was 44.5 per cent (in 1998) (World Bank 2000: 35, table 1.1). In 1997, Bulgaria and Romania had the highest percentage of children living in children's homes among all East European countries (World Bank 2000: 57, figure 1.4). In the first period of the transition (roughly 1990–4) Bulgaria and Romania showed very rapid deterioration of income inequality (World Bank 2000: 140, table 4.1). In the late 1990s both countries faced problems of "deep poverty". They also shared the problem of social exclusion of ethnic minorities (Pomak Muslims in Bulgaria, Roma in both countries). In both countries, social assistance schemes failed to achieve more than a low level of coverage of poor households (World Bank 2000: 296–7, tables 9.1, 9.3). Compared to most OECD and even other post-communist East European countries, Bulgaria and Romania showed relatively small public expenditure in health care, at around 3 per cent of GDP in 1998 (World Bank 2000: 269, figure

8.4). In 1999, life expectancy at birth in Bulgaria was 70.8 years. In Romania it was 69.8 years. Both cases lagged behind the EU average (77.6 years) and most other post-communist East European countries (Government of Romania-CASPIS 2002: 63, on the basis of data from the UN's Human Development Project of 2001).

The first attempts to compare post-transition East European welfare states date from the early 1990s. At that time, Bob Deacon classified the emerging welfare systems of East European transition countries into four "types": post-communist conservative corporatism, conservative corporatism, social-democratic type and liberal-capitalist type (Deacon 1992a: 181). Bulgaria and Romania were classified in the first type, i.e., the post-communist conservative corporatist type, on the grounds of a number of variables (listed below, see table 1). This type implied ideological and practical commitment to socialist values even after the initial transition had taken place and social pacts had been agreed upon between the government and major labour unions (1992a: 182). Such idiosyncratic traits of the Bulgarian and Romanian welfare systems, in turn, were related to the maintenance in power of part of the old guard (the Bulgarian Socialist Party in Bulgaria and the National Salvation Front in Romania). In general, after the transition Bulgaria and Romania were seen as either "late reformers" (by the United Nations Development Programme, the UNDP; see Deacon 2000: 150) or as cases of "limited to modest reform" (by the World Bank, 1996).

Bulgaria and Romania were classified by Bob Deacon as the first type because they were characterized by medium to low economic development, high working-class mobilization, small or no influence of Catholicism on social policy formulation, absolutist and authoritarian legacy, mass character of the revolutionary process that led to the transition to democracy, and medium to low impact of the transition on their welfare regimes.

Still, some of these characteristics were more formal than real. The declared interest of the Bulgarian and Romanian governments to enhance social protection was still not visible at the level of social expenditures, which have been low (see tables 2 and 3). The governments' interest primarily lay in passing legislation and forming new policies. However, in South-eastern Europe statistical figures and official policies often concealed harsh realities, possibly to an extent larger than in other regions of Eastern Europe. For instance, reform projects were announced but may have never been fully carried out, and laws were passed but may have never been implemented. There was a lot of formalism, meaning a gap between official pronouncements and actual developments. Thus, all facts and figures should be read with caution.

A look at social expenditures in Bulgaria and Romania between 1989 and 1995, reveals an initial trend towards an increase and then a reverse trend towards a decrease of expenditures, which was more dramatic in the case of Romania than in the case of Bulgaria. Specifically Romania did not follow other East European transition countries in the pattern of initial large decrease in social expenditures (see table 2), possibly because spending was already too small to be cut further. By the mid-1990s, Romania and Bulgaria were still devoting a smaller share of their GDP to social expenditure than other East European transition countries (see table 3, following after table 2). Later,

Table 1

Emerging welfare regimes in Eastern Europe

	Bulgaria	Czechoslovakia	Germany	Poland	Hungary	Romania	Slovenia	Serbia	USSR
Economic development	M	H	H	M	M	L	H	L	L
Working-class mobilization	H	H	M	H	L	H	L	M	H
Catholic teaching on policy influential	N	L	L	H	L	L	M	N	N
Absolutist and authoritarian legacy	H	L	M	H	M	H	M	H	H
Character of revolutionary process	Ms	Ms	Ms	Ms	Q	Ms	Q	Ms	M
Transitional impact	M	M	H	H	H	L	M	L	L
Emerging welfare state regime-type	1	3	2	1	4	1	4	1	1

Symbols:
M = Medium
N = None
H = High
Ms = Mass
L = Low
Q = Quietude
1 = Post-communist conservative corporatism
2 = Conservative corporatism
3 = Social democracy
4 = Liberal capitalism
Source: Deacon (1992b: 181).

Table 2

Decreases in (public) social expenditure (as % of GDP) in Romania and in
post-communist countries in 1993, in comparison with 1989

Countries in transition	1989	Decrease of social expenditure in 1993, in comparison with 1989 (%)
Average of transition countries	16.7	4.5
Average of European transition countries	20.4	6.6
Romania	14.2	*1.0*
Average of CIS countries	13.6	6.0

Source: Zamfir (1999: 69).

Table 3

Social expenditure as percentage of GDP in Romania and Bulgaria, in comparison with
other countries of transition and the EU

Romania (1995)	16.0% (16.6% in 1998)
Bulgaria (1995)	18.3%
Average of transition countries (1993)	21.2%
Average of European transition countries (1994)	27.0%
Average of CIS countries (1994)	19.6%
Average of EU countries (1995)	28.3%

Source: Zamfir (1999: 69).

towards the end of the 1990s, there was a reversal of the decreasing trends
of both countries (see table 4).

In detail, even though Bulgaria and Romania generally lagged behind
other transition countries in terms of social expenditure, after the first phase
of the transition, during which in both countries there was an increase in
social spending, there was a decrease in public expenditure in health, education and pensions. Public spending then rose in 1997–8 both in total and on
education and health services. Development followed a three-phase pattern:
first an increase in social expenditure, then decrease, later increase again.

There was some differentiation between different services in the general three-
phase pattern. As table 4 shows, in the mid-1990s in Bulgaria the decrease was
more accentuated in education and health expenditures than in pension
expenditures. This is probably related to the skewed "demographic tree" of
the Bulgarian population, a population which is rapidly ageing. By contrast,
in Romania, education expenditures rose—albeit with some fluctuation—
between 1989 and 1996 and pension expenditures also rose between 1989 and

Table 4

Social public expenditures in Bulgaria and Romania, 1989–1999, as percentage of GDP

		1989	1990	1991	1992	1993	1994	1995	1996	1997	1998	1999
Total social expenditures	Bulgaria	20.3	21.2	24.5	27.0	22.8	21.0	18.3	16.3	17	19	21.2
	Romania	14.2	16.6	17.0	16.5	15.2	15.5	16.0	15.7	15.9	17.3	18.4
Education expenditures	Bulgaria	5.5	5.0	5.1	6.1	5.7	4.8	4.1	3.2	4	4	4.4
	Romania	2.2	3.0	3.6	3.6	3.2	3.1	3.4	3.6	3.3	3.3	3.2
Health expenditures	Bulgaria	3.3	4.0	6.4	5.7	5.1	4.2	3.5	2.9	2.9	3.1	—
	Romania	2.5	2.9	3.3	3.3	2.7	3.1	2.9	2.8	2.6	3.1	3.9
Pension expenditures	Bulgaria	8.7	8.7	9.4	10.2	9.5	9.4	8.1	—	—	—	—
	Romania	5.2	6.6	6.1	6.4	6.5	6.5	6.9	6.9	6.9	—	—

Source: Zamfir (1999: 729, 730, 733). For Romania, the original source is UNDP, *National Human Development Report: Romania 2000*, p. 129, and the database of Research Institute for Quality of Life (Romania). For Bulgaria, the source is the TransMonee database.

1995. In the same country, health expenditures rose—with some fluctuation—until 1994 and declined thereafter, until 1998, when they started rising again. In Bulgaria, the reversal, i.e. the downturn in the second phase, was dramatic because of the economic decisions which prompted a severe economic crisis in 1997–8. Such decisions involved the "loosening" of fiscal restraints and of strict monetary policy. These were compounded by the bankruptcy of banks and by growing speculation. Since then, the Bulgarian economy has somewhat recovered, but there were substantial effects on social policies. Child allowances, pensions, sickness, maternity and unemployment benefits were cut sharply, while social assistance spending doubled between 1992 and 1997 (Deacon *et al.* 1997: 117).

Individual Sectors of Social Policy

In what follows, we present a short glimpse at three sectors of social policy in Bulgaria and Romania: public health, pensions and unemployment. Our purpose is to consider the trajectory of welfare state development in both countries after the collapse of communism. Our data are drawn on figures provided by international organizations, national official sources, and some national and EU research projects.

Health care

A first point is that the governments of Bulgaria and Romania probably could not cut down on pension spending, owing to demographic pressures, and instead chose to downsize public health. In that sector, both countries started from a low level of spending before transition. As was mentioned above and as table 5 shows, some health indicators for Bulgaria and Romania, such as life expectancy and infant mortality, were already lagging behind OECD averages. This was probably related to the very uneven quality

Table 5

Some social indicators at the end of the communist regimes (1988), in Romania, Bulgaria and in the OECD

Indicators	Bulgaria	Romania	OECD
GDP per capita (US dollars)	5.633	4.117	14.637
Social public expenditure (% of GDP)	20.3	14.2	22.21
Life expectancy (years)	72.0	70.0	76.0
Infant mortality (per 1,000 live births)	14.0	24.0	8.0
Average pension (% average wage)*	57.3	47.1	—
Social expenditure in education (% of GDP)*	5.5	2.2	5.9
Social expenditure in health (% of GDP)*	3.3	2.5	9.7

* UNDP (1994).
Source: Deacon (1992a: 6).

of medical and hospital services, which had been particularly problematic in Romania. To some extent, this explains the initial enthusiasm of the post-communist Bulgarian and Romanian governments for private or semi-private health care.

This enthusiasm led, however, to sharp reductions in public spending on health. Reduction in public spending was accompanied by a wholesale public health reform, which was promoted by the Bulgarian government which was in power in 1997–2001. The reform was based on a "national health strategy", which introduced a new health insurance scheme, a reform of the medical profession, an emphasis on primary care and the creation of voluntary health insurance funds (GVG-Bulgaria 2002: 148–51). Overall, the strategy was to promote privatization of health care in a coordinated and supervised manner. In 1999 in Bulgaria a National Health Insurance Fund (NHIF) was created. The NHIF had multiple purposes. It was to become the main agency of management and financing of public hospitals, to contract out health care provision to public and private agencies and also to engage in negotiations with the professional associations of doctors and dentists. In particular, in 2000–1, outpatient services were transferred (first stage of reform). For 2002, the NHIF aimed to take up 25 per cent of hospital care costs. The Bulgarian government has planned to raise this share of the new Fund, to redirect 10 per cent of medical activities from hospitals to outpatient providers and to privatize or close down around 10 per cent of public hospitals (second stage of reform; cf. Government of Bulgaria 2002: 7).

However, after the turnover in government in July 2001, the new cabinet of former King Simeon the Second started discussing again some of the principles of the health reform and changed its goals. Some renationalization of health schemes was now envisaged. This caused delays in the implementation of the measures noted above and was met with resistance by the sectoral interests of doctors and dentists.

The reform of health care in Romania also seemed to be a case of incomplete privatization. The aim of the reform was first to improve on primary health care and then to change the health social insurance system. In 1997 a new law reorganizing health insurance was adopted, with an aim to privatize and decentralize health care. New institutions were created on a central and on a district basis (for example, the College of Physicians of Romania). The relevant laws were passed and public expenditure rose from about 2.8 per cent of the GDP in 1997 to 4.1 per cent in 2000 (GVG-Romania 2002: 118–19, 127). However, there were delays in the implementation of the new health insurance scheme, independent health service providers complained of their intense monitoring by and subordination to central authorities and users of the health system were not informed about their new rights (GVG-Romania 2002: 143).

Generally, in Bulgaria and Romania the main problem remained that, with the privatization of health services, access to health provision was influenced by the worsening of the economic situation. Obviously, this affected adversely a large share of the population in both countries. Owing to the division of health services into private and public, many people enjoyed much worse health services than before because they could not afford to pay for private health services, while public health services deteriorated. Poor people in particular had no means to pay health insurance and, thus, had very limited access to medical services.

Pension system

Under communism, Bulgaria used to have a pay-as-you-go system of pensions. This system was characterized by early retirement ages and high replacement rates. During the transition the economic crisis hit incomes from pensions quite hard and the dependency ratio worsened. In 1998 in Bulgaria there were 2.5 million pensioners out of a population of 8.3 million people (30.1 per cent of the population), while the average pension corresponded to 32.6 per cent of the average monthly salary. In terms of purchasing power, in 1998 Bulgarians enjoyed on average approximately one-third of their purchasing power in 1989 (Beleva *et al.* 1999: 10). Shortly after the transition (in 1991), the Bulgarian government reduced the retirement age and set a minimum pension level. However, after the crisis of 1997, policy changes were brought about by Minister of Labour and Social Policy, Mr Neikov, who was in charge of the Bulgarian social security system. The changes had financial, structural and social aspects. Financially, the purpose was to alleviate the fiscal burden placed by the pension system on the public finances of Bulgaria. Organizationally, the idea was to introduce a three-pillar system, diffused by international organizations and also introduced in other East European countries. Socially, the aim was to improve the purchasing capacity of pensioners, whose living conditions had deteriorated after the transition.

In 1999 in Bulgaria, the minimum age for retirement was raised, and regulations for private pension funds were introduced. Most importantly, in August 1999, under the influence of the IMF and the World Bank, the new three-pillar system of pensions was introduced. The system, which is not yet fully operational, is supervised by a "State Insurance Supervision Agency" and consists of a public pay-as-you-go pillar, a mandatory insurance fund-based second pillar, and a voluntary private third pillar (East-Western Institute 2000). The financial aims of this reform are to alleviate the deficit which has threatened the viability of the first pillar and to transfer part of the contributions to the second pillar. Such new measures cannot distort the general picture of the 1990s which is one of general economic decline of pensioners. Two examples may serve to illustrate this point: in 1991 the real average pension in Bulgaria was 51 per cent lower than in 1990; and in 1996, it was 47 per cent lower than in the immediately previous year. Examining the situation every year between 1991 and 1998, we see that the real pension was higher than in the previous year in 1993 (3 per cent), in 1995 (9 per cent), in 1997 (25 per cent) and in 1998 (15 per cent). In all other years (1991, 1992, 1994 and 1996), there were decreases in comparison with the previous year, ranging from 18 per cent in 1992, to 51 per cent in 1991 (Shopov 1999: 71).

In Romania, although the living standards of the old people have generally been very low, there was a more clear rural–urban divide. Among the old, the peasant population has fared even worse than the general population.

Retired peasants were receiving very low pensions already in 1989 and their situation has not improved since (Pop *et al.* 1998: 231). Generally, in the first years of the transition, the practice of handing out pensions fulfilled the function of social dumping and bore the costs of economic restructuring. Among employed Romanians in general, earlier retirement was preferred by many to receiving unemployment benefits. However, over time, employment and thus contributions declined and the debts of the social security budget accumulated. As in the case of Bulgaria, the fiscal burden of the pension system on the public finances of Romania was heavy. To amend the situation, a new law was passed in August 2000, which, as in the Bulgarian case, raised the minimum age for retirement and provided for a three-pillar system (East-Western Institute 2000; GVG-Romania 2002). The new pension law triggered a rise in the social security tax rates. In order to offset this rise, the Romanian government has decided to cut down on other taxes and to incorporate them in the state budget (for example, to incorporate the payroll tax which was channelled to the special fund for handicapped persons; Government of Romania 2001: 4).

Unemployment and labour market policies

Real incomes worsened in both countries while inflation eroded wages and salaries and unemployment fluctuated largely (see table 6). As is well known, in command economies, before the transition there was hidden unemployment. For instance, in 1989 in Romania unemployment was about 3–4 per cent. By contrast, in 1986 in Bulgaria there were more job vacancies than job candidates (Deacon and Vidinova 1992: 70). Generally, in both countries there was job security and equal pay for equal work (albeit, not always for female workers). However, as Bob Deacon puts it, "the advantages of job security for the many did not counter the inadequacy, or absence, of unemployment benefit" (Deacon 2000: 147). In addition, there were wage differences between the two sexes, and party bureaucrats enjoyed various privileges.

Since the collapse of communism, the problem of unemployment has become particularly acute in Bulgaria. The rate of unemployment has fluctuated a lot: it increased until 1993, then declined and then increased from 11.1 per cent in 1995 to reach a record high 16.0 per cent in 1999. This was related to the economic crisis of the mid-1990s in Bulgaria, the effects of which are shown in table 6 also in terms of the rising inflation rate and the falling real wage in 1993–7.

After 1991 in Bulgaria a generous unemployment benefits scheme was developed (Deacon 1992b: 171). The state budget and the employers bore the cost of unemployment benefits. A new fund, the "Professional Qualification and Unemployment Fund", was created. Over time, in the 1990s, a more restricted policy for unemployment benefits was adopted, while in 1998 the share of the long-term unemployed people was 60 per cent of the total number of unemployed. There was also very extended unemployment among the young.

Since 1997, the Bulgarian government has adopted a policy of passive and active measures to combat unemployment. In 1998, passive measures, such

Table 6

Some macro-economic indicators of Bulgaria and Romania in 1990–1999

		1990	1991	1992	1993	1994	1995	1996	1997	1998	1999
GDP per capita (US $)	Bulgaria	—	—	1.014	1.281	1.152	1.563	1.179	1.230	1.490	1.513
	Romania	—	—	859	1.158	1.323	1.243	1.290	1.395	1.845	1.517
Inflation rate (% change from previous year)**	Bulgaria	26.3	333.5	82.0	73.0	96.3	62.0	123.0	104.9	22.2	0.7
	Romania	5.1	170.2	210.4	256.1	136.7	32.3	38.8	154.8	59.1	45.8
Unemployment (% of labour force)*	Bulgaria	1.7	11.1	15.3	16.4	12.8	11.1	12.5	13.7	12.2	16.0
	Romania	n.a	3.0	8.2	10.4	10.2	8.2	6.5	7.4	10.4	11.5
Real wage per capita (1989 = 100)**	Bulgaria	98.3	58.5	60.8	63.2	55.5	49.0	47.8	42.5	51.0	—
	Romania	105.5	85.4	74.6	62.1	62.4	70.2	76.9	59.4	61.5	61.6

Sources: *East-Western Institute (2000).
** Zamfir (1999: 746). An additional source for data after 1999 is Zamfir *et al.* (2001: 20).

as unemployment benefits, absorbed about 60 per cent of the cost of labour market policies. Active measures included training, employment subsidies, hiring for temporary public works, etc. Other measures were targeted towards social categories particularly hit by unemployment, such as the Roma. However, the fall of the Kostov government and the rise to power of the more pro-liberal National Movement of former King Simeon II (NMSS) in 2001, has meant that the old policies to fight against unemployment are under reform. The old legal framework for labour market policy has been abolished and a new, more liberal framework is expected to take its place.

In Romania, unemployment increased sharply until 1993, declined between 1994 and 1996, but rose thereafter. Overall, the levels of unemployment in Romania remained lower than the equivalent in Bulgaria. Massive lay-offs of workers in cases of privatization were accompanied by redundancy payments to the fired workers. The payments ranged between 6 and 12 months' average wage. Active measures to combat unemployment were adopted in Romania in 1997. A special agency, titled "National Agency for Employment Professional Training", was created. Training was organized for unemployed people. Some grants and wage subsidies were offered to small and medium-size businesses to motivate them to hire young people who were unemployed. Active measures to combat unemployment amounted to 50 per cent of the costs incurred by the unemployment policies. Despite all, in 1994–7, only between 2 and 3 per cent of the unemployed people were included in the training programmes (qualification / requalification programmes), while in 1991–6 expenditures for the social protection of the unemployed never surpassed 1 per cent of the Romanian GDP (National Statistical Institute of Romania 1998).

Overview and Discussion

In this paper we have presented a very brief outline of the development of a few sectors of social policy in post-communist Bulgaria and Romania. It seems that after an initial "stop-and-go" attitude, in the very beginning of the twenty-first century the governments of Bulgaria and Romania adopted more liberal and residualist social policies. This trend has varied among the individual sectors of the welfare state. To the extent that we can generalize for the two countries under study, in the health sector there was a rather early shift towards private providers. This shift has not been completed, but it has been accompanied by reductions in public health spending. Some effort to regulate private provision of health services began in 1997 in Romania and in 1999 in Bulgaria.

In the pension system, although both Bulgaria and Romania have tended to adopt the three-pillar system, in the past they had followed different paths. In Bulgaria, after 1992, the fate of pensioners deteriorated. Public spending on pensions decreased at a time when the population was—and still is—ageing. This has caused extended poverty among older people. In Romania, pensions were on the rise until 1995. Afterwards pension expenditures remained rather stable. There was extended poverty among older Romanian farmers.

In the labour market, there was an important difference between the two countries: in Bulgaria, the problem of unemployment has been more acute than in Romania. Recently, both countries adopted active and passive measures to battle unemployment. However, finding a job would not mean the solution of economic problems either for the average unemployed Bulgarian or for the Romanian. Since 1990, real wages and salaries have dropped and low pensions, low wages and low salaries have contributed to income inequality and poverty in both countries. Extended poverty is currently the most important social problem in Bulgaria and Romania.

Is there a pattern in the disappointing performance of the Bulgarian and the Romanian welfare states since the transition from communism? A possible answer is that in these countries during the transition from communism, the government initially chose to increase social expenditures, at least until the cost became unbearable in fiscal terms, as in the case of Greece, Portugal and Spain during the period of their own transition from authoritarian rule. After the initial phase, the Bulgarian and Romanian governments proceeded to abrupt cuts in the mid-1990s (second phase). Such cuts were somewhat reversed only in the late 1990s, in a third phase, during which the social consequences of those cuts became very visible. The transition dilemma explained in the beginning of our paper took a particular twist in Bulgaria and in Romania. The first post-transition governments seemed to neglect to a large extent the macro-economic requirements of transition to the market. These governments did not seem to be keen on competitiveness and efficiency. They were rather ambivalent about what to do, particularly in terms of social policy. This ambivalence reflected a similar lack of vision in economic and fiscal policy. As a study on social protection in Bulgaria has claimed, "a critical factor for the management of budget expenditure was the absence of a clear and consistent vision of mid-term fiscal policy until 1997" (GVG-Bulgaria 2002: 5).

How can the above pattern be explained? There are at least two possible explanations, the first being mainly economic, the second political. The first explanation would be that the fluctuation of welfare policy followed the common boom-and-bust economic cycles. This has been argued particularly with respect to the case of Romania. A study on social protection in Romania observed a pattern of successive cycles of economic recession and recovery, which probably impacted on social policy as well: "The first transformation recession (1990–1992) continued for three years, after which a recovery period that lasted three years followed (1993–1996). The next transformation recession lasted three years as well (1997–1999), and starting with 2000 a period of growth has been registered" (GVG-Romania 2002: 6). Reviewing the performance of the Romanian economy in 1989–2000, a report of the International Monetary Fund has stated: "Romania's stabilization and reform efforts still lag behind those of most other transition countries in Central and Eastern Europe, reflecting mainly the "stop-and-go" approach to reform and macroeconomic stability pursued for much of the past 11 years" (IMF 2000: 2).

If the above claims are correct, then the trajectory of welfare state development was just a reflection of a general "stop-and-go" economic policy. It may be argued that the Bulgarian and Romanian governments did not realize the transition dilemma at all, at least until the mid-1990s when financial crisis and fiscal constraints pushed them in a direction different from the one they had followed in the first years of the transition.

However, the fluctuation of the economy was not the only explanatory variable of this change. A more decisive variable was politics, namely the nature of the transition to democracy and the nature of the governing political elites. It may be argued that transition to democracy and the market in Bulgaria and Romania was delayed and that it did not really start until the mid-1990s. Immediately after 1989, former communist party cadres were able to win the first wave of general elections. They formed governments which applied policies that only nominally (rather than substantively) differed from the policies of the last communist governments before the transition. The first transition leaders did not fully espouse an abrupt break with the past. Former communist cadres remained in power in Bulgaria and Romania until the mid-1990s when a second wave of elections brought about their demise. This was the "two-step democratic transition process" which, according to some analysts, is characteristic of post-communist South-eastern Europe (Diamandouros and Larrabee 2000: 48–9).

Revamped communist parties were able to prevail in the first wave of elections, early in the transition, because the nature of the deposed communist regimes did not permit the incubation of democratic opposition forces before the transition had started. According to one opinion (Diamandouros and Larrabee 2000), compared to Central-European communism, which in the 1980s was "mature post-totalitarian" (for example, the political regimes of Poland or Hungary before the transition), South-eastern Communism was traditional "totalitarian". This meant that

the absence of pluralism and, hence, the pronounced organizational weakness of civil society implicit in this regime type translated into the lack of any significant opposition to the outgoing [communist totalitarian] regime, capable of taking the lead or, at the very least, of playing a central role in the transition to democracy. It is the very absence of credible alternative democratic actors capable of organizing power or of channelling local political participation conducive to a democratic outcome, which imparted in the South-East European transitions their distinctive two-step logic that profoundly influenced the course of their democratization trajectories and left its distinct imprint on them. (Diamandouros and Larrabee: 48)

The meanderings of welfare state development in Bulgaria and Romania between 1990 and the first years of the twenty-first century, probably confirm this thesis. Clearly, much more empirical research and testing of alternative theoretical explanations are necessary. If, however, the general idea of a two-step transition is correct, then it may be that the democratic governments of Bulgaria and Romania are only just beginning to face the transition dilemma which was presented in the beginning of this paper.

Persisting Problems and Outlook of Future Policies

Currently, both Bulgaria and Romania face persisting problems and try to reorient their policies, particularly in the areas of health care and pensions.

To start with public health, in Bulgaria until late 2002 the new government, elected in July 2001, had not led the health sector in a steady course of reform. The large debts of the hospital sector are one of the major problems which require immediate action. In Romania, an increase in the participation of the private sector in health provision is probably a continuing trend. This general trend may be accompanied by other policies towards the attaining of objectives set by the government of Romania. Such objectives include the development of integrated health care services, the expansion of access of non-insured categories of the population to minimal health care, the rebuilding of territorial health care and social assistance, which had been dissolved in the 1990s, and the improvement of mortality and morbidity indicators (Government of Romania-CASPIS 2002: 63).

In the area of pensions, there are common challenges to be faced by Bulgaria and Romania in the near future. The most imminent are of financial nature. In order to improve the sustainability of their pension systems both countries need to enlarge the contributors' group. Both Bulgaria and Romania continue to experience changes which tip the demographic pyramid in favour of beneficiaries. In the same vein, both countries attempt to increase retirement age and to impose tax discipline in order to collect contributions from tax-evading companies and individuals.

Clearly both countries face complex problems. The complexity of the problems is compounded by the fact that welfare state development goes hand in hand with developments in macro-economic indicators and in state capacities. The fine-tuning of the social policies of Bulgaria and Romania is necessary. It would be a mistake to relegate the development of the welfare state to a priority of secondary status and to consider the improvement of social policy an expected result of further overall economic growth. However, social policy improvements will prove inconsequential if the economies of Bulgaria and Romania do not continue to stabilize and grow, in line with the requisites of integration with the EU, and if their state institutions do not become more efficient and transparent.

Acknowledgements

This paper was first presented at the conference "Welfare Reforms for the 21st Century", which was held under the auspices of the programme COST-A-15, on 5–6 April 2002 in Oslo. The authors would like to thank the organizers of the conference and to particularly acknowledge the feedback of Professor Peter Taylor-Gooby, coordinator of the third working group of the above programme.

References

Beleva, I., Tzanov, V., Noncheva, T. and Zareva, I. (1999), *Background Study on Employment and Labour Market in Bulgaria*, Sofia: European Training Foundation (August).

Deacon, B. (1992a), East European welfare: past, present and future in comparative context. In B. Deacon (ed.), *The New Eastern Europe: Social Policy Past, Present and Future*, London: Sage, pp. 1–30.

Deacon, B. (1992b), The future of social policy in Eastern Europe. In B. Deacon (ed.), *The New Eastern Europe: Social Policy Past, Present and Future*, London: Sage, pp. 167–91.

Deacon, B. (2000), Eastern European welfare states: the impact of the politics of globalization, *Journal of European Social Policy*, 10, 2 (May): 146–61.

Deacon, B. and Vidinova, A. (1992), Social policy in Bulgaria. In B. Deacon (ed.), *The New Eastern Europe: Social Policy Past, Present and Future*, London: Sage.

Deacon, B., Hulse, M. and Stubbs, P. (1997), *Global Social Policy: International Organisations and the Future of Welfare*, London: Sage.

Diamandouros, N. P. and Larrabee, F. S. (2000), Democratization in South Eastern Europe: theoretical considerations and evolving trends. In G. Pridham and T. Gallagher (eds), *Experimenting with Democracy: Regime Change in the Balkans*, London: Routledge, pp. 24–64.

East-Western Institute (2000), *Task Force on Economic Strategy for South Eastern Europe: Final Report*, New York-Prague-Moscow-Kiev-Brussels-Helsinki: East-Western Institute.

Government of Bulgaria (2002), Letter of Intent to IMF and Memorandum on Economic Policies. Sofia, Bulgaria, 12 February (in www.imf.org/external/np/loi/2002/bgr/01/index.htm).

Government of Romania (2001), Letter of Intent to IMF and Memorandum on Economic Policies. Bucharest, Romania, 17 October (in www.imf.org/external/np/loi/2001/rom/01/index.htm).

Government of Romania-CASPIS (2002), *National Anti-poverty and Social Inclusion Plan*, The CASPIS Commission report: Bucharest (July).

GVG-Bulgaria (2002), Study of the Social Protection Systems in the 13 Applicant Countries—Bulgaria Country Report, Second Draft, Cologne, Brussels: Gesellschaft fuer Versicherungswissenschaft und Gestaltung (October).

GVG-Romania (2002), Study of the Social Protection Systems in the 13 Applicant Countries—Romania Country Report, Second Draft, Cologne, Brussels: Gesellschaft fuer Versicherungswissenschaft und Gestaltung (October).

International Monetary Fund (IMF) (2000), Public Notice of the Executive Board of IMF—Conclusions of the Article IV Consultation with Romania, 12 December (in www.imf.org/external/np/sec/pn/2000/pn00106.htm).

Maravall, J.-M. (1992), What is Left? Social democratic policies in Southern Europe, working paper 1992/36, Centro de Estudios Avanzados en Ciencias Sociales, Madrid: Instituto Juan March de Estudios e Investigaciones.

National Statistical Institute of Romania (1998), *Annual Statistical Book*, Bucharest.

Pop, L., Dan, A., Campeanu, M., Stroice, S. and Vladescu, C. (1998), The state's role in maintaining welfare during a period of transition, *Calitatea Vietii*, 3–4: 225–59.

Shopov, G. (1999), Legislative reform of social assistance: the philosophy of changes. In G. Karasimeonov and E. Konstantinov (eds), *Social Policy: Philosophy of Reforms*, Sofia: Gorex Press and Fr Ebert Foundation, pp. 69–90.

United Nations Development Programme (UNDP) (1994), *Human Development Report*, New York: UNDP.

World Bank (1996), *World Development Report*, Washington, DC: World Bank.

World Bank (2000), *Making Transition Work for Everyone: Poverty and Inequality in Europe and Central Asia*, Washington, DC: World Bank.

Zamfir, C. (ed.) (1999), *Politici Sociale in Romania: 1990–1998*, Bucuresti: Expert.

Zamfir, C., Kyoko, P. and Ruxandra, S. (eds) (2001), *Poverty in Romania*, Bucharest: Research Institute for the Quality of Life and United Nations Development Programme.

9

Convergence in the Social Welfare Systems in Europe: From Goal to Reality

Denis Bouget

Introduction

Up to the late 1970s, the social welfare systems in many European countries had been extended to the entire population (health, family, retirement). In addition, they had improved both access and the amount of benefits, and had worked towards an equality in entitlements, independent of either the location or the social status of the inhabitants. For this reason, despite the wide differences between the organization of the systems (Esping-Andersen 1990; Ferrera 1998), most systems gradually became based on the universal values of social rights. Europeanization of welfare systems was seen as unnecessary and the principle of subsidiarity legitimized the consistency of the national welfare systems within the European area. As a result, the history of the social welfare systems in Europe in the postwar period appears as autonomous national processes because the construction of Europe, which imposed common rules in many areas, was equally consistent with the national development of social welfare systems, within each national culture. However, the idea of a common system of social protection has always remained linked to political and economic European construction, which would create a more cohesive society.

According to Chassard (2001), even before the Treaty of Rome, the six European countries (France, Germany, Italy and the three Benelux members) were confronted with the problem of the harmonization of the social security schemes (Coppini 1980). However, the proposal for harmonization created several difficulties and was toned down by the compromise in the 92/442/CEC recommendation, on *The Convergence of social protection objectives and policies* (Chassard 1992). Certain proposals were intended to solve the problem of coordination: the "sixteenth state" (Pieters *et al.* 1990), the "European social snake" (Dispersyn *et al.* 1990, 1992) and the "active social fund" (Pochet *et al.* 1998). None of the three proposals has ever been implemented as they have been perceived as tools of harmonization and have never received any strong political support.

In order to find a solution to the management of the social rights of the migrants, especially the migrant workers in Europe, coordination regulations were passed in 1971. They also contain several severe drawbacks (Schoukens 1997; Pieters 1997) which largely explain the continuing attempts at the creation of new social protection schemes or policies at the EU level.

As we can see, both the implementation of an ambitious European system of social protection and the creation of a harmonized system of national welfare systems have always been found to be impossible. However, we simultaneously note a constant reference to convergence as a catch-up process in the comparative evaluation of the national social policies. One decade after the publication of the recommendation on convergence of objectives, Amitsis *et al.* (2003) show the renaissance of convergence as one goal of the modernization of social policics in Europe. In their report, multidimensional convergence is conceived as a historical result (convergence of the South European model toward the continental one), as an objective and target of social policies (convergence through commonly set targets) or as a norm of action through the use of the open method of coordination (OMC) combined with benchmarking. The success of OMC as a new instrument of governance in the EU renewed the notion of convergence. The benchmarking has enhanced the debates on social indicators which become not only explanatory instruments in the evolution of societies but also (at least in the case of some of them) instruments of evaluation of social policies in different countries.

One result of the recent history of social protection at the European level is a new concern governing the assessment of multidimensional convergence. Several domains of social protection can be analysed as becoming convergent or divergent: convergence in policy-making, political convergence, economic convergence, institutional convergence, legal convergence or cultural convergence. All these domains can influence convergence in social protection. Many studies have analysed the trend of specific social policies and their convergence or divergence in Europe. However, these specific analyses have not taken into account the possible phenomena of substitution (André 2003: 8) between social benefits (for example, between passive and active benefits or between unemployed and handicapped people). Furthermore, global convergence is often conceived as resulting from the domestic dynamics of each social risk (2003: 8).

In the paper we assume a different point of view. Even if the maturation or the reforms of each social policy explains the root of the increase in social expenditure, the macro-economic pressure or constraint on public expenditure can fuel the convergent/divergent evolution of social expenditure. According to Malinvaud (1996), from a financial point of view, the convergence criteria laid down in the Maastricht Treaty were global ones. A financial requirement can only be global, thus leaving room for a trade-off between various social transfers (Malinvaud 1996: 240). Following this, convergence in social welfare systems can be assessed by the convergence in total national social expenditure between countries.

The paper focuses on one specific topic: the quantitative evaluation of convergence among the EU and OECD countries at the macro-economic level. This means that we do not refer to the numerous studies on convergence in different social policies (disability, family, employment, health, etc.), or to the financing side (Hagfors 1999; Kautto 2001). In the first section we explain the construction of social indicators which can assess the convergence or divergence of social expenditure in EU and OECD countries. In the following section, we will show the ambiguous evidence of convergence due to many methodological problems and difficulties of interpretation of the social indicators. In the third section we will see that the analysis of national trajectories of social expenditure and the link with economic development can enrich the analysis of convergence in social protection.

In conclusion, despite the uncertainty of certain trends, we will show that convergence in social expenditure does not change the traditional distinction between the regimes of social protection.

Evidence of Convergence

The empirical convergence of social expenditure is generally conceived as a social indicator of convergence, but contrary to the prolific literature dealing with the long-term convergence in per capita GDP, few studies have focused on the evidence of convergence in social expenditure (Alonso *et al.* 1998; Herce *et al.* 1998b; Cornelisse and Goudswaard 2001; Overbye 2003).

Social indicators of social welfare systems

Two main social indicators are used in the quantitative and comparative analysis of the trend of social protection: the per capita social expenditure on the one hand and the share of social expenditure in GDP on the other.

In this paper, social indicators have been designed using OECD data between 1980 and 1998. Social expenditure is limited to public social expenditure. In many countries, the private compulsory social expenditure is very small and does not entail any consequence on the measurement of social expenditure. Sometimes a distortion appears with the difference in public social expenditure or compulsory social expenditure including public and private social expenditure (Germany, Korea, Switzerland, the United States). Sometimes it seems that part of private expenditure is not included when the national scheme is not compulsory (New Zealand). Finally, our concern is the trend of public social expenditure. The social indicators are also constructed using "gross" public social expenditure, not net social expenditure (Adema 1999). This means that we do not take into account the taxation on social benefits, which is sensitive in certain countries (such as Denmark).

The sample of countries is larger than Europe. It consists of 14 out of the 15 EU countries (except Austria, because of a lack of data over a three-year period), and some other OECD countries (Australia, Canada, Japan, New Zealand, Switzerland, Turkey, United States), in order to facilitate comparisons, for example, regarding the idea of an "Americanization" of the societies. Therefore, the OECD sample pools 21 countries. We immediately see the drawback of the analysis of the European countries. For instance, EU15 in 1998 contains countries which were not member states in 1980. This means that it is impossible to obtain a homogeneous institutional sample of EC or EU in the long term because of its gradual enlargement.

Denis Bouget

The data of social expenditure cover the period 1980–98. This period makes it possible to analyse the trend of a more consistent notion of social expenditure. Furthermore, the analysis of this period is of interest because it is generally defined as a period of crisis in the organization of the different national social welfare systems and a period in which most countries implemented structural reforms.

The analysis of the convergence in per capita GDP, since the initial studies of Abramovitz (1986) and Baumol (1986), has developed a large range of different statistical methods: the two well-known σ-convergence and β-convergence, the time-series analysis and co-integration, the panel analysis and the cluster analysis. In this paper, the instruments are restricted to a simple measurement of inequality between the countries. The σ-convergence is defined by the measurement of an indicator of disparity between the countries: any convergence trend has to be assessed by a decrease in the indicator of disparity; any divergence has to be measured by an increase in the index. The σ-convergence is assessed by the variance, the standard deviation or the coefficient of variation.

Micklewright and Stewart (1999: F697) have clarified the use of weighted or non-weighted indicators according to the different size of the nations. Comparison of social protection as an element of individual well-being leads to the use of a weighted index of dispersion, taking into account the difference in the sizes of countries. However, comparison of social protection systems as different national institutions results in the use of non-weighted indexes of dispersion.

Convergence in per capita social expenditure

Alonso *et al.* (1998) studied the convergence in per capita social benefits among the countries of the EU during the 1966–92 period, using the β-convergence, σ-convergence (standard deviation of the logarithm of per capita social protection benefits) and a panel analysis. Between 1966 and 1992, the analysis shows a long-run drop in the disparity in per capita social benefits among the EUR12 countries, whatever the statistical method used. However, the trend of convergence is not a steady one. Between 1974 and 1978 a significant widening in the divergence between countries occurred, followed by a strong convergence during the 1978–92 period. The authors explain this fluctuation in terms of the consequences of the oil crisis for the European countries.

The trend of the coefficient of variation of per capita social expenditure (see figure 1) during a more recent period (1980–98) highlights several features. Firstly, the cross-section disparity in the per capita social expenditure is always lower among the EU countries than among the OECD sample because most non-EU countries have an underdeveloped public sector and public social protection system. Secondly, one striking result throughout the 1980–98 period, compared with the previous one (1966–78) is that, despite all the reforms of the national social welfare systems in the 1980s and the 1990s, the trend of convergence in per capita social expenditure is steady, without any significant fluctuation. Thirdly, despite the effects of economic crises within the 1980s and 1990s, per capita public social expenditure is convergent in the

Figure 1

Coefficient of variation of per capita social expenditure in OECD and EU
countries between 1980 and 1998 (constant prices 1995; PPPs 1995)

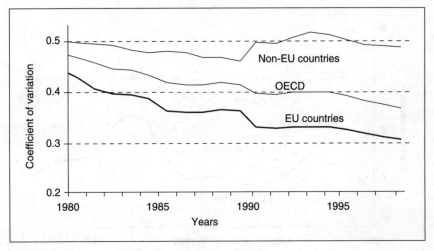

Source: OECD (2003), *Social Expenditure* (Database Edition).

EU, but no clear trend appears in non-EU countries. Finally, OECD countries converge because of the number of EU countries in the sample.

Convergence in social expenditure as a proportion of GDP

This analysis of convergence in social expenditure also makes use of another
indicator—the percentage of social expenditure in GDP. Convergence in the
social expenditure/GDP ratio means that the European construction prompts
a similar national effort to sustain the coverage of the social risks, to cover
the basic needs and/or to reduce individual inequality of well-being.

In order to avoid the problem of international comparison of the per capita
social benefits (parity of purchase power, PPP), Herce *et al.* (1998b) empirically tested the convergence in the percentage of social benefits in GDP.
They used the same kind of data as Alonso *et al.* (1998), among the EUR12
countries for the 1970–94 period. They empirically tested a long-term
convergence process between EU countries on the one hand, and a simple
catch-up (low convergence) with one country, Germany, on the other hand.
They used a time-series analysis. Even if the hypothesis of a long-run convergence was rejected, the study reported finding a catch-up between all countries
and Germany, except Greece.

In this paper, the empirical analysis of the convergence in the social
expenditure/GDP ratios makes use of the same methodology as in the analysis
of the convergence in per capita social expenditure, that is, the σ-convergence.

Denis Bouget

Figure 2

Standard deviation of the percentage of social expenditure in GDP in OECD and
EU countries between 1980 and 1998

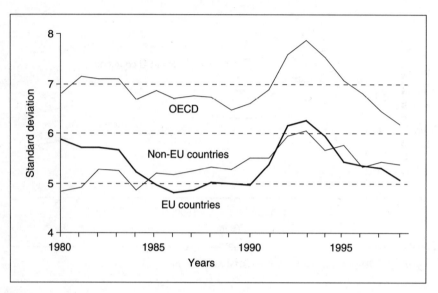

Source: OECD (2003), *Social Expenditure* (Database-Edition).

However, the simple standard deviation (an absolute index of inequality) is used instead of the coefficient of variation.

Figure 2 shows the trend of the standard deviation of the ratio of social expenditure in GDP between 1980 and 1998. Contrary to the previous analysis, the trend of social expenditure of the OECD and EU countries does not lead to a steady convergence. Instead of a fairly steady convergent process, we note a cycle of convergence (1980–90), divergence (1990–3) and convergence (1993–8). In 1985, the process of convergence came to a halt and between 1990 and 1993, a sudden divergence between the EU countries appeared. This divergent trend did not last and, very quickly, convergence reoccurred and has continued until now. To sum up, between 1980 and 1998, only 10 years are clearly years of convergence. Within the general trend of convergence between 1980 and 1998, the short period of divergence (1990–3) is clearly coupled to the divergent reactions from countries which faced international economic recession. Certain countries (Ireland and Luxembourg) remained non-sensitive to the economic recession while other countries (Sweden and Finland) experienced a dramatic increase in the share of social expenditure in GDP.

The convergence in the percentage of social expenditure in GDP has to be linked to the macro-economic policies of the EU member states. Especially since the drawing-up of the Maastricht Treaty, social protection has been considered as a financial burden which blunts the competitiveness of enterprises and fuels the potential public deficit. From this point of view, the extension in social protection is a factor of the enlargement in the public sector. As a result, the percentage of social expenditure in GDP falls under economic supervision even if it is not included in the set of convergence criteria. From the OECD point of view, the constraint on the public sector calls for stricter attention to social expenditure and mainly to the ratio of social expenditure in GDP.

Finally, the use of both indicators leads to different conclusions, which are partly explained by methodological problems, but also by a necessary analysis of their links with economic development.

Convergence and the Uncertainty of Conclusions

The difference of the results between the trend of per capita expenditure and the share of social expenditure in GDP derives from the construction of the statistical assessment of convergence, which is very sensitive to some methodological choices.

The index of the per capita social expenditure in each country leads to serious problems of international comparison, which requires the use of the PPPs to compare the social expenditure between countries, on an annual basis. The second problem is the analysis of each national trend of social expenditure in real terms. The assessment of convergence combines both deflators (PPPs and domestic prices) which can strongly influence the results of the analysis.

The second indicator, the social expenditure/GDP ratio, is often used in international comparison. Its advantage is to avoid the problem of the use of PPPs. However, the use of GDP as a "deflator" is also criticized. In the first place, the indicator becomes very sensitive to any economic shock. Secondly, the use of GDP entails serious problems of evaluation in small countries because a part of GDP is not formed by national factors. There is therefore a problem of distortion between social expenditure and GDP.

Both indicators evaluate the absolute or gross convergence because they do not take into account the difference of structural features of the countries. The conditional convergence hypothesis assesses a convergence among countries that are similar in preferences, technologies, rates of population growth and government policies (Galor 1996: 1057). Conditional convergence and the absolute convergence hypotheses coincide only if all the economies have the same steady rate (levels of technology, propensities to save, population growth rates). Therefore, absolute convergence requires convergence in structural characteristics across countries.

Some authors (Cornelisse and Goudswaard 2001; Overbye 2003) define two types of convergence, an "absolute" convergence when it is measured by an absolute index of inequality (standard deviation for instance) and "relative" convergence when it is measured by a relative index of inequality (coefficient of variation). There are two reasons why this methodological relationship between a type of convergence and its measurement is not very relevant in this case. Firstly, the authors define the type of convergence by a type of measurement. This means that the statistical tool defines the concept (absolute or relative convergence). A second weakness of this measurement has been put forward by Micklewright and Stewart (1999). They explain that the relative indicators of inequality which are commonly used in the analysis of per capita income or per capita social benefits are not an adequate measurement of the disparity in the social expenditure/GDP ratio because the ratio varies between a bottom limit, 0 and a top limit 1. In this case, the use of a standard deviation, for instance, is more suitable than the previous relative dispersion indices because comparisons based on an absolute measurement remain unchanged by the switch to the complementary values. If the index of disparity of the ratio of social expenditure in GDP decreases over time, complementarity will have also to converge. However, the relative indices do not respect this characteristic.

From this general analysis, we can detail the proper contribution of each country in the convergent/divergent process. Tables 1 and 2 show the variation of the dispersion (variance) of the ratio of social expenditure in GDP between two dates of the three periods (1980–90, 1990–3, 1993–8) in OECD countries and EU countries. These tables show the statistical contribution of each country to the convergence or divergence trend. The convergence is measured by a decrease in variance (a negative number in the tables) and the divergence

Table 1

Position of each country in the trend of convergence or divergence in OECD countries

	1980–90	1990–3	1993–8
Belgium	−1.56	−0.13	−0.59
Denmark	−2.57	0.15	−1.84
Finland	1.44	7.33	−7.45
France	1.45	−0.01	0.84
Germany	−1.08	1.45	1.06
Greece	−3.40	0.67	−0.68
Ireland	0.32	0.81	2.77
Italy	1.04	−0.39	0.05
Luxembourg	−1.68	0.04	0.01
The Netherlands	−1.18	−2.03	−2.52
Portugal	0.38	−0.33	−1.76
Spain	−0.25	0.14	0.48
Sweden	−1.03	8.21	−8.46
United Kingdom	−0.17	0.77	−0.40
Australia	−0.31	0.47	−2.41
Canada	−1.29	−0.03	1.31
Japan	2.58	2.49	−5.16
New Zealand	0.10	0.50	−0.30
Switzerland	0.01	−0.03	1.78
Turkey	1.30	4.83	−10.69
United States	2.02	1.03	0.03
Variation of variance	−3.89	25.96	−33.92
	Convergence	Divergence	Convergence

Table 2

Position of each country in the trend of convergence or divergence in EU countries

	1980–90	1990–3	1993–8
Belgium	−0.85	−0.16	0.01
Denmark	−1.95	−0.33	−0.39
Finland	−0.09	3.99	−3.90
France	0.41	−0.16	0.84
Germany	0.07	−0.07	0.83
Greece	−6.38	2.67	−2.51
Ireland	1.30	2.12	2.95
Italy	−0.22	−0.06	0.04
Luxembourg	0.10	1.03	−0.54
Portugal	0.73	0.20	−3.96
Spain	−0.49	0.74	0.13
Sweden	−0.92	5.50	−5.07
The Netherlands	−0.97	−1.69	−0.86
United Kingdom	0.23	−0.31	0.00
Variation of variance	−9.03	13.46	−12.42
	Convergence	Divergence	Convergence

is measured by an increase in the variance (a positive number in the tables). We note that the size of the sample of countries, OECD or EU countries, can change the conclusions but certain stable trends continue to be found in both samples.

As expected, three periods appear clearly (figures in the bottom row in the tables): the decade 1980–1990 experienced a trend of convergence, the period 1990–1993 experienced a rapid divergence in EU countries and the period 1993–1998 experienced another rapid convergence.

In the sample of EU countries, from a quantitative point of view, only six significantly contribute to the cycles of convergence/divergence. Not one country contributed to a permanent convergent trend; but one (Ireland) experienced a divergent process throughout the three periods. The global convergence in 1980–90 comes from the high quantitative contribution of Greece in the variation of the variance; Denmark has also a moderate contribution in the same direction. Neither Spain, Italy nor Portugal significantly contributed to the convergent trend. As a result, we cannot conclude that the decade between 1998 and 1999 was really characterized by the catch-up of the Southern countries.

The period 1990–3 is characterized by a divergent trend between countries. Sweden and Finland largely contributed to the divergent process and Greece and Ireland also contributed at a lower level. The Netherlands experienced a convergent trend. The convergence throughout 1993–8 is different from the convergent trend during the whole of the 1980s. Four countries largely contribute to the convergence, Sweden and Finland on the one hand, Portugal and Greece on the other.

Denis Bouget

Finally, we note that the cycle of convergence and divergence is largely due to certain Nordic countries, especially to the huge variations in Sweden and Finland.

Can we conclude from these data that convergence comes from a process of European integration? All the most generous systems have not experienced a crisis in the distribution of social benefits; all the Southern countries have not experienced a permanent catch-up. Furthermore, Ireland experienced a divergent process throughout the periods.

All these features lead to moderation of the thesis of convergence due to European integration. This does not mean that the process of integration does not exist, but it means that the empirical data on total social expenditure do not easily confirm the thesis of integration.

Trajectories and the Relationship between the Two Indicators

In the previous paragraphs, the indicators of convergence in social protection were presented as an "independent" evaluation of convergence. In different ways, each indicator shows a long-term convergent process but in different ways. However, this interpretation overlooks the relationship between both indicators. In fact, in each country and at each year, the following relationship links both indicators, the per capita social expenditure and the percentage of social expenditure in GDP:

Social expenditure/head = Social expenditure/GDP *GDP/head

This formula sums up the following: the level of per capita social expenditure takes into account the richness of the society assessed by per capita GDP and the national social effort towards social welfare evaluated by the social expenditure/GDP ratio, whatever the regime or the legal rules which define the institution.

This relationship links social protection to per capita income (per capita GDP). Therefore, the evolution of social expenditure also depends on the per capita GDP trend. At this point, we will not develop the vast economic literature on the long-run convergence in per capita GDP (Abramovitz 1986; Baumol 1986; Quah 1992, 1996a, 1996b; Sala i Martin 1996; Dowrick and Quiggin 1997, etc.). Le Pen (1997) has written a review on this literature which started in the mid-1980s and sparked writings from a great number of economists. Finally, this formula means that we cannot interpret the trend of per capita social expenditure solely through the reforms of the social institutions because some of the increase in social expenditure results from the general economic development and from improved household incomes.

According to the formula, the disparity in per capita social expenditure depends on the inequality of social expenditure/GDP ratio, and on the inequality of the per capita GDP. We can thus start to examine the correlation between both variables.

Many publications have presented and explained the cross-section relationship between the percentage of social expenditure in GDP and per capita GDP (ILO 2001: 82; CEC/DGV 1994: 42; CEC/DGV 1996: 60). This relationship has also been interpreted in a causal way and has led to a wide debate on the causal direction of the relation (Atkinson 1995, 1996; Herce *et al.* 1998a, etc.). In 1980 (see figure 4), a positive relationship linked the percentage of social expenditure in GDP with per capita GDP. This relationship was very strong within the EU countries (r = 0.83). This relationship has often been used to explain the link between economic development and social protection. However, this cross-section relationship is not stable in time. Between 1985 and 1994, the coefficient of correlation between the variables plunged and since then, it has been impossible to argue for a strong link between them.

This means that the decrease in the cross-section correlation has had a positive impact on the σ-convergence in social expenditure per head, independently of the effect of GDP/head or of the social expenditure/GDP.

Analysis of trajectories

Alonso and colleagues suggest that the convergence in social protection is related to general economic development. Convergence in per capita social benefits globally reveals the same pattern as in per capita GDP (Alonso *et al.* 1998: 154), during the 1974–92 period. They uphold the idea that an effort by EU countries to reduce the non-wage cost distortion in Europe has facilitated labour mobility. We will see that these explanations contribute to the varieties of national trajectories since 1980.

From 1966 to 1992, there was a relationship between the convergence/divergence trend of per capita social benefits and the trend of per capita GDP. This relationship disappeared within the 1980–98 period because there is not any convergent process of per capita GDP. In fact, we note a divergent trend of per capita GDP in Europe but this divergence is first and foremost due to the rapid economic growth in Luxembourg and the effect of the extension of the financial economy within this period. Therefore, the convergence in social protection cannot be the direct consequence of a catch-up process in the economic sphere as Alonso *et al.* suggested for the period 1966–1992.

The convergence could be a consequence of the process of European integration but the statistical observation is not as simple. The decrease in the correlation between social expenditure/GDP and GDP per head is measured on cross-national data and does not mean that there is no link between them. In order to understand the process of convergence, we need to examine the trajectories of this pair of variables between 1980 and 1998 for each country of the OECD sample and EU countries.

The relationship between the three variables of the formula can easily be illustrated in figures 3 and 4(a–c). Per capita GDP is indicated on the horizontal axis; the social expenditure/GDP ratio is indicated on the vertical axis. One point on the figure represents one country. Figure 3 describes the position of countries in 1980 and 1998; an arrow shows the long-term trend between 1980 and 1998 for each country and the tips of each arrow are the positions of 1980 and 1998. A horizontal arrow means that an increase in the social per capita expenditure is uniquely due to the increase in per capita GDP; a

Figure 3

Trajectories of the variables between 1980 and 1998

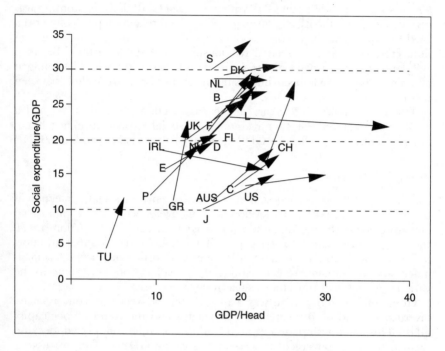

vertical arrow means an increase in the per capita social expenditure derives from an increase in the social expenditure/GDP ratio without any economic growth.

From the graphical properties of the figure, we can immediately see a surge in the per capita social expenditure in all countries, even in Ireland. All the countries which had a low level of social protection in 1980 experienced a significant development in social protection throughout the period (Turkey, Portugal, Greece, Japan, Australia, Canada, United States and Switzerland). Among the high-protection countries, the trends are more diversified. Belgium, Luxembourg and Denmark experienced stability or a slight increase in the share of social expenditure.

Unlike the cross-section analysis in 1980, and also contrary to a common idea which relates the development of social protection to economic development, we note that the long-run trend (1980–98) of social protection is not always coupled to the increase in per capita GDP. The correlation between the variation of the percentage of social expenditure and the growth rate of per capita GDP becomes very low. For two decades, economic development has not systematically fostered a development of social protection, within this sample of the most developed countries. In order to present the relationship between the evolution of the ratio of social expenditure in GDP and GDP

Table 3

Variation of the percentage of social expenditure per point of growth rate of per capita
GDP between 1980 and 1998 (increasing values)

Countries Group 1 Weak sensitiveness	Ratio	Countries Group 2 Medium sensitiveness	Ratio	Countries Group 3 High sensitiveness	Ratio
Ireland	−0.02	New Zealand	0.09	Australia	0.18
Luxembourg	−0.01	Japan	0.09	Italy	0.19
The Netherlands	−0.01	Portugal	0.11	Finland	0.20
United States	0.03	United Kingdom	0.11	Germany	0.20
Denmark	0.04	Turkey	0.12	France	0.26
Belgium	0.05	Sweden	0.14	Switzerland	0.77
Spain	0.08	Canada	0.17	Greece	0.80

Sources: OECD (2003), *Social Expenditure* (Database-Edition).

per head, we have classified the countries according to the long-term sensitiveness of social protection to economic growth (see table 3).

Group 1 contains the countries in which the share of social expenditure in GDP is hardly sensitive to economic growth. The perfect example is Luxembourg, which experienced very high economic growth but stability in the ratio of social expenditure in GDP. Figure 4(a) presents the yearly trend of the pair of variables (GDP/head and social expenditure/GDP) for each country of group 1. The second group gathers countries which are characterized by a medium sensitiveness of social protection to economic evolution (figure 4(b)). Countries of the third group are characterized by a significant change in the share of social expenditure in GDP (figure 4(c)).

The pattern of the relationship between the percentage of social expenditure and per capita GDP is not a steady one between 1980 and 1998. One striking feature is the similarity of the trajectories of many countries in the short run. They show a spiralling in the percentage of social expenditure in GDP, without any increase in per capita GDP around 1990 and often for a period of four years. For instance, the share of social expenditure in Sweden suddenly increased from 1990 to 1993 while the country fell into an economic recession (vertical part of the trend in figure 4(b)). That short-run change can be explained as follows. In the late 1980s, the economic recession prevented the steady increase in per capita GDP and, consequently, the increase in the income of the households (here the per capita GDP). Unemployment also worsened. Simultaneously, the social protection system worked in two different directions. Some of the increase in the social expenditure/ GDP ratio originates from the increase in the protection of individuals as a reaction in the wake of the impoverishment of a section of the population (increase in unemployment). Another part of the increase comes from the

Denis Bouget

Figure 4

Trajectories of the variables between 1980 and 1998

(a) First group of countries

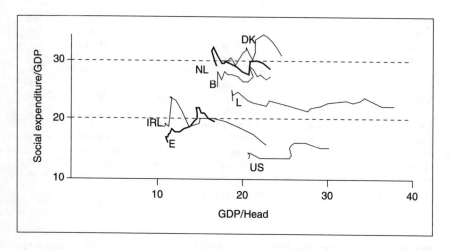

(b) Second group of countries

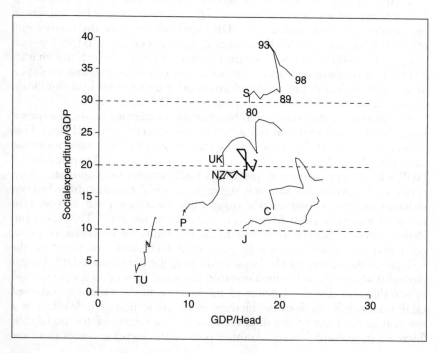

Figure 4 (*Continued*)

(c) Third group of countries

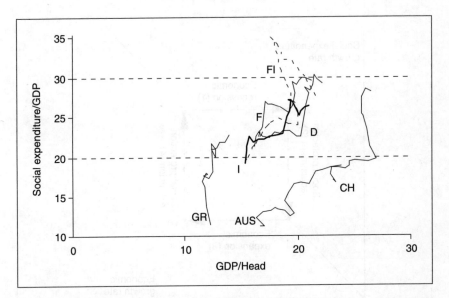

Explanatory note: The trajectories are constructed on the basis of yearly data for the period 1980–1998. A national curve represents the yearly relationship between two variables, the per capita GDP and the percentage of social expenditure in GDP. Very often, the starting point represents 1980 and the final one 1998 (see the example of Sweden in figure 4(b).

non-stop development of the pension schemes linked to the maturity of the schemes, which is hardly sensitive to economic seesawing and arises from the higher demand for health care services, which also remains largely independent of the economic cycle. Throughout this international crisis, each country experienced a particular economic shock (Finland for instance).

This sudden and dramatic increase added to several macro-economic black spots and mainly to the public deficit. Faced with this increase, either because some countries were candidates for EMU, or simply because of an orthodox economic policy, or under the pressure of international institutions (OECD, IMF), several countries tried to put a stop to this increase and, sometimes, to curb the share of social expenditure (Finland, Sweden, Canada). When economic development permitted an increase in the per capita GDP, the shock of the increase in the social expenditure ratio seemed to be absorbed without too many difficulties (Japan, United States). When economic crisis followed, that is, when the GDP/head did not increase, even in the second half of the 1990s, strict reforms in social protection then lowered the proportion of social expenditure in GDP.

The similarity of the evolution of numerous countries leads us to propose a cycle which links total social expenditure to economic growth. In the

Denis Bouget

Figure 5

Cycle of social expenditure

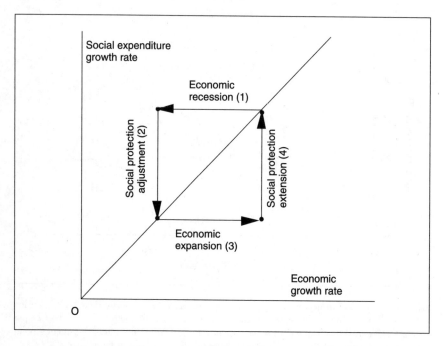

developed countries, economic growth almost immediately entails an increase in social expenditure. When an economic crisis occurs, the rate of economic growth decreases but the rate of growth of social expenditure remains stable or increases, due to the reasons we have accounted for earlier in the paper. This is the first phase of the cycle (see figure 5). The distortion between the two growth rates entails a deficit of the budget. Since the late 1980s and the early 1990s, the national restrictive economic policies and the refusal of any adjustment through increase in taxation pressure has led most of the governments to constrain the evolution of social expenditure and to reduce the growth rate of social expenditure (Phase 2). After the crisis, economic growth again entails a moderate or a proportional growth to social expenditure. In this case, the ratio of social expenditure either slightly decreases or remains stable (Phases 3 and 4).

In the late 1980s and early 1990s, the sudden increase in the percentage of social expenditure in GDP was explicitly or implicitly conceived as a catastrophe because it was often correlated to a budgetary deficit. The stabilization of social expenditure partly stemmed from a rationing process on the financing side (Kautto 2001). Kautto also highlights the asymmetric situation between expenditure and financing. "While control of expenditure remains in the hands of the government, the revenue side is increasingly affected by factors beyond the control of nation-states" (2001: 236). As a result, European integration, driven by its key engines, the European Commission, EMU and the Single Market, and tax policy coordination is thrusting member states' financing solutions towards a similar mould (2001: 237).

The cycle of social expenditure shows that a part of convergence is not due to any convergence in social policies. Nor is it necessary to make any reference to maturation or needs-covering to find an explanation of convergence of aggregate social expenditure.

As figure 3 clearly shows, we do not find any convergence towards the bottom because in the long term we do not see any clear tendency to the reduction of social expenditure in the developed countries. However, since the late 1980s, most nations have been under a double pressure: slow economic growth and a chronic deficit in the budget. Macro-economic pressures (with or without the Maastricht criteria) have entailed new social policy reforms, which are converging. Therefore, the convergence we note in specific social policies results from the economic pressures which entailed new reforms and different types of recalibration (Ferrera and Hemerijck 2003).

Conclusion: Towards a Typology of Trends?

In the late 1980s and the early 1990s, the trend of social protection was interpreted in a very pessimistic way (austerity, dismantlement, cost containment, retrenchment of the national systems). However, the analysis of long-term trends of social protection shows that the period of retrenchment of social policy has not entailed a final race to the bottom.

The long-run convergence or divergence of social welfare systems leads to the question of the link between the regimes of social protection and the different trajectories. From the different figures and tables, it is impossible to note any similarity between the trajectories and the regimes. According to table 3, countries often classified as "liberal" experienced a rather sluggish increase in the percentage of social expenditure per point of growth in per capita GDP. However, the trend of Australia does not correspond to the idea of the retrenchment of the social protection sector. Within a Scandinavian and "social-democratic" context, Denmark experienced a rather different trajectory than did Sweden and Finland. In the continental tradition, France and Germany are close in the table while Belgium is not. As is shown in the table, there is no link between the type of regime and the long-term type of trajectory. Furthermore, the short-term and medium-term analyses show a spiralling link between the trend of social expenditure and economic development, and the existence of cycles.

Therefore, a second question appears: do the differentiated trajectories modify the classification of the countries within the regimes (shift of a country from one cluster to another), or the notion of the regime (new types of regimes)? Figure 3 shows that a sustainable regime entails not a decrease in the per capita social expenditure, as the consequence of a kind of retrenchment of social protection in the country, but an increase in per capita benefit which is mainly derived from economic development. From this point of view, the sustainability of a regime comes from the harmony between economic development, the enlargement of social protection and the national institutions. The case of Turkey is of interest because it shows the case of a poor country which simultaneously experienced economic development and a fast development in its social protection. The case of Greece looks more complex, given that the dramatic development of social protection in the long run is not linked with any economic development. Finally, the long-term convergent trend of social expenditure and its cycles have not blurred the distinction between the systems during the previous decades.

This conclusion confirms other results of comparative analysis on the convergence in social protection (Kautto 2001). Inspired by the definition (Hall 1986) of three types of public policies, Palier (2002) distinguishes the quantitative changes in benefits and financing, the instrumental changes in social policies and the institutional changes. Our empirical analysis supports the idea of "adjustment" reforms rather than radical changes in a transitional period, from old systems of social protection to new ones, but do we have to accept the criticism of Taylor-Gooby (2002), who has claimed that the quantitative approaches tend to overemphasize stability, just at a point when radical changes are on the cards?

References

Abramovitz, M. (1986), Catching-up, forging ahead, and falling behind, *Journal of Economic History*, 46, 2: 385–406.

Adema, W. (1999), *Net Total Social Expenditure*, Paris: OECD.

Alonso, J., Galindo, M. A. and Sosvilla-Rivero, S. (1998), Convergence in social protection benefits across EU countries, *Applied Economics Letters*, 5: 153–5.

Amitsis, G., Berghman, J., Hemerijck, A., Sakellaropoulos, T., Stergiou, A. and Stevens, Y. (2003), *Connecting Welfare Diversity Within the European Social Model*, report, Athens: Ministry of Labour and Social Security.

André, C. (2003), Ten European systems of social protection: an ambiguous convergence. In D. Pieters (ed.), *European Social Security and Global Politics*, The Hague: Kluwer Law International, pp. 3–44.

Atkinson, A. B. (1995), The welfare state and economic performance, *National Tax Journal*, 48: 171–98.

Atkinson, A. B. (1996), Growth and the welfare state: is the welfare state necessarily bad for economic growth, *New Economy*, 3: 182–6.

Baumol, W. J. (1986), Productivity growth, convergence and welfare: what the long run data show? *American Economic Review*, 76: 1072–85.

CEC/DGV (1992), *Convergence of Objectives and the Policies of Social Protection*, Suppl.5/1992, Brussels, Luxembourg.

CEC/DGV (1994), *Social Protection in Europe 1993*, Brussels, Luxembourg.

CEC/DGV (1996), *Social Protection in Europe 1995*, Brussels, Luxembourg.

Chassard, Y. (1992), La Convergence des objectifs et politiques de protection sociale: une nouvelle approche. In *La Convergence des Objectifs et des Politiques de Protection Sociale*, Bruxelles: CEC, *Europe Sociale*, Suppl.5/92.

Chassard, Y. (2001), European integration and social protection: from the Spaak Report to the open method of coordination. In D. G. Mayes, J. Berghman and R. Salais, *Social Exclusion and European Policy*, Cheltenham: Edward Elgar.

Coppini, A. (1980), *Les Dépenses de la Sécurité Sociale et les Facteurs démographiques dans les Pays de la Communauté Européenne, 1965–1995*, Brussels, CEC report, Social Policy Series.

Cornelisse, P. A. and Goudswaard, K. P. (2001), On the convergence of social protection systems in the European Union, *International Social Security Review*, 5 (July–September): 3–17.

Dispersyn, M., Van der Vorst, P., De Falleur, M., Guillaume, Y., Hecq, Ch., Lange, M. and Meulders, D. (1990), La Construction d'un serpent social européen, *Revue Belge de Sécurité Sociale*, 12.

Dispersyn, M., Van der Vorst, P., De Falleur, M., Guillaume, Y., Hecq, Ch., Lange, M. and Meulders, D. (1992), La Construction d'un serpent social européen, étude de faisabilité *Revue Belge de Sécurité Sociale*, special issue, 4, 5, 6 (April–June).

Dowrick, S. and Quiggin, J. (1997), True measures of GDP and convergence, *American Economic Review*, 87, 1 (March): 41–64.

Esping-Andersen, G. (1990), *The Three Worlds of Welfare Capitalism*, Cambridge: Polity Press.

Ferrera, M. (1998), The four social Europe: between universalism and selectivism. In M. Rhodes and Y. Meny (eds), *The Future Of European Welfare: A New Social Contract?* Basingstoke: Macmillan, pp. 79–96.

Ferrera, M. and Hemerijck, A. (2003), Recalibrating Europe's welfare regimes. In J. Zeitlin and D. Trubek (eds), *Governing Work and Welfare in a New Economy*, Oxford: Oxford University Press.

Galor, O. (1996), Convergence? Inference from theoretical models, *Economic Journal*, 106 (December): 1056–2132.

Hagfors, R. (1999), The convergence of financing structure 1980–1995. In *Financing Social Protection in Europe*, Helsinki: Ministry of Social Affairs and Health, Publications, no. 21.

Hall, P. (1986), *Governing the Economy: The Politics of State Intervention in Britain and France*, New York: Oxford University Press.

Herce, J. A., Sosvilla-Rivero, S. and De Lucio, J. J. (1998a), Social protection benefits and growth: evidence from the European Union, *FEDEA, Documento de Trabajo* (January).

Herce, J. A., Sosvilla-Rivero, S. and De Lucio, J. J. (1998b), A time-series examination of convergence in social protection across EU countries, *FEDEA, Documento de Trabajo* (April).

ILO (2001), *Social Security, A New Consensus*, Geneva: International Labour Office.

Kautto, M. (2001), Moving closer? Diversity and convergence in financing of welfare states. In M. Kautto, J. Fritzell, B. Hvinden, J. Kvist and J. Uusitalo, *Nordic Welfare States in the European Context*, London: Routledge, pp. 232–61.

Le Pen, Y. (1997), Convergence des revenus par tête: un tour d'horizon, *Revue d'Economie Politique*, 107, 6 (November–December): 715–56.

Malinvaud, E. (1996), Is the European welfare state unsustainable? In M. Baldassarri and L. Paganetto, *Equity, Efficiency and Growth, The Future of the Welfare State*, London: Macmillan Press, pp. 237–55.

Micklewright, J. and Stewart, K. (1999), Is the well-being of children converging in the European Union? *The Economic Journal*, 109 (November): F692–714.

Overbye, E. (2003), Globalisation and social policy convergence. Communication in the Forum on *Social Protection in a Widening Europe*, DREES-MIRE, Paris, 20–22 March.

Palier, B. (2002), *Gouverner la Sécurité Sociale*, Paris, Presses Universitaires de France.

Pieters, D. (1997), Towards a radical simplification of the social security coordination. In P. Schoukens, *Prospects of Social Security Co-ordination*, Leuven: ACCO, pp. 177–223.

Pieters, D., Palm, W. and Vansteenkiste, S. (1990), Le treizième état, *Revue Belge de Sécurité Sociale*, December.

Denis Bouget

Pochet, P., Antoons, J., Barbier, C., Moro Lavado, E. and Turloot, L. (1998), Union européenne et processus de convergence sociale, *Revue Belge de Sécurité Sociale*, 40, special issue.

Quah, D. (1992), International patterns of growth: I. Persistence in cross-country disparities, Working paper, London School of Economics.

Quah, D. (1996a), Twin peaks: growth and convergence in models of distribution dynamics, *The Economic Journal*, 106 (July): 1045–55.

Quah, D. T. (1996b), Regional convergence clusters across Europe, Discussion Paper no. 1286, Centre for Economic Policy Research, January, p. 24.

Rassekh, F. (1998), The convergence hypothesis: history, theory, and evidence, *Open Economies Review*, 9, 1 (January): 85–105.

Sala i Martin, X. (1996), The classical approach to convergence analysis, *The Economic Journal*, 106 (July): 1019–36.

Schoukens, P. (1997), Introduction. In P. Schoukens, *Prospects of Social Security Co-ordination*, Leuven: ACCO, pp. 11–13.

Taylor-Gooby, P. (2002), The silver age of the welfare state: perspectives on resilience, *Journal of Social Policy*, 31, 4 (October): 597–622.

Zeitlin, J. and Trubek, D. (eds) (2003), *Governing Work and Welfare in a New Economy*, Oxford: Oxford University Press.

Index

Index

Index

Index

Index

Index

Index

Index

Index

private pensions 8
privatization, health care systems 122–3
Professional Qualification and Unemployment Fund (Bulgaria) 124
professionalization, care services 25
PROGNOS study (1999) 40
public health, policies 15

qualified majority voting (QMV) 12, 13, 14

racial discrimination 10, 15
  legislation 23
Raffarin, Jean-Pierre 89
Rassemblement pour la République (France) 88
recalibration 18
reciprocity 5
re-commodification 18
Red–Green government (Germany) 41, 42
reddito minimo di inserimento (RMI) (Italy) 104–5
redistribution, vs. regulation 79, 80–1
refugees 14
Regional Fund 8–9
regulation
  use of term 55
  vs. redistribution 79, 80–1
rehabilitation programmes 13
Rendimento Mínimo Garantido (RMG) (Portugal) 106–7
renta activa de inseción laboral 108
rentas mínimas de inserción (Spain) 109
restructuring, processes 2
retirement age 25, 27
  Bulgaria 123
  early 88
  Finland 43
  Germany 39, 42
  Romania 124
retirement income policies
  multi-pillar approach 42–3
  one-pillar approach 42
  see also pension schemes
reunification 39
Revenue Minimum d'Insertion (RMI) 87–8, 91, 101
Ricardo, David 4
rights
  employment 14
  equal 71–2, 77
  workers 9
  see also social rights
RMG (*Rendimento Mínimo Garantido*) (Portugal) 106–7
RMI (*reddito minimo di inserimento*) (Italy) 104–5
RMI (*Revenue Minimum d'Insertion*) 87–8, 91, 101

Roma people 126
Romania
  economic characteristics 116–17
  economic indicators **125**
  health care systems 116–17, 121–3
  labour market policies 124–6
  life expectancy 117
  pension schemes 123–4, 126
  political transitions 115–16, 117–21, 127
  retirement age 124
  social expenditure 117–21
  social indicators **121**
  social policy 121–9
  social tourism 24
  unemployment 124–6, 127
  welfare state development 116–21; future trends 128–9
Rome (Italy) 104
RSI (Social Insertion Income) (Portugal) 107
Russia, primary care reforms 57

Scandinavia
  care services 27
  citizenship 50
  primary care reforms 58
  social expenditure 147
  welfare states 85
  see also Nordic countries
Schumpeter, Joseph Alois 7
  Capitalism, Socialism, and Democracy (1942) 3–5
Schumpeterianism 7, 9, 15
SEA (Single European Act) 8, 14
Second World War 25
selectivism 48
self-help programmes, disabled persons 75–7
sex differences *see* gender differences
SHI countries *see* social health insurance (SHI) countries
Simeon II, King 122, 126
Simon, H. A. 69
Single European Act (SEA) 8, 14
Single Market 147
single-parent families
  employment 91–2
  poverty rates 85
single-parent households 27
Social Action Programmes 9, 13
social assistance *see* social security systems
Social Charter (1988) 9, 12, 13, 14, 23
social democracy, and welfare state 17
Social Democrats (Finland) 44
Social Democrats (Germany) 38, 39, 41
social dumping 24
social exclusion 12, 88, **90**, 103
  ethnic minorities 116

Index

Index

Index